Praise for *No Place for a Woman*

"The exclusion, marginalization, mistreatment and oppression of women lies at the very heart of the systemic and deep-seated crisis of the abuse and misuse of power within the Church over many centuries. This powerful book combines research and analysis with far-reaching experience and testimony to show what has gone wrong and what needs urgently to change, both practically and theologically. For many in the Catholic Church and beyond this book will make difficult and painful reading. Its message, while rightly unflinching and uncompromising in calling out spiritual and power abuse, is ultimately hopeful and positive. But only if those in positions of influence are willing to engage with root and branch reform, to give up privilege themselves, and to put the voices and authority of women at the centre of a major reversal in the way power is understood and exercised by the Church."—**Simon Barrow**, Director, Ekklesia thinktank

"Meticulous research, presented in an accessible style, presenting a compelling apologetic for the urgent reform required, to ensure gender equality, at every level of ecclesiastical life, as Jesus intended. The author provides vital information to empower the countless women, whose genuine vocations are being suppressed, to continue to bear witness to Christ's call to them. *No Place for a Woman* exposes the shocking and systematic exclusion of women, by men throughout history, in contrast to the positions of authority to which Jesus had appointed them, and that they enjoyed in the early Church. Every Christian should equip themselves with the facts that this shrewd book reveals, to enable them to play their part in ensuring the church evolves, to comprehensively integrate women in the apostolic holy orders, mission, and magisterium of the church."—**Archbishop Jonathan Blake**, Open Episcopal Church

"In this rigorously researched and brilliantly written book, Debra Maria Flint examines the historic treatment of women by the Catholic Church. She documents the prominence women once had and explores the causes of the destruction and erosion of female influence, including disordered attitudes towards God, human nature, and sexuality. Flint challenges the Church to make radical changes and to rid itself of its entrenched misogyny if it is to survive as a faithful witness to Christ in the world."—**Rev. Christina H. M. Rees CBE**

"Debra Maria Flint has masterfully woven her viewpoint from her lived experience into a timeline of historical events using the Holy thread of inspiration. Flint's writing is clear and accessible. Her message is unmistakable. The Spirit of her work should cause pause in anyone seeking to understand how women experience a world created by and for men. If this book isn't the impetus for immediate change to our current paradigm of perception and action in the world, then the people holding hostage all the worldly power, who have hoarded and who guard the resources needed for moving with the Spirit, are not in the Holy Space of listening and acting in God's name. The action taken by those claiming the ultimate authority should resemble the embrace from the arms of a loving Mother, with Her support in all forms, to let Her children grow into independence so they can embrace both their Parents from a place of complementary equality. Debra Maria Flint's work should be widely disseminated and used for contemplation by all people of God and especially by those claiming any sort of authority over another with the understanding that true authority comes from letting go and finding our own beginning and ending in the company of each other. This book helps us do this by offering a viewpoint that hasn't been considered; a woman's viewpoint, the viewpoint of the conquered. We need this because where two or more are gathered in Christ is where God lives in this world. It's not 'two or more gathered,' no matter how many there are, if the 'two or more gathered' aren't sharing the story from their unique perspectives. Debra Maria Flint's book is an invitation to see with different eyes, to be open to Christ and to bring God's love to our actions in this world."
—**Rev. Jill Striebinger**, Association of Catholic Women Priests

"Sadly, Christians are having to become ever more familiar with the concept of spiritual abuse, as we are being forced to recognize that beliefs can and have been used to manipulate and control. Up to now the concept of spiritual abuse has tended to be applied to the behavior of individuals towards individuals. In this sweeping and searing analysis of the place of women in the Roman Catholic Church, past and present, Debra Maria Flint argues that the institution is guilty of spiritual abuse towards half the human race. It is an argument that will shock and disturb many, but it cannot be ignored, particularly at this crucial point in the history of the Roman Catholic Church when, under the leadership of Pope Francis, it seeks to become a listening and inclusive Church."
—**Elizabeth Stuart**, Professor Emeritus, University of Winchester

"Debra Maria Flint has researched a complicated subject extensively: The current marginal position of women within the Roman Catholic church when it comes to policies and a religious life and the power abuse, spiritual abuse, and sexual abuse they still risk today that are sustained by a hierarchal power structure of celibate, male and mostly old clergy.

No Place for a Woman unravels the heralded ideas behind the harsh and hostile degrading threads of misogyny that led to the current situation where women have the least place in the Roman Catholic church in its history despite the fragile steps by Pope Francis to instigate the synod on synodality and the inclusion of some women in an assembly of thousands of bishops.

Flint debunks false 'biblical' and 'traditional' claims that whitewash misogynous decisions regarding the role and position of women. Once read, the authority of the Roman Catholic Church lies in tatters. Her arguments are strengthened by the examples where the other church of all ages, the Eastern Orthodox Church, has steered clear of numerous pitfalls. For example, neither women diaconate nor marriage are forbidden fruits but canonized.

No Place for a Woman broadens the current debate on women's ordinations beyond yes or no through a well-researched historical overview of the many forms that gave women a religious place in the church and where women held positions of influence. Although several forms of religious life were restored in modern times the regard of women as teachers, thinkers or spiritual directors is but a bleak shadow of the influence and positions held in earlier times.

Having been a member of the flock Flint is also compassionate for the Roman Catholic Church to become again a church fitting the people of this day and age. When human rights and women's rights are upheld by numerous organizations worldwide and abuse in its many forms can no longer be hidden behind cloaks of pseudo respectability the Roman Catholic Church faces the challenge to engage with the world or to wither.

It would be a brand-new day when the words of Flint, 'Time and time again, the hierarchy have shown that they will stop at nothing to destroy the core of someone's being in order to maintain their control on dogma,' will be obsolete.

Having faced spiritual abuse herself, and being ordained deacon in another Catholic denomination, Flint unravels the conditions by which this and other forms of violence against women are sustained to this very day.

Flint's recommendations to end all forms of power abuse contain inclusion of women in the hierarchy, a vow of respect instead of obedience along with open and accountable procedures in case of any abuse, freedom of conscience, and freedom of debate for all church members.

No Place for a Woman is a brave, intelligent and well-written book for all who advocate a religion with a heart and soul. A must read for all women who have a calling for religious life to make informed choices."
—**Bishop Paula-Willemijn van Rooijen**, Old Catholic Apostolic Church, diocese Europe

The Spiritual and Political
Power Abuse of Women
Within Catholicism

No Place
—FOR A—
Woman

Debra Maria Flint

Lantern Publishing & Media ● Woodstock and Brooklyn, NY

2024
Lantern Publishing & Media
PO Box 1350
Woodstock, NY 12498
www.lanternpm.org

Cover design by Taha Shahzad

Printed in the United States of America

Library of Congress Cataloging-in-Publication Data

Names: Flint, Debra Maria, author.
Title: No place for a woman : the spiritual and political power abuse of women within
    Catholicism / Debra Maria Flint.
Description: Woodstock, NY : Lantern Publishing & Media, [2024] | Includes
    bibliographical references.
Identifiers: LCCN 2023028101 (print) | LCCN 2023028102 (ebook) | ISBN
    9781590567227 (paperback) | ISBN 9781590567234 (epub)
Subjects: LCSH: Women in the Catholic Church. | Catholic women—Abuse of.
Classification: LCC BX2347.8.W6 F57 2024 (print) | LCC BX2347.8.W6 (ebook) |
    DDC 282.082—dc23/eng/20231130
LC record available at https://lccn.loc.gov/2023028101
LC ebook record available at https://lccn.loc.gov/2023028102

This book is dedicated to the memory of Bertram William Flint, a broad-minded Catholic theologian and poet with whom I lived for twenty-nine years in Clevedon, Somerset.

> The Danube to the Severn gave
>   The darkened heart that beat no more;
>   They laid him by the pleasant shore,
> And in the hearing of the wave.
>
> There twice a day the Severn fills;
>   The salt sea-water passes by,
>   And hushes half the babbling Wye,
> And makes a silence in the hills.
>   Alfred, Lord Tennyson, "In Memoriam A.H.H." (1850)

Tennyson is believed to have written this poem over a period of seventeen years in Clevedon, the town from which his best friend Arthur Hallam hailed. Both Arthur Hallam and Bertram William Flint are buried on the grounds of St. Andrew's Church Clevedon.

We've had enough exhortations to be silent. Cry out with a thousand tongues—I see the world is rotten because of silence.

St. Catherine of Siena

The lack of consciousness of belonging to God's faithful people as servants, and not masters, can lead us to one of the temptations that is the most damaging to the missionary outreach that we are called to promote: clericalism, which ends up as a caricature of the vocation we have received. A failure to realize that the mission belongs to the entire Church, and not to the individual priest or bishop, limits the horizon, and even worse, stifles all the initiatives that the Spirit may be awakening in our midst. Let us be clear about this. The lay persons are not our peons, or our employees. They don't have to parrot back whatever we say. Clericalism, far from giving impetus to various contributions and proposals, gradually extinguishes the prophetic flame to which the entire Church is called to bear witness.

Pope Francis

Contents

Foreword

Deborah Jones

This is a dangerous book. If it were safe, it would not be worth reading. Don't worry! There is no jeopardy to Catholic faith or morals here, but books on similarly challenging and forbidden subjects, such as women's ordination, have been banned and even burned!

Among the uncomfortable concerns raised is the lack of accountability in the church—that is, not the "whole People of God" meaning of the word "church," but the institutional hierarchical organization led exclusively by celibate men. It is particularly that last characteristic that seems the core of the problem facing many faithful, committed women in the church. The sort of women who feel called to give themselves in service to the living Body of Christ that constitutes all the baptized. The sort who would live consecrated lives—if they knew what they were and how to go about it. And crucially, if they were permitted to do so by those who have the power to accept and allow them.

In the persecuted early church there was a slave, an *ostiarius*, or gatekeeper, whose job was literally to tend the doors of the house churches (often owned and led by women) during eucharists. They were to secure the safety of the worshipping community from intruders who could betray the Christians to their state enemies. After the era of persecution, that role became the first, or lowest, of the four stages, or minor orders, before a person could have conferred on him one or more of the three major orders—those now of deacon, priest, or bishop (previously subdeacon, deacon, and priest/bishop, but let's not get into that).

Now gatekeeping is assiduously performed at every level by those endowed with a major order. At parish level, the person who decides what information is transmitted to the parish, what biblical interpretation and message to preach, and who is to minister what and for whom, is the priest. In the diocese, the bishop holds the reins over all church activity, finance, and personnel. Above them all are the Vatican officials and heads of departments, led or guided by cardinals—who, before 1917, included lay men in their number. Now every role of authority and leadership is occupied by a celibate man.

Of course, there are exceptions, Catholic married priests who were once Anglican, and permanent deacons. Still, the rule holds well—as complaints by those in the latter group about the limits put on them by their priests, demonstrate. Pope Francis is making occasional appointments of women within Vatican offices, women who tend to be vowed religious and with exceptional expertise. This is a commendable effort on his part, confronted as he is by vociferous conservatives objecting to his every move and insulting him in unprecedented ways in the media and elsewhere.

But it does not tilt the boat. She continues to sail onward—toward the precipice.

If change does not come, if, like any living organism, it does not adapt, the church faces extinction. It may not disappear entirely, but could exist in the future simply as a hard-core remnant of traditionally minded members of an exclusive cult. It is haemorrhaging women and young people in the West and in Latin America, and appeals mainly now to those who identify with clear-cut, black and white, absolutist values. In other words, in a troubled world it offers hard, definitive answers that comfort the insecure but not those who look for the compassionate, non-discriminating approach of the Jesus of the Gospels. It is driving away just those very women who could, were they given the chance, lead the church into being the solution, rather than the problem.

After all, the major change called for is the church's whole approach to women. The two main reasons for holding back in women's ordination, into the diaconate or the priesthood, are, first, the historic assertion that

Jesus chose only men to be apostles and their successors—bishops and, eventually, priests. Of course, in a first-century Roman outpost, only men would have had any autonomy or authority. Yet this overlooks the numerous examples of women, from Mary of Magdala to Phoebe and many others, who despite the restrictions on them were acknowledged as agents of the Christian gospel. The ancient female diaconate has been well attested, and we await the present papal commission's findings and authorization of women deacons in the near future. The fact that the first apostles were all circumcised Jews has not stopped the church from expanding the ethnic field from which they have been since recruited.

The second claim is the symbolic resemblance of the priest to Christ, specifically Jesus at the last supper, so that the male Jesus is ministering to the female *ecclesia*. In other words, a man looks like Jesus in his maleness. As if that matters! What matters, surely, is that God incarnated as a human is represented by a human. Had Christ been a woman, nobody would have heard a word about her. But the role of Jesus is not a sexual one, tradition insisting that he did not have a sex life, so the sex or gender of Jesus is irrelevant. The church's being "female" is also an irrelevant metaphor unless one adheres to the outdated notion that a woman must be led by a man, as the church is by Christ. But does anyone seriously think that such a figure of speech should determine policy?

Separating clergy from laity by stating that they differ "essentially and not in degree" (*Lumen Gentium* n.10) encourages the very clericalism, the pedestal-building elevation of the male clergy, that has proved so fateful in both infantilizing the laity and, in the clergy, making room for the abuse scandals that have rocked the church. The arrogance of a late foremost cardinal who said that in respect to ordaining women we "may as well try to ordain a potato" is breath-taking. The sheer misogyny among many of the clergy can only be countered by continued informed discussion, undeterred by the threat of excommunication of anyone broaching the subject. Do the training and culture of the male priests lead to the misogyny, or do the misogynists, many of whom are closet or openly gay, find retreating into priesthood a form of escape from, perhaps, peer and family pressure to "get married."

The argument against change does not hold up. The church has adapted to society from the earliest days, namely by taking on Roman civic vestments for liturgical use, organizing itself on medieval feudal court structure, and embracing the twentieth-century liturgical reforms. In many other ways too, the church has changed its opinions and practices: slavery, once condoned (see the papal permission in *Dum diversas* of 1452 of Portuguese enslavement of captured Saracens and pagans) then condemned; capital punishment deemed "inadmissible" in every situation only in 2018; apologies in 1992 to Galileo Galilei for his treatment at the hands of ignorant churchmen; celibacy for clergy only enforced in the twelfth century; the burning of witches and heretics no longer acceptable; previous support for, now condemnation of, antisemitism, and even within one century, the *volte face* in canon law between the 1917 and 1983 editions whereby illegitimacy, which once debarred a candidate from priesthood, now is no obstacle.

So, the last great change required of the church is to listen to half its population. Really listen. Listen and act. Not token gestures, not just niceness and friendliness. We have had those for decades. What is needed is a wholescale overhaul of the structures of the church to make it more accountable and more relevant. If it means opening up the ordained ministries to women, so be it. If it means letting women's scholarship and experience be heard from pulpits, so be it. If it means absolution can be channelled through women, especially spiritual directors, so be it. If it means changing approaches to fertility and reproduction (which affects women in ways it cannot the celibate clergy), so be it. Whatever is the *sensus fidelium*, discerned not just by synodal bishops but also by the whole church, let that be the source of change, trusting that the Holy Spirit is there in the collective voice of all members of the church.

Closed minds, resistant to reason and to change, and hearts closed to empathy with the victims of power and control unfairly used, are dangerous. Not only do they harm others, they also harm the institution they claim to love and support. The Catholic Church, an effective if not consistent means of transmission of the Gospel of love for two millennia, is in peril of becoming irrelevant and ultimately discarded by the society, the human beings, it exists to serve.

Now retired, Dr. Deborah M. Jones has been a lecturer, editor of a religious newspaper, and a member of the Bishops' Conference Committees for Ministerial Formation and Theology.

www.deborahmjones.co.uk

Introduction

We often hear Roman Catholic clerics talking about women. They talk about what should be done for women or what should not be done for women; what ministries should be open to women or what ministries should not be open to women. In all these conversations women are discussed as if they are a pressure group that should be given a little bit more attention. They are actually half of the human race but are allowed no role in the decision-making process of the Catholic Church and no part in the defining of faith and morals. What kind of religion sweeps aside half of the human race as irrelevant? What kind of religion allows only men to make decisions about women? Is this the religion of the historical Jesus?

Of course, many clerics will deny that they sweep women aside and, in some cases, this is actually true. There are some clerics who genuinely try to not sweep women aside and to treat them as equals. However, there are many others who try to justify and uphold a model of the church that is blatantly discriminatory. *We don't sweep you aside,* they say. *We value and respect your femininity. It is just that your vocations are different to ours.*

Yes, very different. Have you noticed how it is always women who are cleaning and decorating the church, making the teas, and acting as parish secretaries? Many clergy say that they value a woman's femininity, but how do they see that femininity, exactly? Are the attributes of femininity purely those of a domestic servant? And even if our femininity were to be valued, what about our intellect? The Catholic Church has thirty-six doctors of the church but only four of them are women. Catholic women today are also stereotyped by the church in a very different way to men, and this often comes through in the way that the female consecrated life is pictured. For example, generally speaking, consecrated women today are still expected to live in groups in convents. There are some exceptions, such as the restored vocation of consecrated virgin and the fairly new vocation of membership to a secular institute, but there has been a resistance to promoting these vocations by some bishops because it is still believed by many clerics that women are better off herded together in a convent. Women are thought to need each other's company in order to survive the consecrated life. The Catholic Church of today doesn't seem to like the idea of independent consecrated women very much. However, when it comes to the male priesthood the perceptions are very different. The male diocesan priest is expected to live independently in his own home. He doesn't need to live with anyone. He is a man and well able to look after himself. It seems he can also be trusted to keep his vows while living alone but perhaps a woman can't be trusted. Of course, in reality, many priests have not kept their vows.

I've heard some priests say that they "believe in" women priests. *Women will be admitted to the priesthood one day,* they say—*it's just that now is not the right time.* I've also heard priests preach about the great female mystics and state how much they value the intellect and spiritual contributions of women. But what happens if an intelligent woman joins their parish? Do they value women then? It has been the experience of many intelligent women that some priests feel uncomfortable having intelligent women in their parishes. They do not really know how to deal with the female theologian, the female head teacher, or the female writer. They prefer the female cook or the female cleaner. In Catholic parishes it can often be the female teacher, writer, or theologian that is the subject of victimization. Actually, the Catholic clergy has no understanding of women at all because none of its members are women. Just think about the number of deacons, priests, bishops, archbishops, and cardinals there are right now across the world. Apparently, there are around 200 cardinals, 5,600 archbishops and bishops (known as the College of Bishops), 414,400 priests, and 48,300 deacons in the world today, but none of them are women. Interestingly, there are actually more consecrated women in the world than there are cardinals, bishops, priests, and deacons put together, but the consecrated women of course have no real influence as they do not vote at synods and councils of the church. All those who vote at synods and councils of the church are cardinals and bishops, and, since the ninth century, there haven't been any women voting among them, although, at the time of writing, Pope Francis has promised a small number of women will vote at the forthcoming Synod on Synodality. Synods and councils determine the church's teaching authority, but for hundreds of years no one who has sat on these councils has known what it is like to be a woman. They haven't known what it feels like to live and think as a woman, and yet they have seemingly issued statements on faith and morals that appertain to women. That can't be right, can it?

In the New Testament accounts of Jesus, we read of his care and concern for women. Jesus valued women and gave them the same respect that he gave to men. In many ways he was actually very radical in his treatment of women. For example, in New Testament times a woman would be stoned for committing adultery, but the same sentence would not be given to a man who had done the same. In John 8 (1–11), Jesus seems to challenge this. A woman has been caught in adultery, and the Pharisees bring her to him. They say that in the Jewish law it states that such a woman should be stoned, and they ask Jesus what he thinks about this. Jesus states, "Let the one who is guiltless be the first to throw a stone at her," and all her accusers walk away one by one. It is interesting that Jesus deals with the woman like this, because of course there would have been a man who had committed adultery with her. Jesus is pointing out that men commit this same sin, as well as other sins, and so they have no right to point a finger at this woman.

On other occasions in the Gospel of John, Jesus is criticized for the way he treats women by his own disciples. For example, in John 4:1–42, Jesus has a long discourse with a Samaritan woman but when the disciples find him talking to her, they are surprised and ask him what he wants with her. Later (Matthew 26:6–13; Mark 14:3–9; John 12:2–9), Mary anoints either the feet or the head of Jesus (there is a difference in the Gospel accounts) with a costly ointment. The disciples challenge Jesus on this, stating the ointment could have been sold and the money given to the poor, but Jesus tells them to "leave her alone," as she has prepared him for his death. This story is interesting because Jesus is well able to identify with the feelings of the woman in making such an extravagant gesture. Actually, this gesture does seem to be a more feminine one. It is quite difficult to imagine a man carrying out a similar gesture. Jesus seems to understand the way women think and feel and to enjoy their company. There is another element to this story as well. It was common Jewish practice to anoint both priests and kings and also to anoint bodies before burial. Mary seems to be recognizing Jesus as both a priest and a king and one who will ultimately go to his death. The male disciples who are present at this event do not have this insight.

After the resurrection, the first person to whom Jesus appeared was a woman, St. Mary Magdalene, and it was she who was instructed to tell the disciples that he had risen. Sadly, today, the church has not given this fact the attention it deserves, just as it has also conveniently forgotten the words of St. Paul in his letter to the Galatians (3:26) where he states, "There can be neither Jew nor Greek, there can be neither slave nor freeman, there can be neither male nor female for you are all one in Christ Jesus." Well, in the twenty-first century church there are certainly male and female, the males being the ones who are allowed to have the ministries of deacons, priests, and bishops or to be honored with the title of cardinal, and the females being the rest. But did Christianity begin like this? I shall argue both from scripture and other sources that it did not.

In my first book, *Look Back to the Future: Consecrated Women in Britain 597 AD to Date*, I demonstrated how women in the pre-Reformation Church of Britain held much more influential roles in that church than women do in the Catholic Church of today. In particular, during the Anglo-Saxon period, female religious were established in double houses of men and women, which were almost always presided over by a woman. These women, who were known as abbesses, received the same education as monks and went on to be teachers and theologians. They also voted at synods. For example, St. Hilda both hosted and voted at the Synod of Whitby. This synod was of national importance in England because it sought to resolve a conflict between the Celtic and the Roman churches as to when Easter should be celebrated. However, St. Hilda, a woman, was a pivotal figure at the synod. There were also other Anglo-Saxon women who voted at church synods, such as Aelffled, who was a key figure at the Synod of Nidd. The influence of women began to wane in the European church, but even so women were still far more influential in the pre-Reformation church than they are today. For example, the Italian St. Catherine of Siena carried out a long correspondence with both Pope Gregory XI and his successor, Pope Urban VI, and could actually be described as giving them both spiritual counsel. The English mystic Julian of Norwich was also renowned for the wise counsel she gave to eminent people within her own country.

Within this work I will be looking at the waning of female influence within Catholicism not only in Britain but also in the rest of the world. I will examine female influence within the church from New Testament times to date more widely, and I will demonstrate how women, who were certainly authoritative in the early church, were slowly and gradually eliminated from all influential positions during the course of history. This elimination of women achieved its height at the time of the Reformation; and while other Christian traditions such as the Anglican one have now rectified this, the Catholic Church has yet to do the same. It had been hoped, of course, that Vatican II would bring about a change that would enable women to be more involved in the decision-making processes of the church, but sadly this has never happened. Women are not even ordained as deacons within the Roman Catholic Church despite the fact that there is indisputable evidence that women were ordained as deacons in the early church. Due to this evidence, the Orthodox Church began to restore the female diaconate in 2017, but the Catholic Church has not done the same and remains entrenched in a position that goes against all the evidence.

I perceive the elimination of women from positions of influence within the Catholic Church to be both spiritual and political power abuse. I will therefore define spiritual and political power abuse before demonstrating how the use of both has, throughout history, not only caused direct discrimination against women but has also slowly and gradually eliminated the influence of women within the church. I will then look at the current hierarchy of the church and demonstrate how this model differs from earlier models. Catholic bishops today have much more power and much greater influence than they did in earlier centuries, and this is alarming because power can be dangerous. I believe that the current hierarchical model of the church is abusive and therefore all women in the world today are, in a general sense, victims of spiritual abuse by their exclusion from the decision-making processes of the church. Following on from this I will then look more specifically at the spiritual and political power abuse of women within the structure of the Catholic Church today. I will examine the consecrated vocations that are currently open to women and will illustrate how it is possible for women to be victims of spiritual and political power abuse within these vocations. I will also examine the vocations that are not open to women and illustrate how denying women access to these vocations is both spiritual and political power abuse. I will then look at the current synodal process. Will it achieve anything? Is it flawed?

There are some very disturbing misogynistic trends within the Catholic Church of today, but can these be eradicated? I believe that these trends are symptomatic of a much more ingrained misogynistic culture, and it will be difficult to eradicate misogynism without a complete overhaul of the church and the way it perceives its own history.

Lastly, there is a sense in which many women can be unaware of the abuse that they can encounter within the church today because they themselves have never directly experienced it. I will look at some modern women who have experienced spiritual abuse and I will examine the effects this abuse has had on their lives.

Finally, I myself have also been a victim of spiritual abuse for reasons I have never actually been able to fathom. I was seriously ill at the time and had certainly done nothing to warrant the treatment I received. This experience has completely changed my life and my view of the church because I was treated in an unjust manner by a prelate of the church. Of course, all of us have had some bad experiences in our lives, and he was not the first person to treat me badly. However, this experience was different from other bad experiences of mine because it appeared to be deliberate on the part of the prelate and I also felt that it was completely undeserved. With other bad experiences I may have had in my life there was at least a sense in which the person may not have fully understood what they were doing to me, or a sense in which I was also to blame through my own actions. On this occasion I felt that neither applied. I was treated unjustly by a prelate who was not subject to any accountability and therefore believed that he could treat me as less than human for reasons known only to himself. I will examine this experience toward the end of this work, and I will also detail how I overcame it.

The conclusion of this book looks at the possible actions that are necessary to bring about reform in the Catholic Church and whether laypeople can do anything to bring about these actions. The Catholic story is not just a negative story. The Catholic Church has, during the course of history, also made some great contributions to civilization. The problem is that it is currently losing all credibility. This is due to its increasingly desperate attempts to keep power and influence in the hands of celibate men. Modern society won't buy this anymore. Our understanding of women and of celibacy has developed and evolved. As numbers of church attendees in the West decline, the hierarchy bury their heads in the sand, stating that the church will never end because it was instituted by God. An initial version of the church may have been instituted by God; but God will not condone corruption and elitism. Perhaps the hierarchy should see the demands for change as the call of the Holy Spirit.

This book is not intended to be an anti-Catholic book as, although my most recent experience of the church has been negative, there is also a part of me that still remains both Catholic and indebted to the church. This is due to the influence that many good Catholic people have had on my life. However, the Catholic Church of today cannot survive without reform, and therefore this book is necessary. The church must reform or die because patriarchy itself has already died.

I converted to Catholicism in the wake of the Second Vatican Council, and the church had a very positive influence on my life for thirty-nine years. It was my rock and gave me stability, education, and a good Catholic husband. Sadly, an incident that occurred nearly four years ago led me to encounter a side of the church that I had never seen before—its dark side. One cruel or unthinking action by a member of the clergy has the potential to seriously damage a person's life, and I only survived due to my own inner faith and strength and also the love and care of friends. Within this book I will be stressing the need for the church to make bishops accountable for their actions. There are currently no official procedures in place in any diocese for someone to make a complaint against a bishop unless that complaint is one of sexual abuse. The only way to complain is to write to the Pope himself or to one of his ambassadors, a process that could take years. This lack of accountability enables some bishops to act like authoritarian despots within their own dioceses and to treat people as dispensable. Sexual abuse has been a great scandal within the church and is now being addressed, but other issues of power and spiritual abuse are not being addressed. While there are of course some good bishops within the church, there are also those who do not act justly and fairly or who make mistakes. The lack of accountability of these bishops is a cancer that is eating away at and destroying the soul of modern Catholicism.

CHAPTER ONE

Definitions of Spiritual and Political Power Abuse

The existence of the abuse of power has been acknowledged across the world for centuries, and here, within the United Kingdom and Ireland, we will all be aware of various examples. However, often when power abuse is a factor in any given situation, it will be noted that this form of abuse is not the only one that is occurring in that situation. Usually, this form of abuse will occur alongside other forms, such as physical, sexual, or emotional abuse and, more recently, a newly defined form of abuse that we term spiritual abuse.

There are several definitions of "power abuse." One of the best ones is found in Black's *Law Dictionary* (2nd edition):

> A misuse of power by someone in a position of authority who can use the leverage they have to oppress persons in an inferior position or to induce them to commit a wrongful act.

Another definition of "power abuse" is found in *West's Encyclopedia of American Law* (2nd edition):

> Improper use of power by someone who has that authority because he or she holds a public office.

Now, in both of these definitions of power abuse we have an example of one person in authority oppressing another person or persons, or inducing another person or persons to commit a wrongful act. But an abuse of power can go far beyond one authoritarian or corrupt individual using his/her power to oppress or mistreat another person or people. Abuse of power can also be organizational, institutional, and political. Institutional or organizational abuse is the maltreatment of a person or people through a system of power. This form of abuse occurs when an organization or institution adopts widespread policies that are contrary to human rights. Human rights are moral principles for certain standards of behavior that are protected in international law. They are understood to be inalienable rights to which a person is inherently entitled simply because he or she is a human being. They are universal and egalitarian in the sense of being the same for everyone. These rights include the right to life; the right to be equal with others before the law; the right to a fair trial; the right to privacy; the right to freedom of movement; the right to seek a safe place to live; the right to a nationality; the right to marriage and family; the right to own possessions; the right to freedom of thought; the right to public assembly; the right to democracy; the right to food and shelter; the right to education; the right to be recognized as an individual born free and equal to other individuals; and the right to a fair and free world.

An example of an organizational and political abuse of power that violated these human rights would be the events of the Holocaust during World War II. Under the Nazi regime, policies were legalized that isolated the Jews from civil society. Early policies led to the boycotting of Jewish businesses, but as time passed more and more inhuman policies were legalized, which eventually resulted in the policy of extermination of the Jews, known as the Final Solution to the Jewish Question.

Organizational abuse can be prevented by policies that seek to outlaw it but, as can be seen from the preceding example above, problems arise when policies actually enshrine the abuse. Problems also occur when there are no policies at all to counter the abuse because it is assumed that the abuse cannot occur. This is the case with the church today in regards to bishops. The bishop who is head of a diocese is not a delegate of the Pope. Instead, he has of himself primary teaching, governance, and sanctifying responsibility for the diocese for which he has been assigned bishop. There are no procedures in place to make complaints against bishops other than safeguarding procedures for sexual abuse. However, these procedures are relatively recent and only came into being because in the past bishops had been able to cover up sexual abuse due to the fact that no complaints could be brought against them. Today, complaints can be brought against them for sexual abuse (or for covering up sexual abuse), but it is not possible to complain about a bishop for any other matter. As bishops have failings like everyone else, this enables bishops to carry out spiritual and political power abuse.

The concept of spiritual abuse is a relatively recent one, and there has been some debate as to whether spiritual abuse is a separate category of abuse distinct from other forms of psychological or emotional abuse or whether it should be incorporated into the category of psychological and emotional abuse. Lisa Oakley, in her article "Understanding Spiritual Abuse," has argued that spiritual abuse should be incorporated into the category of emotional and psychological abuse and defines "spiritual abuse" as follows:

> Spiritual abuse is a form of emotional and psychological abuse. It is characterised by a systematic pattern of coercive and controlling behaviour in a religious context. Spiritual abuse can have a deeply damaging impact on those who experience it.
>
> This abuse may include: manipulation and exploitation, enforced accountability, censorship of decision-making, the requirement of secrecy and silence, coercion to conform, control through the use of sacred texts or teaching, the requirement of obedience to the abuser, the suggestion that the abuser has a "divine" position, isolation as a means of punishment, and superiority and elitism.

David Johnson and Jeff Van Vonderen, authors of *The Subtle Power of Spiritual Abuse*, explain the term this way:

> It's possible to become so determined to defend a spiritual place of authority, a doctrine or a way of doing things that you wound and abuse anyone who questions, or disagrees, or doesn't "behave" spiritually the way you want them to. When your words and actions tear down another, or attack or weaken a person's standing as a Christian—to gratify you, your position or your beliefs while at the same time weakening or harming another—that is spiritual abuse.

This work concentrates mainly on power abuse and spiritual abuse because these seem to be the two forms of abuse within the Catholic Church that are rampant at the moment and that are not being addressed. However, it is important to point out that it is very rare to find one stand-alone form of abuse taking place within any given situation. In any situation there are normally several forms of abuse taking place at the same time, and this is clearly seen in Brian Devlin's book, *Cardinal Sin*.

Within his book, Devlin describes how he was groomed as a naïve and vulnerable seminarian by his spiritual director, Keith O'Brien, at the seminary where he was training to be a priest. This spiritual director would later become a cardinal of the Catholic Church. Brian Devlin looked up to Keith O'Brien, and O'Brien took advantage of this by slowly grooming him for a sexual relationship. This started with inappropriate "hugs" and eventually resulted in O'Brien's sexually assaulting Devlin one night after dinner. Devlin refused O'Brien's advances. Already there are three forms of abuse here. Firstly, there is sexual abuse, but there is also both spiritual and power abuse. O'Brien has taken advantage of his position of spiritual director to groom Devlin, and he has also abused his power over Devlin by trying to coerce him to commit a wrongful act. Any sexual act is wrong here because both men have taken vows of celibacy and are going against the rules of their organization. So, sexual, spiritual, and power abuse are all seen in this scenario, but it doesn't end there. There is also institutional and organizational abuse in Devlin's account of events. He initially feels unable to report the abuse because he thinks that no one will believe him. Later he leaves the priesthood because he is asked to work for O'Brien and cannot stomach working for his former abuser. The fact that Devlin felt forced to leave the priesthood illustrates the tremendous damage that any form of abuse can do. Devlin had trained to be a priest and had no other qualifications to enable him to take up any other form of employment. He also had no formal qualification in theology despite studying the subject for six years. This was because the seminary did not issue any formal certificate to its students. So, Devlin was forced to leave with nothing, retrain, and rebuild his life. Years later, Devlin discovered that other seminarians had been abused by O'Brien, and he teamed up with three other victims to try to bring O'Brien to account within the church, but they were obstructed both by the Catholic Church within Scotland and by Rome. Eventually, they saw no option but to go to the press due to a lack of policies and procedures within the Catholic Church to enable them to bring O'Brien to account.

What is particularly sad about Devlin's situation is that it is apparent even now that the church has no real time for him. True, O'Brien was made to resign and vanished from public life, but no one in the church has ever really acknowledged the harm that the abuse did to Brian Devlin and his fellow whistleblowers. No one has ever fully apologized to Devlin or sought to make amends for the harm done to him. There is a sense in which he is treated as a betrayer of the church because he dared to expose its wrongdoing. He states that the Pope has never contacted him. All of this illustrates that the Catholic Church is still very far from being a transparent organization that is willing to learn from its past mistakes. Yes, there are now policies and procedures in that which seek to prevent sexual abuse, but spiritual and political power abuse continue, and the main victims of that are, of course, usually women.

CHAPTER TWO

The Erosion of Female Influence in the Early Christian Church

This chapter will examine how the influence of women within the early Christian church was progressively eliminated in the early centuries. It will be argued from the New Testament accounts that Jesus treated women equally and indeed chose a woman who had followed him throughout his ministry, St. Mary Magdalene, to be the first witness to the resurrection. Scholars agree that by the time Luke wrote his Gospel, he was already making minor changes to the narrative in Mark's Gospel, as well as other changes to the various accounts of the resurrection. Some of these changes already began to undermine women. The Gospel of Mary Magdalene will also be examined. This Gospel demonstrates that a church had developed and grown around the persona or teaching of Mary even if she, herself, did not actually write or dictate this Gospel. The Gospel of Mary was almost certainly suppressed by the early church fathers. I will also demonstrate through references to the New Testament and through references to the early church fathers and others that there can be no doubt whatsoever that there was an order of female deacons within the early church. There is also strong evidence from the writings of the early church fathers that women were being ordained in early Christendom and that it was these fathers who suppressed these ordinations. I will argue that, in doing so, these fathers were moving further and further away from the original church that had been created by Jesus.

From the Gospels of the New Testament, it can be devised that many women followed Jesus through towns and villages where he preached the "Good News of the Kingdom of God." Luke is quite clear (Luke 8:2–3) that Jesus made his way through towns and villages not only with the twelve but also with certain women including Mary Magdalene, Joanna, Susanna, and others. In fact, Luke's Gospel contains some information and accounts of women and Jesus's dealing with women that is different to the other Gospels, which is interesting of itself as it would suggest that already, at the time of the writing of this Gospel, some differences were beginning to emerge in regards to the importance of women within Christianity. However, even so, all the accounts of Jesus's dealing with women in all of the Gospels are positive and nondiscriminatory. Most of the narratives are details of actual events that occurred during Jesus's ministry, and there are also details of the women who accompanied Jesus right up until his death on the cross and who later witnessed the resurrection.

In regards to the narratives of events during Jesus's ministry, some of these detail Jesus healing either a woman herself or the offspring of a woman, and in these incidents there is often a strong correlation between healing and faith. For example, Jesus tells the woman with a hemorrhage, "Courage, my daughter, your faith has saved you" (Matthew 9:22); and when he heals the daughter of the Canaanite woman, he says, "Woman, you have great faith. Let your desire be granted" (Matthew 15:28).

There are also details of Jesus's encounters with widows, and with these women Jesus is both empathetic and radical. Luke tells us that Jesus felt sorry for the widow at Nain who had lost her only son, and this appears to be his primary reason for restoring the dead man to life (Luke 7:11–17). However, in the accounts of the Widow's Mite (Mark 12:41–44; Luke 21:1–4), a radical Jesus is encountered. This Jesus is described as sitting opposite the treasury watching the people put money into it. Many of the rich put in a great deal of money, but then a poor widow came along and put in only two small coins that are the equivalent of a penny. Jesus tells his disciples that she has given more than anyone else because others gave only what they could spare but this woman gave everything she had. Thus, Jesus elevates the poor but sincere widow above the rich and the powerful, which would have been a very radical thing to do in his day. Other narratives that detail both Jesus's empathy with women and his radical approach to them include his encounter with the Samaritan woman (John 4:1–42) and the anointing at Bethany (Mark 14:3–9; John 12:1–11; Matthew 26:6–13).

Jesus's encounter with the Samaritan woman is particularly radical because during New Testament times the Jews and Samaritans were enemies from different cultures and did not interact with each other. In addition to this, the Samaritan woman with whom Jesus interacts is not only a woman but also a sinner. Jesus is aware that she has had five husbands. However, despite her dubious status of being both a sinful woman and a Samaritan, Jesus is happy to have a long conversation with her. Such an interaction simply did not occur in Jewish society, and when the disciples return, they challenge Jesus about it, saying, "What do you want with her?" Jesus has shown by his interaction with this woman that he values sinners, foreigners outside of his own race, and women. This event is of course a forerunner of the ultimate good news of the Gospel—that salvation is not just for the Jewish people but for all people.

There are three different accounts of the anointing at Bethany (Matthew 26:6–13; Mark 14:3–9; John 12:2–9), which differ slightly, but the theme is the same. A woman, whom John alone identifies as Mary, pours some very costly perfume over Jesus while he reclines at a table. Matthew and Mark state that the oil is poured over his head, while John states that it is poured over his feet. The reaction in all three Gospels is the same. Some of the disciples are indignant, stating that the perfume could have been sold and given to the poor. However, Jesus defends the actions of the woman, stating that she has done him a good deed as the poor will always be with them but they will not always have him. Jesus not only understands the woman's extravagant gesture as a loving one but also sees it as symbolic. Expensive perfumes were used by the Jews for anointing priests and kings and also for anointing the dead for burial. In these three accounts the woman is therefore demonstrating an insight into Jesus's identity and purpose. She sees him as a priest and king who will ultimately die. This is interesting because this anointing at Bethany precedes Jesus's passion and resurrection and shows this woman to have a better insight into Jesus's person and mission than the disciples. They do not understand the significance of the anointing.

Later, during the passion, it is the women followers of Jesus who are depicted in the Gospels as being the most loyal. They would also have been the bravest of his disciples. They follow Jesus to the cross and stand near him as he is crucified while the male disciples run away. Mark identifies these women as Mary of Magdala; Mary, the mother of James the Younger and Joset; (Mary) Salome; and many others. He tells the reader that these women had followed Jesus when he was in Galilee (Mark 15:40–41). Matthew identifies the women as Mary Magdala; Mary, the mother of James and Joseph; and the mother of Zebedee's sons (Matthew 27:55–56). John identifies the women as Jesus's mother; his mother's sister, Mary the wife of Clopas; and Mary of Magdala (John 19:25–27). So, the Gospels state quite clearly that during Jesus's passion the female disciples never left him, while the male disciples were nowhere to be seen.

Following on from the death of Jesus, one of the main reasons why the narratives of the resurrection ring as true and authentic is the fact that all the Gospels have Mary of Magdala as being the first witness to the resurrection. There are some slight variations in the different Gospel accounts, but all have the same central features. Matthew has Mary of Magdala and "the other Mary" going to visit the sepulcher and encountering an Angel of the Lord who tells them that Jesus is risen and that they should run and tell the disciples. As they run off to inform the disciples, they encounter the risen Lord, who tells them that they should tell his brothers they must leave for Galilee, where they will see him (Matthew 28:1–10). Mark has Mary of Magdala; Mary, the mother of James; and Salome going to the sepulcher and encountering a young man in a white robe. He tells them that Jesus is risen and that they must go and tell the disciples that Jesus is going ahead of them to Galilee and they will see him there. Initially, they run away, as they are frightened, but Jesus then appears to Mary of Magdala (Mark 16:1–11). Luke has Mary of Magdala, Joanna, and Mary, the mother of James, going to the tomb and encountering two men in brilliant clothes, who advise them that Jesus is risen. In this account the women do not encounter the risen Lord but are the first to hear that he is risen from the two mysterious men. (Luke 24:1–11). John has Mary of Magdala going to visit the tomb and finding it empty. She runs to tell Peter and "the disciple that Jesus loved" that the tomb is empty. The disciples visit the empty tomb and go home, but Mary stands outside the tomb weeping. Then she sees two angels sitting where the body had been who ask her why she is weeping. On turning around, she also sees Jesus, whom she does not immediately recognize until he says her name. Mary is then instructed to find the brothers and tell them that Jesus is ascending to the Father (John 20:1–18).

While all Gospel narratives differ in various details, Mary of Magdala is always the first person to hear of or witness the risen Lord, and the reason why this makes the Gospel accounts seem authentic is because, of course, Mary was a woman. Had the Gospels been a work of pure fiction or greatly embellished stories of a man who had simply lived and been crucified, it is reasonable to assume that one of the central figures in this story would not have been a woman. Women were second-class citizens at the time of Jesus and were not regarded as reliable witnesses. Therefore, making a woman the first witness of the resurrection would have only served to make the story less likely to be believed. A fabricator would surely have made a man the first witness of the resurrection. However, all the Gospels are insistent that Mary of Magdala was the first to either witness or hear of the resurrection, and this gives credence to the fact that there were some remarkable events occurring at this time that were first witnessed by a woman. So, Jesus chose a woman, not a man, to be the first witness of his rising from the dead. What does this mean theologically? Sadly, there has never been a great deal of reflection in the church of today on this question. It has been suggested that Mary was the first apostle, but the church has always sought to avoid any scholarship around this proposition, preferring to proclaim that only the male disciples and St. Paul were apostles. Recently, however, Pope Francis did raise the level of Mary's liturgical memory from that of a memorial to that of a feast, stating that she should be referred to as the "Apostle of the apostles."

While the Gospel accounts of the resurrection give the story of Jesus rising from the dead some credence, due to the primary first witness, being a woman, there is already at this early stage some evidence of the story being changed. This can be seen in Luke's account of the resurrection.

Most scholars agree that the Gospel of Luke was written after the Gospels of Mark and Matthew and that its primary source was the Gospel of Mark itself along with other sources, such as a sayings collection known as Q and material not found in other Gospels, which is often referred to as the L source. Scholars are also in agreement that Luke eliminated from his narrative anything that reflected poorly on the male disciples. For example, he omits the sentence in Mark about the parable of the sower where Jesus asks the disciples if they understand the parable: "Do you understand this parable? Then how will you understand any of the parables?" Presumably this is omitted because it is not seen to put the disciples in good light. He also omits Peter's rebuking Jesus (Mark 8:32) in regards to the prophecy about the passion, and he omits the sentence in Mark stating that all of the disciples deserted Jesus at the time of his arrest (Mark 14:50). Bearing in mind these and other details that Luke has omitted from his Gospel, there is a strong case for arguing that Luke deliberately omitted from his account the details of Mary Magdalene's encounter with the risen Lord.

Luke's Gospel is the only Gospel to state that although Mary Magdalene was the first person to be told that Jesus was risen, she was not the first person to witness the risen Lord. This account does not ring true. Why would an angel appear to Mary first to tell her Jesus was risen if she was not to be the first witness of the resurrection? Luke's account of the resurrection is therefore probably one of the first examples of something being eliminated from Christian history in order to put men in a better light than women. Mary Magdalene's witness of the resurrection was deleted. Now it is generally agreed that Luke used Mark's Gospel when writing this account of the resurrection and the manuscripts of the Gospel of Mark have a number of different endings. Some do not mention the resurrection appearances at all. However, those that do state that Mary Magdalene was the first witness of the resurrection, and, that Luke has changed this. But this was just the beginning. There is now strong evidence that there existed in the early church an early Christian community that grew up either around Mary Magdalene or around the teaching of Mary Magdalene and that this community was suppressed.

In January 1896, one Carl Reinhardt purchased the Berlin Gnostic Codex. This important and well-preserved Codex had been discovered somewhere near Akhmim in upper Egypt. It contained Coptic translations of three very important early Christian Gnostic texts, and one of these was the Gospel of Mary. This Gospel had been lost for over fifteen hundred years, and the copy that Reinhardt purchased was not the complete Gospel but only half of it. It was missing pages 1–6 and 11–14 and, as no other copies of the complete Gospel are in existence, the Gospel in its entirety is probably lost forever. This particular Codex dates back to the fifth century, but since then two Greek fragments of the same Gospel have been discovered that date back to the third century. Karen King, author of *The Gospel of Mary of Magdala: Jesus and the First Woman Apostle*, states that it is unusual for several copies from such early dates to have survived, and therefore the attestation that the Gospel of Mary is an early Christian work is unusually strong. Most early Christian literature has survived because it was copied and then recopied as the materials on which they were written wore out. It is quite remarkable that three parts of different copies of this early Gospel have survived; but there are no known copies of this Gospel after the fifth century, which would suggest that it may have been suppressed.

There has been some debate as to which of the New Testament women named Mary is the central character of the Gospel of Mary. Some scholars have suggested that the central character may have been Mary, the mother of Jesus, or a sister of Jesus who has been lost in history. However, the main consensus of scholarly opinion is that the central character of this Gospel is Mary Magdalene. This is due to the fact that Mary Magdalene was known to be a follower of Jesus who accompanied him on his journeys and was present at the crucifixion. More important, she was the first witness of the resurrection.

It is not known whether the original Gospel of Mary was dictated by Mary herself or was initially written after her death by a community that had either grown up around her or had grown up around her teachings. The date that the Gospel was written is also unknown. The earliest fragments in existence are the two Greek fragments, which date back to the early third century, but that does not mean that there were not earlier copies of the Gospel written in the late first or second century. Christianity in its early stages was made up of a variety of communities around the eastern Mediterranean that were often isolated from each other. It is highly unlikely that all these communities possessed the same documents. What is more likely is that different church traditions grew up around different groups and individuals, some of which may have possessed some of the same texts. These church traditions sometimes had very different perspectives on essential elements of Christian belief and practice.

In regards to the Christian perspective of the Gospel of Mary, this is a Gnostic Gospel that emphasizes Jesus's teachings as a route to personal spiritual knowledge. It does not particularly stress Jesus's suffering and death as a route to eternal life but instead offers a utopian vision of spiritual perfection that Jesus has given to Mary through a vision. It is this different version of the Gospel that Mary would wish to be preached, but the disciples are presented as being afraid to preach the "Gospel of the Kingdom of the Son of Man" due to fear of receiving the same fate as Jesus. Mary encourages them not to be irresolute. Of particular interest in this Gospel is the fact that Peter is presented as saying, "Did he really speak privately with a woman and not openly to us? Are we to turn about and all listen to her? Did he prefer her to us?" It is not particularly surprising that Peter should speak in this way, as it has already been noted that there are occasions in the canonical Gospels when the disciples question Jesus's dealings with women, such as when he has a long discourse with the Samaritan woman. However, in this Gospel Levi defends Mary, stating that the savior had known Mary very well and had loved her more than the disciples. Before he defends Mary, though, he states that Peter is "contending against the woman like the adversaries." This statement makes it very clear that even if this Gospel was written after Mary's death, it was well known that there were already people in her lifetime who were not happy with her status and teaching. In this Gospel, Mary is presented as both a visionary and a mystic, and there is no suggestion whatsoever that she was a prostitute. There is, of course, also no suggestion that Mary was a prostitute in the New Testament. However, this idea does seem to have been suggested at some time in Christian history, with some scholars suggesting that she may have been the woman caught in adultery in John's Gospel. There was never any evidence for this whatsoever, as the woman caught in adultery is not named. The presentation of Mary in this Gospel as a Gnostic woman with a distrust of the flesh strengthens the case against her ever having been a prostitute, and one cannot help but wonder if this idea about her may have been put around in the early church to undermine her credibility.

Christian Gnosticism is known to have flourished until the second century, when the fathers of the early church began to denounce it as heresy. Jesus was identified in Gnosticism as an embodiment of the supreme being who became incarnate to bring gnosis (spiritual knowledge) to earth. Early Christianity was diverse, and Gnostics and proto-orthodox Christians shared some beliefs, and initially these groups were hard to distinguish from each other. Early Gnostic writings included the Gospel of Thomas; the Dialogue of the Savior; the Gospel of Philip; Pistis Sophia; the Apocryphon of John; as well as the Gospel of Mary. Most of these other Gnostic writings also portray Mary as an apostle. This would suggest that Mary was very highly regarded in some areas within the early church even though we hear nothing of her in the canon of the New Testament outside of the four Gospels.

St. Irenaeus (AD 130–202) became the Bishop of Lyons in AD 177, and he began to write against Gnosticism, declaring it a heresy. St. Hippolytus of Rome (AD 170–235) also wrote against Gnosticism. Christian Gnosticism was suppressed in the third and fourth centuries, but it is interesting to note that some of its ideas were incorporated into mainstream Christianity. For example, Irenaeus regarded the Shepherd of Hermas, which certainly contains some Gnostic elements, as a canonical Gospel. In addition to this, the scholar Raymond E. Brown has argued that the Gospel of John contains some Gnostic elements, particularly in the prologue (John 1:1–18). However, if, as is very likely, Mary was indeed a Gnostic, then very few traces of her theology have filtered through into orthodox Christianity, even though the movement around her must have been very strong to have survived the early persecution of the Gnostics. The main copy of the Gospel of Mary that we have dates back to the fifth century, and this means that it was copied over a hundred years later than the condemnations of Gnosticism by Irenaeus and Hippolytus.

The elimination of the teaching of Mary Magdalene or of those who followed a tradition that grew up around her is not the only example of women's being suppressed in the early church. There is indisputable evidence that women in the early church were ordained deacons and that female deacons were accepted for some centuries. Women were also consecrated into an order of widows, a practice that continued right up until the Reformation, when it was finally suppressed. Today, this order of widows has been partially restored by the Catholic Church, but it is still not written into the Code of Canon Law. There is also evidence that women were being ordained as priests in the early church. This practice was suppressed in the early third and fourth centuries, but by the time it was finally eliminated it would have been going on for at least three hundred years—and probably even longer. Following are some examples of the evidence for the ordination of women to the diaconate and the priesthood as well as examples of the consecration of widows.

In the New Testament, St. Paul writes, "I commend to you our sister Phoebe, a deacon of the church at Cenchreae; give her, in the Lord, a welcome worthy of God's people and help her with whatever she needs from you—she herself has come to the help of many people, including myself" (Romans 16:1–3).

It is also worth noting here that all of Paul's letters are often translated as being addressed to "brothers," but the Greek word *adelfoi* (αδελφοί) is used in all the letters. This word actually means "brothers and sisters." In addition, Paul uses the same word for female deacons as for male deacons—*diakovos* (διάκονος)—and so translations that refer to female deacons as deaconesses are incorrect. Also to be noted is the fact that Paul often uses the word *diakovois* (διάκονοις) when referring to many deacons. This Greek word grammatically means deacons of both sexes. If he were referring to male deacons only, a different word would have been used: *diakovous* (διάκονους). Therefore, we can be sure that when Paul addresses the deacons at the start of his letter to the Philippians (Philippians 1:2), he is referring to both male and female deacons and not to male deacons alone. Unfortunately, New Testament exegesis has been plagued by scholars with a very poor understanding of Greek.

The first evidence that is found for the existence of female deacons outside of the New Testament is a letter written by Pliny the Younger. Pliny the Younger (AD 61–113) was a lawyer, author, and magistrate of ancient Rome. He wrote hundreds of letters, of which 247 survive. In one of his letters to the emperor Trajan, he writes of two female deacons whom he arrested and tortured.

The early church fathers also write of the order of female deacons, of which they approved at the time, and also of female presbyters (priests), of which they did not approve and suppressed; following are some examples. It would seem that the main role of the female deacons in the early church was to baptize women and to keep the Holy Gates, which may have been the central doors of the iconostasis. In the early church (and still in the Orthodox Church of today), Mass was said behind the iconostasis. However, there is absolutely no reason why female deacons, if restored today, could not carry out weddings and funerals as well as baptisms, as do the male deacons. This question will be examined further in a later chapter.

> I salute the keepers of the holy gates, the deaconesses in Christ.
> (Ignatian letter to the Antiochians)

> It is true that in the Church there is an order of deaconesses, but not for being a priestess nor for any kind of work or administration, but for the dignity of the female sex, either at the time of baptism, or of examining the sick or suffering, so that the naked body of a female may not be seen by men administering sacred rites but by the deaconesses. (St. Epiphanius of Salamis)

Appoint, O Bishop, a female deacon faithful and holy, for the ministering of women. For sometimes it is not possible to send a male deacon into certain houses of women, because of unbelievers. A female deacon is of use to us also in many other situations. First of all, in the baptising of women, a male deacon will touch only her forehead with the holy oil and afterwards the female deacon herself anoints them; for it is not necessary for the women to be gazed upon by men. (1231 Apostolic Constitutions of the Holy Apostles by Clement)

A deaconess does not bless, but neither does she perform anything else that is done by presbyters and deacons but she guards the doors and greatly assists the presbyters when they are baptising women. (1236 Apostolic Constitutions of the Holy Apostles by Clement)

In addition to the writings of the early church fathers, recent excavations in Israel uncovered a Byzantine basilica that contained the graves of many female deacons. Many of the women deacons in this basilica are actually named. Some of the tombs discovered included the remains of Theodosia the deaconess, Gregoria the deaconess, and Severa the deaconess.

In regard to the ordination of women to the priesthood, we begin to read of the criticism of women's being involved in active ministry in AD 200 when Tertullian wrote the Demurrer Against the Heretics. However, his written opposition to the involvement of women in ministry is not a balanced argument at all, but rather a misogynistic rant that illustrates that by the beginning of the third century misogynism was on the rise within Christianity. The fact that Tertullian found it necessary to rant about women in such a shameful way at this time would suggest that there must have been many women involved in ministry by the beginning of the third century—otherwise he would not have had any reason to write anything. It is therefore possible to postulate that following the death and resurrection of Christ, women were originally very much involved in the church in the way that Jesus would have wished; but as time progressed, they were squeezed out by discriminatory misogynism. This is illustrated on the next page, where it seems the women were called heretics merely because they wanted to exercise ministries. Tertullian also refers to their ordinations as "casual, capricious and changeable." The fact that he refers to female ordinations taking place in AD 200 would suggest that these ordinations had probably been happening for over a hundred years at his time of writing and were eventually squeezed out by his misogynism and the misogynism of others.

> All are puffed up, all offer knowledge. Before they have finished as catechumens, how thoroughly learned they are! And the heretical women themselves, how shameless are they! They make bold to teach, to debate, to work exorcisms, to undertake cures and perhaps even to baptise. Their ordinations are casual, capricious and changeable.

We would do well here to remember Johnson and Van Vonderen's definition of spiritual abuse, as the tone of Tertullian's writing certainly fits it:

> [Being] so determined to defend a spiritual place of authority, a doctrine or a way of doing things that you wound and abuse anyone who questions, or disagrees, or doesn't "behave" spiritually the way you want them to. When your words and actions tear down another, or attack or weaken a person's standing as a Christian—to gratify you, your position or your beliefs while at the same time weakening or harming another—that is spiritual abuse.

Later, sometime after Tertullian's diatribe in AD 312, the emperor Constantine converted to Christianity. Constantine called the first ecumenical council of the church, the First Council of Nicaea, in AD 325. Constantine invited eighteen hundred bishops to attend this council, but it is not known exactly how many attended. The bishops did not travel alone and were given permission to bring with them two priests and three deacons. This council did not discuss the place of women in the church, as it was called to achieve a consensus on Christian beliefs across Christendom (the Nicene Creed): however, it is significant to note that the council prohibited younger women to live in the houses of clerics. This would suggest that female deaconesses may have been doing so and this prohibition may have undermined their status.

It was the later Council of Laodicea, the exact date of which is unknown but which is thought to have taken place sometime around AD 360, that not only ruled out the ordination of women but also stated that women were not to come anywhere near the altar. This council was a regional, rather than ecumenical, council, but its authority seems to have been accepted by the universal church. It had therefore taken the church over three hundred years to prohibit the ordination of women. As the ordination of women was not prohibited until the mid-fourth century, I would postulate that for three hundred years women were clearly being ordained. If they were not being ordained, there would have been no reason for this council to issue these canons. These canons in effect show that it is not true that the church never ordained women. There were clearly some women priests in existence at this time, as they are referred to as "the so-called presbyteresses." It could be argued that this council politically abused women in the mid-fourth century by banning their already well-established ordinations and also by preventing them from approaching the altar, as these ordinations had clearly taken place for over three hundred years.

> That the so-called prebyteresses or presidentesses are not to be ordained in the Church. (Council of Laodicea, Canon 11)

> That women are not to come near the altar. (Council of Laodicea, Canon 44)

The preceding canons enshrined a spiritual abuse of women into the law of the time and are therefore also an example of organizational power abuse. They are certainly not in keeping with the teaching of Jesus. These canons obstructed women from approaching the altar. Jesus had never obstructed any women from approaching him.

There was, however, another female order that did initially survive this misogynistic onslaught, and that was the order of widows. This order is mentioned in the New Testament (1 Timothy 5:9–15). Consecrated widows took vows of chastity and devoted their lives to the service of the church. They lived independently in their own homes and served their local Christian communities. Timothy states that to be enrolled in this order a widow had to be at least sixty years of age and known for her good works. The main duty of consecrated widows was to pray for the people and for the church, but as time passed, they also became known for their good deeds. This vocation survived right up until the Reformation when it, too, was finally eliminated. Consecrated widows are mentioned by St. Hippolytus of Rome, who describes them as "being appointed for prayer" (The Apostolic Tradition 394f). Although Pope St. John Paul II approved the restoration of this order in *Vita Consecrata* (Vatican, 1996), it has still not been fully restored by the current church as it has not been written back into Canon Law.

There is one other early Christian female order that was never politically eradicated but eventually waned and died out only to be later restored in the twentieth century, and that is the order of consecrated virgins. This order is mentioned by St. Paul in 1 Corinthians where he suggests a special role for unmarried women in the church. Chastity was praised as a religious virtue in the New Testament, and it is believed that a consecration was imparted to virgin women by their bishops since the time of the apostles. The first known formal rite of consecration is that of St. Marcellina in AD 353. Initially, consecrated virgins lived independently, like consecrated widows, but this did not continue for long, probably because they did not have the financial means to be self-funding. These vocations were eventually absorbed into monastic life. During the medieval period, women were still consecrated as virgins, but by that time the consecration of virgins was maintained by nuns in monastic orders. From that time onward, women were not able to be consecrated independently as virgins until 1970, when this vocation was finally restored by Pope St. Paul VI in the wake of Vatican II.

In conclusion, the New Testament accounts of the historical Jesus clearly show that Jesus was radical in his dealings with women and treated them equally. There is evidence of some early changes to historical events regarding the historical Jesus and the accounts of the resurrection. For example, Luke is the only Gospel to state that Mary Magdalene was not the first witness of the resurrection. In the early centuries, a variety of different Christian churches grew up around the Mediterranean, and each of these had different traditions. However, over time some of these churches were suppressed by proto-orthodox

Christians. It is likely that a church that grew up around the persona or teaching of Mary Magdalene was suppressed. There is strong evidence that women were ordained as both priests and deacons in the early church. The ordination of women as priests was suppressed by the Council of Laodicea in the fourth century. The ordination of women as deacons is not believed to have ever been suppressed but rather to have slowly died out. It is thought it probably died out when infant baptism became the norm, as baptizing women had been one of the main roles of the early female deacons.

CHAPTER THREE

The East–West Schism and Its Effects on Women

This chapter examines the East–West Schism of 1054 that separated the Orthodox Church in the East from the Roman Catholic Church in the West. I argue that this schism had a very damaging effect on the Catholic Church because it enabled the hierarchy of that church to pursue, from henceforth, a policy of enforced celibacy for the male priesthood. The Orthodox Church had, in the main, always opposed enforced celibacy, but once it was separated from the Catholic Church, there was nothing to prevent the hierarchy of the Latin Church from foisting celibacy onto its clergy. I argue that it was this policy of enforced celibacy that created a culture of ingrained misogynism and perverse sexuality within the Latin Church.

For several hundred years before the East–West Schism in 1054, the churches in the East and the West were developing very strong and distinct cultural and theological differences. Prior to the East–West Schism, five patriarchs held authority in different regions: Rome, Alexandria, Antioch, Constantinople, and Jerusalem. The patriarch of Rome (the Pope) held the honor of "first among equals," but he did not possess authority over the other patriarchs. For many years the church in the West had been pushing for the patriarch or bishop of Rome to have universal jurisdiction and authority. However, while the other patriarchs in the East agreed to honor the patriarch of Rome, they believed that ecclesiastical matters should be decided by a council or synod of all regions, and they would not grant universal jurisdiction and authority to the bishop of Rome. The Eastern churches would not accept that any central authoritarian figure, i.e., the bishop of Rome, could have an absolute last word on church doctrine, which would have meant that many Latin practices would have been forced upon them. This was because the churches of the East and those of the West were already very far apart in terms of practice due to major differences in theology.

Latin thought was strongly influenced by Roman law and a developing scholastic theology, whereas in the East, theology was comprehended through philosophy and the context of worship. In addition, the Eastern churches developed Greek rites using the Greek language in their religious ceremonies. The New Testament, of course, had been written in Greek, while the Old Testament was written mostly in Hebrew. However, the patriarchs of the East produced a Greek Septuagint translation of the Old Testament. In the Church of Rome, churches conducted their services in Latin and their Bibles were translated into Latin as per the Latin Vulgate. This led to the churches of the East continuously stating that many practices of the Latin Church were heretical due to errors that resulted from their lack of understanding of the New Testament in its original Greek.

Apart from their differences in regard to the authority or jurisdiction of the bishop (or patriarch) of Rome, some of the other theological differences between the churches of the East and the West revolved around the following: the nature of the incarnate Christ; clerical celibacy; fasting; anointing with oil; the use of unleavened bread by the churches in the West for the Eucharist; the reverence of St. Augustine by the Latin Church (many in the Eastern churches believed him to be bordering on heresy); and the procession of the Holy Spirit. As this is a book focusing on the effect of the East–West Schism on women in particular, the theological differences that will be examined here will only be those that had a strong effect on women.

In regard to the procession of the Holy Spirit, this dispute centered around the doctrine of the Trinity and whether the Holy Spirit proceeded from God the Father alone or from both God the Father and God the

Son. The Eastern church insisted on keeping the original wording of the Nicene Creed, which stated that the Holy Spirit proceeded from God the Father only, whereas the Western church had begun to state that the Holy Spirit proceeded from both God the Father and God the Son. The Eastern church believed this view of the Western church to be based erroneously in Augustinian thinking, which it considered to be unorthodox and bordering on the heretical. The Eastern church's rejection of Augustinian thinking is very interesting not only due to the position of Augustine on the procession of the paraclete but also because it can be argued that Augustine had a very perverse and unhealthy view of sexuality, and due to that alone his reverence by the Latin Church has had many repercussions.

Augustine of Hippo (AD 350–430) would be seen by modern psychologists as an unbalanced man who suffered from what is known as the Madonna-whore complex. Men who suffer from this complex see women either as saintly Madonnas or as debased prostitutes. They also see love as being either sacred or profane, and they categorize women into two groups—women they can admire or women they find sexually attractive. There can be, for these men, no integration between the two. These men are unable to have a healthy sexual relationship with a woman, because ultimately they see sex as being something dirty and disgusting rather than something that is beautiful and God-given. They are therefore unable to develop a holistic long-term sexual relationship of mutual enjoyment and love with any woman but instead seek a series of sexual thrills that they perceive to be cheap, exciting, and dirty. This perverse sexuality is thought to be caused by the male's having been raised by an overprotective mother.

Augustine did have an overprotective mother, and in rebellion to her continuous warnings about the sins of the flesh, he began to lead a very hedonistic lifestyle. He was involved in many sexual exploits before becoming involved with a woman of a much lower class than himself, much to the chagrin of his mother. He did not marry her, and she had an illegitimate child who was known to be Augustine's son. He eventually ended his relationship with this woman and agreed with his mother that he would marry someone "more suitable"—but in the meantime he procured another mistress. However, eventually, at the age of thirty-one, Augustine converted to Christianity. Following this conversion, his thought swung from extreme hedonism to extreme puritanism. Augustine became a celibate, and he developed a perverse theology of sexuality stating that sex could not be a beautiful act of love but instead was a dirty evil result of the fall. He stated that evil inevitably accompanied sexual intercourse and that even a marital sexual act which was carried out merely to procreate was in itself evil. He went on to argue that the only way to avoid the evil caused by sexual intercourse was to take the "better" way, abstain from marriage and become a celibate. Sadly, Augustine's theology of sexuality was embraced by the Latin Church, which seemed to have forgotten the words in Genesis "and the two shall become one flesh" (Genesis 2:24) and the Jewish view of marriage as the ideal state where two halves become one, completing each other.

By the time of the East–West Schism, Augustine's views on sexuality had grown in the West, with a considerable number of priests attempting celibacy. However, in the East the sexual views of Augustine were in the main rejected and priests continued to marry. The Eastern churches, of course, did not reject celibacy per se. They recognized that celibacy could be a good thing but only if it was voluntary. They rejected enforced celibacy. Priests were allowed to marry in the East as long as they did so prior to ordination. This issue was one of several festering bones of contention within the relationships between the churches of the East and the West.

At the time of the East–West Schism, Michael Cerularius was the patriarch of Constantinople, while Pope Leo IX was the patriarch of Rome. Problems sprang up in southern Italy, which was part of the Byzantine Empire and followed the patriarch Michael Cerularius. Norman warriors had conquered the region, and they were replacing Greek bishops with Latin ones. When Cerularius learned that the Norman warriors were forbidding Greek rites in southern Italy, he retaliated by shutting down the Latin churches in Constantinople. The two patriarchs eventually declared each other to be heretics, and the East–West Schism was sealed.

The East–West Schism was very unfortunate for women in the Catholic West because it meant that as the Eastern churches were now no longer in communion with Rome, the Latin Church was now free to follow a policy of enforced celibacy. This policy, based on the theology of St. Augustine, was not good for women because it created a misogynistic culture and also began to create a cult of celibate men who were seen to be separate, elite, "special," and above the rest of humanity. Women began to be perceived as a temptation that threatened this pure, "special" status of the celibate priest, and they came to be seen as a second sex to be avoided at all costs by the male clergy. Of course, this developing misogynistic attitude toward women was entirely at odds with the original teachings of Jesus, who had freely mixed with women and had treated them as equals.

In 1122, almost seventy years after the East–West Schism, Pope Callixtus II convoked the First Council of the Lateran. This was the ninth ecumenical council of the Catholic Church. Canon 21 of this council not only forbade clerics to marry, it also stated that the marriages of priests that had already been contracted should be dissolved. This showed that the Latin Church was now developing a very low view of marriage and a very perverse view of a human being's beautiful God-given sexuality. To force priests who had contracted valid marriages to separate from their wives was not only barbaric and completely out of keeping with the original teachings of Jesus, it was also very demeaning to women, who could be officially discarded by the official, "special," cultish cleric.

Later, in 1139, the Second Council of the Lateran was convened by Pope Innocent II. This council reaffirmed the First Lateran Council's condemnation of marriage among priests, subdeacons, and deacons, as well as introduced other sexist practices that confirmed the superior and cultish status of celibate men over the "inferior" second sex of women. For example, the council prohibited nuns from singing the Divine Office in the same choir as monks.

The East–West Schism led to the creation of a misogynistic culture in the Western church and also to the creation of a perverse sexuality that had no roots in Judaism or in the teachings of Jesus. This theology of St. Augustine has always been regarded with suspicion by the Orthodox Church, and modern psychology would state that the sexuality of Augustine is the sexuality of an unbalanced man who had some serious personal issues. The founder of psychoanalysis, Sigmund Freud, would have regarded Augustine as a sufferer of Madonna-whore syndrome. Later psychologists such as Carl Rogers and Abraham Maslow have stated that the fulfillment of sexual needs is absolutely essential to enable a fully rounded person to achieve self-actualization. Modern psychologists also state that other things essential for a healthy personality to grow and develop are self-worth and a positive self-image.

The theology of St. Augustine has made it very difficult for many Catholics to develop a positive self-image, as this theology has taught individuals to feel guilty about their sexuality and to see sex as both "dirty" and disgusting. Many Catholics throughout the centuries have come to loathe themselves because they have sexual desires; and many Catholic men, priests in particular, have come to loathe women because they have wrongly seen women as being, through their very existence, responsible for the creation of their own "dirty desires." Therefore, the theology of Augustine has been responsible for the suffering of many women throughout the ages. Today, feelings of guilt around sexuality are often referred to as "Catholic guilt," and this kind of guilt is very destructive because it is mired in self-loathing and the loathing of one's very own God-given and created humanity.

The perverse theory of sexuality that was created by St. Augustine and firmly taken up by the Latin Church after the East–West Schism is a theme that we'll return to again and again in this book. This is because enforced celibacy turned the clergy into a celibate sect. From the time of the East–West Schism (until very recently, when married priest converts were allowed to be ordained as priests in the Latin Church), no members of the clergy in the West were married or female; they were all male and celibate. This made it very difficult for the clergy to relate to or understand women or married people, as they did not associate with them closely. It also led to the development of a misogynistic culture. The misogyny of the Catholic hierarchy is rooted in Augustine's perverse sexuality, as are the encyclicals of many later popes. It has had a pervasive effect that has become ingrained within Catholic culture.

This is in contrast to the Orthodox Church, where the clergy have the choice to be either married or celibate. Within Orthodoxy, members of the diocesan priesthood are married, while members of the religious orders are celibate. This has led to the Orthodox's having a more well-rounded and healthier view of sexuality and much more positive images of women. The Orthodox do not view sex as evil or as purely for the purposes of procreation, and the use of some forms of contraception (those that are not abortifacient) is regarded as normal within Orthodox culture.

CHAPTER FOUR

The Erosion of Female Influence in Pre-Reformation and Reformation Britain

This chapter will examine the arrival of Christianity in Britain and the initial flourishing of women within Christianity there. Sadly, due to a variety of factors, which included invasions, conquests, and, ultimately, the Reformation, the influence of women within the British church declined over the centuries. The female consecrated life was almost completely eradicated at the time of the Reformation and did not begin to reappear in Britain until the eighteenth century.

It is not known exactly when Christianity first came to Britain because during the first, second, and third centuries very little was written down. The first strong evidence as to the existence of Christianity in Britain is from St. Bede, England's first historian. He reports that in AD 156, during the reign of the Roman emperor Antoninus, a British king named Lucius wrote to Pope Eleutherus in Rome requesting instruction in the Christian faith. It is therefore very likely that by this time Christianity had reached Britain and may have become well established. During the first and second centuries, merchants from all over the Roman Empire came to Britain, and some of them would certainly have brought Christianity with them.

St. Alban was Britain's first Christian martyr; he was executed in a town called Verulamium in AD 304. This town eventually became known as St. Albans, and an abbey was built there and dedicated to the saint. However, in AD 312, only eight years after St. Alban's death, Constantine the emperor of Rome experienced a vision while at the Battle of Milvian Bridge. Apparently, he saw a cross of light in the sky and the Greek words *Ev Toutw Nika* (pronounced "on touto nika"), which means "with that conquer." Constantine adorned his troops with the Christian symbol, and they were victorious. As a result of this, in AD 313 Constantine granted an edict of tolerance to all religions, including Christianity, and the persecution of the Christians ceased.

In AD 597, St. Augustine of Canterbury, who was a Benedictine monk, brought the Benedictine rule to England. By this time monasticism had been flourishing in Europe for some time so there were quite a few monasteries as well as some nunneries. There were also female deacons and consecrated widows in Europe. Some consecrated widows, such as Paula and Marcella, eventually established religious communities for women. There were not, however, any women priests in Europe at this time, as these had been suppressed in the fourth century by the Council of Laodicea. After Christianity arrived in Britain, the tradition of consecrating widows (known as vowesses) became strong in Anglo-Saxon England, and there are early records of this in the penitential of Theodore of Tarsus, archbishop of Canterbury (668–690), and the confessional of Egbert, archbishop of York (732–766). The community religious life also became strong in Anglo-Saxon England, although its formation was not the same as elsewhere.

The formation of community religious life and the establishment of the same was different in England compared to all other countries, with the exception of some parts of France, Belgium, Ireland, and Germany. This was because in England, while there were some all-male religious communities, there were no all-female religious communities. Female religious were housed in double monasteries, which consisted of monks and nuns living side by side in separate dwellings. These houses were almost always led by a woman who was known as the abbess. Female abbesses enjoyed great power and prestige and had far more influence than any woman has in the Catholic Church today.

Anglo-Saxon female abbesses were women of high birth who ruled over a community of nuns and a parallel community of priests. These women were not priests, as the Council of Laodicea and others had suppressed the ordination of women in the fourth century. Therefore, they did not say Mass or administer the sacraments. Nevertheless, their ability to administer the sacraments in no way affected their prestige and influence. They presided over abbeys of great learning and from their monasteries brought about a cultural rising of the people. Abbesses received the same training and learning as monks and were extremely well educated. Most of them taught theology to priests, and some of them, such as St. Hilda, taught future bishops. Abbesses were also sought out for their spiritual counsel, and when Aldfrith, king of Northumbria, died, he chose two abbesses to whom to convey his last words and instructions. In the later church it would have been the bishop who received such a prestigious call, but in Anglo-Saxon England it was often the abbess.

In his 1943 book *Anglo-Saxon England*, Frank Stenton described Anglo-Saxon England as led by all-powerful women, and this is illustrated by the fact that some of these women not only had the synodal vote but were also highly influential at the church synods where they voted. For example, St. Hilda, the abbess of Whitby, was hostess to the famous Synod of Whitby, which was presided over by King Oswy. This synod was of national importance because it sought to resolve a conflict between two different strands of Christianity (known as the Celtic and the Roman) as to the date Easter should be celebrated. Hilda supported the Celtic dating at the synod, although she accepted the Roman dating when this was eventually decided. Hilda was succeeded as abbess of Whitby by Aelffled who was also literate, independent, and powerful. She was involved in the public lives of kings, abbots, and bishops and was sought out for her advice. Aelffled also attended a church synod. She supported Bishop Wilfrid's restoration to the See of Northumbria and she attended the Synod of Nidd in order to express her views. She spoke at this synod and persuaded King Aldfrith to change his mind and restore Wilfrid to the bishopric. This is particularly interesting as it demonstrates that Anglo-Saxon women not only had a say in who was elected as a bishop but could also have a very strong influence overall on this election. As time has progressed, female influence in the Catholic Church has decreased, and these rights have long since been denied to women. For hundreds of years women had no influence whatsoever on the appointment of bishops, although recently Pope Francis did appoint three women to the committee that advises him on the selection of bishops. This was a welcome first move toward beginning to involve women again, although their influence remains small.

All of the Anglo-Saxon abbesses of the early seventh to the late ninth century enjoyed an education on a par with that of men, and many were highly regarded as theologians. They studied ancient law; rules of allegory (in order to interpret the scriptures, which would suggest that they also preached); grammar; spelling; punctuation; and meter (for composing verses in Latin). The abbesses were well versed in Latin, which was the language of the church. We know this because St. Leoba, a female missionary from England who became a German abbess, sent verses in Latin that she had composed to her friend, relative, and mentor St. Boniface. She was a highly educated and influential woman who was consulted by the bishops in Fulda, Germany, on issues of monastic rule. The status of this woman again illustrates how the influence of women in the Catholic Church has declined over the centuries.

Unfortunately, the influence of the Anglo-Saxon abbesses did not last, mainly due to the disappearance of their monasteries as a result of the Danish raids. Viking raids began in England in the ninth century, and these monasteries were targeted due to their wealth. The first monastery to be raided was Lindisfarne in AD 793, and from then on the Vikings continued to raid Britain for almost a hundred years. The monasteries were looted and destroyed, and a great many shrines dedicated to the female Anglo-Saxon saints were lost. The great abbesses were disposed of and with them went their unique and influential role. English women were never again able to achieve within Catholicism the status and responsibilities that they had in Anglo-Saxon England. This was almost certainly due to the fact that their demise was in many ways convenient to a Rome that was sadly becoming increasingly misogynistic in its attitude toward women.

While the influence of Catholic women in England was diminished following the demise of the Anglo-Saxon abbesses, English women were still more influential in the church up until the Reformation than they are today. The matriarchal abbesses were gone; but women were still consecrated as independent vowesses, and a new form of consecrated life was also beginning to emerge in England: that of the anchoress.

In regard to the vowesses, these women were widows who took vows of chastity alone. They did not take the monastic vows of poverty and obedience. They were mature women of faith who took part in the Eucharist; prayed with psalms, hymns, and meditations; and were also known for their intercessory prayer. They existed in Britain from the Anglo-Saxon period right up until the Reformation. Vowesses were answerable to their diocesan bishops, and from Anglo-Saxon times up until the Reformation wore a particular attire of a cloak, mantle, and ring. Generally, these women lived in their own homes and often loosely attached themselves to nearby monasteries. They did a lot of good work in the community, often at their own expense. It is possible that the founder of the Walsingham shrine, Richeldis, may have been a consecrated widow.

Walsingham was a famous shrine that existed in England from the eleventh century up until the Reformation, when it was destroyed by King Henry VIII. The date of the foundation of the shrine is disputed but is likely to have been 1061. It was founded by a mysterious widow who is known only as Richeldis. This widow had a vision of the house in Nazareth where the holy family had once lived. She believed that she was asked to build in Walsingham an imitation of this house in which the annunciation of the archangel Gabriel had occurred. This shrine became very famous over the centuries and was visited by many dignitaries of royal blood, including Richard Coeur de Lion; Edward II; Isabella of France, dowager queen of England; Edward III; Queen Johan, widow of Edward IV; Henry VII; and lastly King Henry VIII in 1511. Sadly, King Henry VIII later ransacked and destroyed the shrine, and with its destruction went most details of its founder, Richeldis. The influence of this woman had been remarkable, and she was, perhaps, the last of the Anglo-Saxon women of influence.

The Walsingham shrine was eventually restored in the late nineteenth and early twentieth centuries when Catholic and Anglicans built two new separate shrines around the site of the original one.

In regard to the anchoresses, the anchorite movement had its roots in the very early church with St. Thecla of Iconium. Thecla was said to have been converted by St. Paul himself. She refused her parents' wishes to marry in order to follow St. Paul, and as a result was sent to the amphitheater to be eaten by the beasts. Thecla managed to escape before the beasts attacked her and then retired to live in a cave for seventy-two years. This kind of withdrawal became widespread in the late third century and arrived in Britain in the late seventh century. The anchorite movement did not initially flourish when it arrived in Britain but began to grow more after the destruction of the Anglo-Saxon monasteries. This was because, as the religious communities had been destroyed, the only path left open for Christian women was one of spiritual independence.

During the twelfth and thirteenth centuries, there were at least two hundred anchoresses living in England; and as this movement continued to grow, a rule was eventually written for them. This rule was known as the "Ancrene Riwle" of 1229. The rule consisted of eight parts. Parts one and eight related to the anchoress's exterior life, and parts two to seven related to her interior life. Anchoresses lived in single cells that were built against one of the walls of a village church. These cells had windows through which the anchoress could view the altar or provide spiritual counsel. The anchoresses became particularly renowned for their wisdom and spiritual direction. The most well-known anchoress was Julian of Norwich, who was one of the later anchoresses.

Paul Molinari, in his 1958 book *Julian of Norwich: The Teaching of a 14th Century English Mystic*, dates Julian's birth at around 1342. But apart from this, very little is known of her life. Her true name is also unknown, as the name Julian, by which history describes her, derives from the fact that her anchoress's cell was built onto the wall of the Church of St. Julian in Norwich. It was common at that time for anchoresses to take the name of the church to which they were attached. The fact that Julian's anchor-hold was at St. Julian's Church, Conisford, Norwich, is established by three wills dated 1405, 1415, and 1416. This anchor-hold belonged to the Benedictine monastery at Carrow, and due to this there has been speculation that Julian may have been a Benedictine nun. However, the consensus by scholars today seems to be that she was a widowed laywoman who became an anchoress and would have been consecrated a widow/anchoress after her visions. These visions occurred when she was seriously ill, and author Sheila Upjohn states that it is significant that while Julian was ill, she did not send for a priest but for "the parson, my curate, to be at my end. He came with a little boy and brought a cross." Upjohn also finds it significant that Julian's mother was present during this illness rather than any abbess. She argues that this illness may have been the plague and that Julian may have lost her husband to the same illness while she survived. It was when she recovered from this illness that Julian wrote her book, *Revelations of Divine Love.*

Julian of Norwich's book *Revelations of Divine Love* is believed to be the first book written in English by a woman. There are two versions, which are known as the short text and the long text. The short text survives in only one manuscript, which is the mid-fifteenth century Amherst Manuscript. The long text survives in several versions, one of which is known as the Paris Manuscript. The first version of Julian's book (the short text) was written shortly after her recovery from her illness, while the second version was written some years later. Molinari states that the second version is the most definitive, as it describes what Julian felt about her visions after twenty years of reflection, thought, and prayer. This second version of her book has also led to Julian's being regarded as one of the greatest Christian mystics of all time.

Mysticism is a form of spirituality that is concerned with the pursuit of perfection and union with the absolute, and it can be found in Eastern religions such as Buddhism and Islam as well as in Christianity. Julian was not unique in her time in being a Christian mystic, but her teaching on mysticism differed from that of her contemporaries, and it is probably due to this that she has become renowned.

The mystical path within the Eastern religions was in many ways a path of negation, and the mystical path of Christianity during Julian's time was very similar. However, Julian was not a follower of the negative path. Her mysticism did not involve negativism and mortifications in order to achieve unity with the divine. Instead, she taught the second conversion and the possibility of uniting fully with God in this world rather than the next. Man or woman, moved by grace, sees the desire of his/her grace and begins to desire the absolute fervently. This desire for God leads to the mystical life, which Julian saw as having three stages. The first stage is longing for God, the second is uniting with God, and the last is beholding. "Beholding" means that an individual's whole life is directed toward the force of love that has possessed it. This love has taken hold of the individual, and nothing other than this love is acceptable as a mode of living.

Julian also spoke of the "motherhood of God," and with this concept she was again breaking new ground. St. Anselm had first fermented the idea of the motherhood of God with his teaching that Christ gave birth to the human person by his dying on the cross and bringing the human person to life. However, this idea of the motherhood of God had never really been developed in Christianity prior to Julian and has not since been developed in any great detail following her passing. She writes:

> I understood three manners of beholding of motherhood in God; the first is grounded in our kind making; the second is taking of our kind—and there beginneth the motherhood of Grace; the third is motherhood of working—and therein is a forthspreading of the same Grace; of length and breadth and of height and of deepness without end.

Julian also writes of the love of God as feminine motherhood as follows:

> The kind loving mother that witteth and knoweth the need of her child, she keepeth it full tenderly as the kind and condition of motherhood will.

Julian's feminist doctrine was almost certainly not disagreed with by the English Church in her day. This can be discerned because it is known that Julian was very highly regarded in her time and her counsel was sought out by many far and wide. We know that Julian was acclaimed in her day due to the autobiography of Margery Kempe, who was a minor female mystic. Margery narrates how she paid a visit to Julian in search of spiritual wisdom. She states that she particularly sought out Julian because she was an expert in divine revelations and was known to give good counsel.

Julian is commemorated in the Church of England, the Episcopal Church, and the Evangelical Lutheran Church, but has never been beatified or canonized in the Roman Catholic Church despite being popularly venerated by Catholics as a holy woman of God. Unfortunately, this does raise the question as to whether this has been due to her feminism.

Following the rediscovery and flowering of the female vocation due to the anchorite movement, there was again a resurgence of female spirituality, and the female community religious life in England was recreated. Many new nunneries were founded, and a great many of these had their roots in the anchorite movement and began with women who were previously anchoresses. It should be pointed out, however, that the women living in these new religious houses had nowhere near the influence that previous consecrated women had enjoyed in Anglo-Saxon England. These women were not all-powerful matriarchs. They were simply enclosed nuns. They also did not attend or vote at synods of the church. The female consecrated life was restored, but the influence of women within the church continued to wane.

One example of a priory that was built to accommodate women who had been anchoresses but now wanted to live a communal enclosed life was Sempringham Priory. This priory was built by Gilbert of Sempringham. He initially built a cell for the women attached to his parish church, and this marked the beginning of the Gilbertine order, which became famous prior to the Reformation. Gilbert soon realized that if the nuns were to be enclosed, they would need to be served by others and, as a result of this, he placed some village girls under a simple vow to fetch and carry for the nuns. This decision of his, to include girls under simple vows, marked the beginning of what is now known as a third order in England. In regard to Sempringham, this order continued to spread, and to safeguard its possessions regular labor was needed. This led to lay brothers, being added to the movement. Augustinian canons were later added to govern the women, and Sempringham became a double monastery. However, this double monastery bore no resemblance to the double monasteries of the earlier Anglo-Saxon period. During that period double monasteries were, in the main, presided over by matriarchal women. In this case, it was men who governed the order, while women were its backbone. Sempringham became a priory in 1139, and it was at this time that an associated house near Sleaford was also established. By the time Gilbert died there were nine double monasteries, and his order had achieved wide renown.

In addition to the anchorite movement's leading to the foundation of double monasteries and other nunneries, some other female religious houses were also founded due to some Norman monasteries, being granted land in England as a result of the Norman Conquest, which intensified links between English and continental monasteries. Some monasteries in England were linked with greatly acclaimed monasteries overseas, such as Fontevrault.

Fontevrault was a French order founded by Robert of Arbrissel and was, from the very beginning, concerned with the female vocation and ministry. The order bore the name of the motherhouse where, in the very beginning, Robert's concern for women had led him to found a monastery for their special care. Robert included men in his order, but they were subservient to women; and he chose a widow, Petronella, as abbess of the first monastery in the village of Fontevrault, near Chinon in France. The abbey consisted of four separate communities of men and women, all of whom were subject to the abbess of Fontevrault. This abbey was very similar to the double monasteries that had existed in England in the Anglo-Saxon period. The order spread to England, and three nunneries were founded at Westwood, Nuneaton, and Amesbury, but these nunneries were not double monasteries. Therefore, English nuns did not enjoy the same prestige and influence at these nunneries as women enjoyed in the original foundation.

Fontevrault is just one example of a continental order that established nunneries in England during the early period of the Middle Ages. There were also others—Cluny, Citeaux, Arrouaise, and Premontre—which did the same. The Cistercians, who were initially hostile to women, also later welcomed them, and over twenty-seven nunneries in England originated from or became Cistercian.

While English women in the early Middle Ages did not have the same influence in the church as women in earlier periods, this was nevertheless a fairly good period spiritually for women. In contrast to this, the later Middle Ages saw a decline in both the popularity of the female religious life and the number of people seeking consecration either as vowesses and anchoresses or within enclosed religious communities. Ascetism was no longer an ideal in the later Middle Ages, and romantic love now seemed to be the desire of most young women. In addition, many enclosed nuns no longer lived lives of particular sacrifice, and some heads of houses lived in great luxury and enjoyed great freedom of movement despite the Papal Decretal Periculoso of Pope Boniface VIII. This Bull, issued in 1298, stated that nuns should be strictly enclosed, but it was widely ignored in pre-Reformation England. However, there was one religious house that practiced very good observance prior to the Reformation, and this was Syon Abbey.

Syon was the only Bridgettine house in England, and it was also a double monastery and a throwback to the earlier Anglo-Saxon times. The first stone of this monastery was laid by Henry V on February 22, 1415. The Bridgettine Order was a modified order of St. Augustine with particular devotions to the passion of Christ and the honor of the Virgin Mary. The original foundation consisted of one abbess, fifty-nine nuns, one confessor general, twelve priests, four deacons, and eight lay brethren. The order grew and became extremely wealthy. The nuns were known for their very good observance and informed devotional life based on the English mystics of the 1300s. These nuns were also extremely well educated, and the monastery had a large, magnificent library that was renowned for its intellectual distinction. There was no crisis of vocation within this religious community, and it housed over sixty nuns right up until the Reformation. Many of these nuns came from well-known families and had aristocratic connections. There were also independently consecrated vowesses who were attached to Syon in a looser way. These were the consecrated widows who took vows of chastity without the accompanying monastic vows of poverty and obedience. They were free to own their own property and to live where they pleased but often chose to live near a large and active monastery, and Syon was particularly favored by them.

Syon Abbey was presided over by a woman, and by the time of the Reformation there had been eight abbesses. The last abbess was Agnes Jordan (1520–1539). The legal corporate identity of Syon was "The Abbess and Convent," which could transact business by affixing its corporate seal. The convent consisted of the abbess and nuns together with the confessor and all religious men. The abbess was the overall presiding officer. In the case of Agnes Jordan, she was the last bastion of female authority in the English Catholic Church before the Reformation.

In England the Reformation came about due to Henry VIII's desire for an annulment in order to marry Anne Boleyn. Henry had grown tired of his first wife, Catherine of Aragon, and was also disappointed that she had not given him a son. Henry argued that his marriage to Catherine of Aragon was invalid because he had been forced into the marriage by others for political reasons. He had married his deceased brother's wife and tried to argue that there had been immense pressure on him to do this. He stated that the marriage was invalid, and he believed this to be the reason why there had been no male heirs.

Henry VIII first raised the question of his marriage with Rome in 1527 and almost certainly assumed that an annulment would be granted. However, the Pope was not convinced of Henry's case, and Henry became increasingly angry. In 1531 he publicly separated from Queen Catherine of Aragon but still received no communication from the Pope that his annulment had been granted. Thus, in January 1533 he went through a form of marriage privately with Anne Boleyn. This marriage was solemnized publicly in April of the same year, and in June Thomas Cranmer, archbishop of Canterbury, granted Henry the annulment independent of Rome. Pope Clement VII promptly declared the second union of Henry invalid, and declared his first marriage to Catherine of Aragon the valid one. Henry was furious. In 1534 the Act of Supremacy was passed, declaring the king and his successors head of the English Church. The split from Rome was definitive.

Once the breach with Rome had taken place, Henry was free to do as he wished with the English Church. He could have taken over the monasteries and allowed them to continue. This is clearly what the last abbess of Syon, Agnes Jordan, had expected him to do, because the nuns of Syon immediately sent a message to Cromwell stating that they hoped he would "be a good maister unto thaim and to thaire house as thaire special trust is in you." Unfortunately, King Henry had no intention of allowing the monasteries to survive and had already begun a campaign to suppress them. This had probably been decided because the king's wars in France had emptied his treasuries and he was bankrupt. The monasteries were an obvious source of wealth, and for this reason Henry seized them in stages and sold most of the monastic land. Surprisingly, despite evidence of bad practice in some monasteries and nunneries, the majority of religious women in England did not want to be released from their vows. However, it was simply not possible for women to withstand the power of King Henry VIII and his new state. Persuasion, manipulation, and the hard logic of the times brought the most die-hard religious women to capitulate, as there were no other options open to them. Those who did not wish to surrender fled overseas, and that is what happened to many of the Bridgettines of Syon.

Once the religious had either capitulated or fled, the monasteries were dissolved and all their wealth was transferred to the king. Plate and silver were sent to the royal treasury and the furniture was auctioned. Lead, woodwork, benches, grates, locks, and other things were sold on the spot or sent to London. The churches were pulled down, as were the steeples, cloisters, and chapter houses. A significant part of English heritage disappeared, and the female consecrated life was eradicated. It is also worth noting that it was not only the consecrated women who lived in community who were eradicated. There were a significant number of vowesses (consecrated widows) and anchoresses at the time of the Reformation, and they also were eradicated. The religious profession of widows was halted and the cells of the anchoresses were destroyed. They were never seen again in Britain until recent times, when a few women in England have been consecrated as widows despite the lack of a universal rite, and a few women have also been consecrated as hermits. Consecrated hermits lead a similar life to the pre-Reformation anchorites, and this form of consecrated life was fully restored by the Catholic Church in 1983.

The most unfortunate result of the Reformation for women, not only in Britain but also in Europe, was that it caused the destruction of many records of the Catholic Church from pre-Reformation times. Monasteries were regarded as centers of learning in pre-Reformation times, and it is likely that they would have held many ancient church records, which would have been burned and destroyed. As has been noted, the famous shrine at Walsingham was also looted, pillaged, and plundered, and all records of the visionary were destroyed. This destruction of past records pretty much allowed the Catholic Church to begin again with a clean slate and to conveniently forget the history of women within the earlier church. As we shall go on to see, the status of women within Catholicism has never recovered from the Reformation. Since the Reformation, women within the Catholic Church have pretty much lost all influence and have never recovered it. This was in many ways due to the Council of Trent, which followed the Reformation and was the Catholic Church's response to the Reformation. This council, which will be examined later, virtually "deified" the clerical state and gave no place to women within its doctrines. At the time of the Reformation the Protestants treated women no better, but they have since gone on to incorporate women into holy orders. The Orthodox Church, of course, never had a Reformation after the initial East–West Schism, but nevertheless the female influence in that church had declined due to the falling away of the ordination of female deacons. However, the Orthodox are now in the process of restoring the female diaconate and, as we will go on to see, it is only the Catholic Church that today refuses to give any place to women within its hierarchy or to attempt to return to women the influence they had pre-Reformation. Pope Francis has recently announced that women can lead various Vatican departments, known as dicasteries, but these appointments involve only a handful of select women and are in no way a major reform. As previously noted, Pope Francis has also given a small number of women the vote at the forthcoming Synod on Synodality, and he has appointed three women to the committee that advises the Pope on the selection of bishops. These are welcome first steps from this Pope but there is still a very long way to go in order to restore to women the influence they had pre-Reformation.

CHAPTER FIVE

Post-Reformation Centralization and the Revival of the Female Consecrated Life

This chapter looks at the further decline of female influence within the Catholic Church from the time of the Reformation and the later revival of the female consecrated life, which began in the late eighteenth century. In this chapter I examine the teachings of the Council of Trent; the foundation of active female religious congregations by Mary Ward; the flourishing of these new movements; and their effects on the growth of the Catholic Church in Europe. I will argue that although there was a revival of the female consecrated life in the late eighteenth, nineteenth, and early twentieth centuries, women still remained second-class citizens within the church overall. They have never recovered the status they had pre-Reformation.

The Council of Trent was the nineteenth ecumenical council of the Roman Catholic Church and was convened in Trent for three periods between December 13, 1545, and December 4, 1563. This council was convened as a response to the Reformation. The Council of Trent embodied the ideals of what is known as the Counter-Reformation, and its decrees were signed by 255 members. These members included 4 papal legates, 2 cardinals, 3 patriarchs, 25 archbishops, and 168 bishops. There were, of course, no women at this ecumenical council, and it is doubtful whether women have ever attended any of the ecumenical councils of the Roman Catholic Church, except perhaps the first. It is possible that some women deacons may have accompanied the bishops to the First Council of Nicaea, as bishops were allowed to take deacons with them and there were women deacons at the time in the early church.

When examining the decrees of the Council of Trent, it is necessary to bear in mind that the council was responding to what it saw as the threats of Protestantism and the teaching of Martin Luther in particular. Luther was a Roman Catholic who became an Augustinian priest but went on to dispute various tenets of the theology of his time. He believed that salvation was not earned by good works but was entirely received as a free gift of grace. He also challenged the authority and office of the Pope by teaching that the Bible is the only source of divinely revealed knowledge. Luther also believed that the Bible should be studied in its original languages of Hebrew and Greek and translated into the vernacular languages of the people. In addition to this, he disagreed with the church on the books to be included in the canon of Scripture. He rejected the elevation of priests to a superior status (known as sacerdotalism) and believed all Christians to be part of a holy priesthood. Luther did not agree with enforced priestly celibacy and married a nun, Katharina von Bora. He also rejected the church's teachings on indulgences.

Sadly, Luther was extremely anti-Semitic.

The main canons and decrees of the Council of Trent were to reaffirm the Niceno-Constantinopolitan Creed; to create the canon of the New and Old Testaments; to declare that the official Bible was the Latin Vulgate and that the church's interpretation of the Bible was final; to reaffirm the practice of indulgences but to bring about various reforms in regards to them; to reaffirm the veneration of the saints and the Virgin Mary; to declare that justification was offered on the basis of faith and good works; and to reaffirm the seven sacraments.

In regards to the seven sacraments, the council gave its greatest weight to these because it wanted to stress that they were necessary vehicles of grace in opposition to Luther's view that justification was by faith alone. It pronounced the Eucharist to be a true propitiatory sacrifice as well as a sacrament and confirmed the practice of withholding the cup from the laity. Ordination was defined to imprint an indelible character on the priest's soul and priestly celibacy was reaffirmed. Marriage was defined to be a sacrament, but the council made clear that celibacy was a superior state. It also, sadly in the case of divorce, denied the right of the innocent party to marry again. This was a right that had existed pre-Trent and which continues to exist in the Orthodox Church. The idea that the Catholic Church has always allowed only one marriage is therefore a fallacy.

If one looks back at history with hindsight and from a twenty-first-century perspective, it can be seen that the differences between the teachings of Luther and the official church of his day were not really differences between one man and the Catholic Church. They were differences between many Catholics. Luther was originally a Catholic for whom Catholicism had gone sour due to, among other things, the increasing elitism of the clergy, and he was supported by many people—all of them Catholics. In the end, due to the popularity of his teachings, he brought about a schism of the church. The teachings of Luther and the teachings of the Council of Trent were greatly opposed to each other, and both of them in various different ways are, in some areas, a long way from the Jesus of the New Testament. It is a pity that the two opposing camps could not have dialogued and brought about a synthesis of their respective theologies. Instead, the Council of Trent chose to oppose one extreme with another extreme, and some of its decrees were not only unbiblical but also greatly damaging. They were damaging because they elevated priests to the status of demigods, which resulted in the belittling of both laypeople and women in particular.

The teaching that the ordination of a priest placed an indelible character on the priest's soul was unfortunate because it confirmed the elevation of priests to a superior status above the rest of humanity. As has already been noted, by the time of the Council of Trent, only celibate men could become priests in the Catholic Church due to the marriage of priests having been banned by the earlier First Council of the Lateran in 1122. However, Jesus had never said that his disciples could not marry, and it is clear from the synoptic Gospels that Peter was actually married

(Matthew 8:14–16; Mark 1:29–31; Luke 4:38–39) and had a son (1 Peter 5:13) The Gospels tell us that Jesus healed his mother-in-law, and Peter himself refers to his son Mark. Some Western scholars have tried to say that this son was a spiritual son, but the Greek word *uios* is used, and this word has always meant biological son. After the East–West Schism the Orthodox Church continued to ordain married men (and continues to do so to this day), while the Roman Catholic Church later banned this practice. As the Council of Trent reaffirmed the Latin Church's decision to prevent priests from marrying, and declared that the ordination of a priest placed an indelible mark on his soul, it in effect stated that ordained male celibate priests were superior to the rest of humanity. Both married men and women could not be ordained as priests, and therefore they could not access this "indelible character" on their souls and were second-class citizens.

This decree of the Council of Trent seems completely contrary both to the teachings of Jesus in the Gospels and to the letters of St. Peter and St. Paul in the New Testament. New Testament scholars are in agreement that Mark is the earliest Gospel, and throughout this Gospel Jesus is presented as being totally against the so-called superiority of the "clerics" of his day. For example, we read:

> Beware of the scribes who like to walk around in long robes, to be greeted respectfully in market squares, to take the front seats in the synagogues and the places of honor at banquets; these are the men that devour the property of widows and for show offer long prayers. The more severe will be the sentence they receive. (Mark 12:38–40)

The writer of St. Peter's letters (some scholars argue that the writer was not St. Peter) does not favor an elite priestly caste either, and saw every Christian as part of the priesthood. In this letter, we read:

> But you are a chosen race, a kingdom of priests, a holy nation, a people to be a personal possession to sing the praises of God who called you out of the darkness into his wonderful light. Once you were a non-people and now you are the people of God; once you were outside his pity; now you have received his pity. (1 Peter 2:9–10)

St. Paul wrote nothing about any special elite priesthood either as there was, in fact, as we have seen in a previous chapter, no particularly exclusive priesthood in his time. Most of his letters are addressed to a variety of people in different ministries in various early church communities, all of which are clearly the people of God. For example, 1 Corinthians is addressed to

> the Church of God in Corinth, to those who have been consecrated in Christ Jesus and called to be God's holy people, with all those everywhere who call on the name of our Lord Jesus Christ, their Lord as well as ours. (1 Corinthians: 1–3)

The decree of the Council of Trent that the ordination of celibate men places an indelible character on the priest's soul therefore smacks of organizational and political power abuse, as the Gospels tell us no such thing. The Gospels tell us that everyone through Christ is called to have an indelible mark on their souls, as we are all "a kingdom of priests." Here we have a church that has moved very far, over the centuries, from the original Gospels of the New Testament and is fighting to maintain its worldly power—a worldly power that Jesus had condemned in the Gospels, stating "I am not of this world" (John 8:23). In addition to this, the decree that the Latin Vulgate should be the official Bible of the church and that only the Catholic Church could authoritatively interpret scripture also smacks of power abuse. The Bible was not written in Latin. The Old Testament was written mainly in Hebrew, and the New Testament was written in Greek. However, no one was now officially allowed to translate this Bible other than priests and bishops of the church, who might not be well versed in either of these languages. Furthermore, they were only allowed to translate this Bible into Latin and not into the vernacular. These decrees in effect removed the original teachings of Jesus further from the people and were clearly about power. They were not about the message of Jesus at all. The Council of Trent was seeking to remove the message of Jesus from the people in order to protect an elitist version of Christianity that had grown up in a version of Christendom that was now being challenged by half of the Catholic world.

The reaffirming of the requirement of a priest to be celibate was also highly unfortunate and could today be classed as a breach of human rights, seeing as the right to marry is today classed as an inalienable human right. The idea that celibacy was a superior state had never been particularly promoted by Jesus, and there is also strong evidence from outside of the New Testament that two of his apostles were married. Clement of Alexandria writing in the second century is quite clear that both Peter and Phillip were married and had children, and he condemns enforced celibacy as scorning the apostles. The concept of priestly celibacy as a higher state was developed at a much later stage by St. Augustine partly due to the writings of St. Paul in 1 Corinthians 7, where he stated that marriage was an acceptable state but it was better to be celibate. However, Paul's writings have to be understood in context. It is quite clear that Paul thought that the second coming of Jesus was imminent and that the world was passing away, and this was really the main reason why he promoted this teaching (1 Corinthians 7:29–31). St. Paul was also living in a period when there was a very poor understanding of human sexuality, and in fairness to the Council of Trent it has to be said that the same thing also applied at the time of this council. Sadly, however, the imposition of enforced celibacy on priests in the Latin Church has done a great deal of damage both to many priests themselves and to others over the centuries.

It is now understood that being sexualized is part of being human, and psychologists, such as Abraham Maslow, have stated that love, belonging, and sexual intimacy are essential needs that must be met in order to achieve wholeness or self-actualization. This does not necessarily mean that every human being must have sex in order to be fulfilled; each human being has a different libido. But it does mean that each human being needs to feel a sense of love and belonging, and for many human beings this will need to be expressed in a sexual relationship. Enforced celibacy denies priests the ability to physically express love, and this can be psychologically damaging. This is not to say that celibacy is wrong, as there are some people who do not have a high libido and for whom physical intimacy is not that important. These people are able to take up celibacy happily and without any difficulty. It is to say that enforced celibacy is wrong because it forces some men, who would wish to serve God as a priest, to take up a way of living that is alien to them and not really what they want. This can have many ill effects on a person, such as loneliness, sexual deviancy, sexual perversion, and depression. Enforced celibacy is also damaging to the church and to wider society because it holds up a way of life that is essentially unnatural as an ideal. Denying an essential part of one's humanity is held up as being better than being fully human, and this creates a cult of men who are different to the rest of humanity and out of touch with the people they are meant to teach and serve. An elitist band of celibate men sit in councils and pronounce on the morality of the masses when many of them have no idea what it is like to be a member of these masses. They have no idea what it is like to be married, and they have no idea what it is like to be a woman. It could even be argued that some of them have no idea what it is like to be a real "fully human" being. Of course, there are some celibate men who are very human and able to be very empathetic. This is usually because they have lived a full life before choosing to become a celibate priest and may have perhaps previously enjoyed a sexual relationship. However, the fact remains that there are a large number of celibate priests who are not only out of touch with the people that they seek to serve but are also out of touch with their own selves. Some of these men struggle with issues to do with sexuality that they are not able to fully comprehend or to resolve. These men are struggling due to a tradition at foisted celibacy onto them in the eleventh century and that was reaffirmed by Trent in the sixteenth century.

While the Council of Trent was sitting in Europe, Elizabeth I came to the throne in England in 1558. At this time Catholicism had been briefly revived in England by Mary I, who was Henry VIII's Catholic daughter. Mary had attempted to restore the female consecrated life in Britain, and the Bridgettines of Syon, who had fled to Europe from her father, had returned to England once again and made a brief attempt at reestablishment. The Dominican nuns had also returned. However, when Elizabeth succeeded to the throne, these religious women were again forced to flee, and the sanctification of the clerical state with the exclusion of women was as unabated in Protestantism as it was in Catholicism. The Reformation gave no real role to women at all other than being a "holy wife" married to a priest. In fact, the Reformation was very demeaning to women, as no options were left open to them outside of marriage. It was not possible to be consecrated in Elizabethan England, and to attempt to do this was to place one's life in danger; but despite this, the female consecrated life was not to totally die out in England. It was to continue due to the determination of one Englishwoman. Her name was Mary Ward.

Mary Ward was born in 1586 to a well-off northern Catholic recusant family, and apparently two of her relatives were involved in the Gunpowder Plot. In 1595, her family home was burned down in an anti-Catholic riot and the children were saved by their father. She later developed the desire to enter a religious order and, as there were no religious orders left in England, she fled to the low countries. In 1606, Mary entered a Belgian convent of the Poor Clares but found that the contemplative life was not for her. She again tried her vocation at a second Poor Clare convent, but this also did not work, out and she returned to England in 1609. It was after her return to England that Mary developed the idea of an active religious order for women that, like the Jesuit order for men, would teach and perform charitable works. She managed to obtain the consent of Jacques Blaise, bishop of St. Omer, and in 1615 opened a first branch of what was later to be known as the Mary Ward Institute in St. Martin's Lane, London. She later sent to Paul V the scheme of the institute and received a favorable reply. She then founded a second convent at Fountains Abbey. This was later moved to Heworth and then to Bar, York. However, the life of Mary and her sisters was not easy in England. On occasion they were imprisoned, and on another occasion the Bar Convent was in danger of being destroyed by a fanatical mob.

The persecution of the new congregation in England was not the only hardship Mary and her sisters faced. The tide was also turning against them overseas. In 1629, the Congregation of the Propaganda suppressed Mary's institute, stating that religious women should be enclosed and not active. Mary herself was imprisoned for some time in the Anger convent at Munich but eventually managed to obtain the permission required for some sisters to continue their apostolate in England. Sadly, this was under the condition that they lived private vows. Mary's new congregation did not receive official recognition until its rule was eventually approved by Pope Clement XI in 1703. The institute itself was not given formal approval until 1877 by Pope Pius IX. This was 232 years after Mary's death.

Mary had given the female consecrated life a resurrection as at the time of the Reformation all active forms of female religious life had been destroyed. Technically, at the time of the Reformation, the female religious orders were enclosed; however, there were other forms of consecrated life that were active, such as the individually consecrated vowesses. These had been wiped out, along with the anchoresses who, although enclosed, received visitors to whom they gave spiritual direction from windows in their cells. Following the Reformation, the Catholic Church had not bothered to encourage the restoration of these forms of religious life. This meant that the only form of consecrated life available to women was the enclosed one, but Mary changed all that. Now women could be consecrated as sisters, and they could therefore combine a reformed life of prayer with an active religious life.

In the seventeenth century many women who had wanted to live a consecrated life had fled England and moved to Europe, but with the arrival of the French Revolution monasteries were destroyed in France, Belgium, Germany, Italy, and Spain. This persecution did not last, and within a generation the monasteries were restored in Europe. However, the French Revolution was important for Catholic women in Britain because it was during the course of that revolution that consecrated women once again returned to British shores. Catholic women who had fled Britain in search of a place to live out their vows now fled continental Europe for Britain for the same purpose, as by this time the country was becoming more receptive to having religious women in its midst. Thus, in 1792 the Benedictine nuns of Montargis arrived in England and a home was found for them. In addition to the Benedictines, other enclosed orders began to arrive and establish themselves, including the Canonesses of St. Augustine; the Canonesses of the Holy Sepulcher; the Carmelites; and the Dominicans.

After the French Revolution, the female religious life began once again to flourish in Europe, and it was at this stage that Mary Ward's idea of the active religious life began to take root, and many new active religious congregations began to spring up across the continent. Within Britain both active religious congregations from the continent and new home-grown congregations began to spring up and grow. These congregations were devoted to carrying out works of charity and also to providing a Catholic education for the young. Many of the young women who joined them at this time desired to live active and innovative lives in the world as bearers of reform. Initially they were to bring about many great reforms, although during later times they were to become tainted with the more unfortunate effects of institutionalization.

Within Britain in particular the sphere in which the active religious women were to have the most effect was the sphere of education. There was a great determination emanating from the religious communities to build schools for the Catholic community, and they made available an education for girls that had not previously existed except, perhaps, for the female children of the aristocracy. By 1850, mainstream England had no public schools for girls and its universities were closed to the female sex, but within the Catholic community a formidable number of convent schools had opened. These schools concentrated on providing an education for girls that equaled that of boys. Later, in 1868, the Schools Enquiry Commission emphasized the poor quality of female education overall—but by this time in Catholic circles the picture was very different. There were over twenty different congregations of religious sisters engaged in teaching, and they offered an imposing selection of convent schools for the Catholic girl that were the envy of mainstream England. Moreover, the education of girls was not the only area in which these new active sisters were pioneers. Congregations such as the Sisters of Charity of St. Vincent de Paul also specialized in helping those with special needs and paved the way in the process of informing society of the value of all human beings regardless of disability. These teachers opened schools for children who were deaf, speechless, and blind, as well as schools for children with learning disabilities. The

Dominican Sisters of St. Catherine of Siena also sought to assist and educate children with learning disabilities.

While female religious women in Britain had found and developed their own careers by choosing to follow the celibate path, they were also eager to ensure that women who did not wish to become sisters or nuns would also be able to have their own careers. For this reason, religious women were instrumental in establishing teacher training colleges, which would enable women to become teachers without becoming religious sisters. In 1901 La Sainte Union opened a teacher training college at Southampton, and by 1950 there were eleven such teacher training colleges in England that had been established by different religious congregations.

The founding of independent Catholic convent schools and the establishing of Catholic teacher training colleges had a great effect on the growth of the Catholic faith in Britain as a whole but particularly in England. By 1950 there were twenty-seven thousand Catholic girls educated in convent schools in England as well as several thousand boys. As 43 percent of those who attended Catholic schools were non-Catholic, this naturally resulted in an increase in the number of Catholics in England because many of the non-Catholics who attended these schools later went on to convert to the Catholic faith. Up until the 1960s there was a steady growth in the number of priests, churches, schools, and convents in England, and one of the main factors behind this growth were the active religious women. Therefore, by 1961, 12.7 percent of all marriages in England were Catholic and 10 percent of the nation was practicing Catholic. This was a remarkable turnabout considering that the Catholic Church had ceased to exist at all in England at the time of the Reformation. However, even though women had done a great deal to assist with the growth of the Church in England and other European countries, this in no way elevated their status.

It would not be right to assume that because consecrated women had instigated a period of growth in the church, they were now highly influential. Women were still second-class citizens within the church itself. For example, while the established Church in England aided and funded the establishment of teacher training colleges for men, the female religious received no such help with the funding of their own teacher training colleges and had to raise the money themselves. In addition to this, the only full-time consecrated vocations that were open to women were the enclosed or active forms of the religious life. But vocations to the female consecrated life were to again decline in the later twentieth century, and when they did so there would be very few other opportunities open to Catholic women. Women remained second-class citizens because they could not be ordained either as deacons or priests, and they also could not participate in church synods. As we have already noted, the Council of Trent had declared that ordination produced an indelible character on the soul, and this had immediately given both women and married men an inferior status to celibate men as they could not access this indelible character. There was also a sitting of another ecumenical council in the nineteenth century that placed a further stranglehold on the power of the church, and this was the First Vatican Council.

The First Vatican Council was the twentieth ecumenical council of the Roman Catholic Church and was convened by Pope Pius IX. This council sat between December 8, 1869, and October 20, 1870. Its main teaching was to condemn rationalism, secularism, naturalism, modernism, materialism, and pantheism and also to pronounce that the Pope was infallible. The dogmatic constitution stated that the Pope had "full and supreme power of jurisdiction over the whole Church" and that when he "speaks ex cathedra, that is, when, in the exercise of his office as shepherd and teacher of all Christians, in virtue of his supreme apostolic authority, he defines a doctrine concerning faith or morals to be held by the whole Church, he possesses, by the divine assistance promised to him in blessed Peter, that infallibility which the divine Redeemer willed his Church to enjoy in defining doctrine concerning faith or morals."

Sadly, the deliberations and pronouncements of this ecumenical council again read as a blind and rigid determination to hold on to power at all costs. Many new ways of learning and thinking were about in the world, but the church had no desire to think about or engage with them. It had no desire to explore whether it could learn anything from these ways of thinking. It simply condemned them. In regard to the infallibility of the Pope, as has been noted in earlier chapters, this had been something that the Western church had wanted to declare for some time, mainly as a means of universalizing its power. However, it is hard to see how the Pope could suddenly now in 1870 become infallible when no Pope had previously been defined as infallible since the death of Christ at around AD 33. The early church would not have understood such an idea, and this council, in promulgating such a teaching, was surely using this to achieve its own purposes and protect the power of the church. It is also impossible to understand how any figure can be infallible when defining a doctrine of faith and morals that is to be held by the whole church when half of the church, namely women, have not been consulted due to their inability to sit on ecumenical councils, which in effect prevents them from having any voice. The First Vatican Council was certainly not speaking for the whole church in its dogmatic constitutions, seeing as half of the church was not consulted on this matter, and, indeed, half of the church had never been consulted on any teaching for hundreds of years. This council was speaking only for men, and celibate men at that, and with its triumphant legalism it further entrenched clericalism.

CHAPTER SIX

Vatican II and Later Disappointments

This chapter will examine the teachings of the Second Vatican Council and their initial and later effects on the church and on women in particular. The opposition to Vatican II by devotees of the Council of Trent and the Society of St. Pius X will also be examined. These opponents of Vatican II are often referred to as "traditionalists," but I will argue that they are not traditionalists. This is because this group of people is true only to the teachings of the relatively late Council of Trent and is not true to the teachings of the historical Jesus or the teachings of the early church. This chapter will also examine various disappointments that occurred following Vatican II, including the encyclicals *Humanae Vitae* and *Ordinatio Sacerdotalis*; the rushed canonization of Pope St. John Paul II; and the sexual abuse scandals that have occurred within the church. I will argue that following an initial period of great hope after Vatican II, many people later went on to leave the church. This is most likely due to the fact that the promises of Vatican II were never fully brought to fruition. Women and, to a lesser extent, married men remained second-class citizens within the church. I will argue that women have far less influence in the Catholic Church today than they have ever had in any previous historical period.

The Second Ecumenical Council of the Vatican, usually known as Vatican II, was the twenty-first ecumenical council of the Roman Catholic Church. The Council was opened on October 11, 1962, by Pope St. John XXIII and was closed on December 8, 1965, under Pope St. Paul VI. The Council met for four periods lasting between eight and twelve weeks in the autumn of each of the four years that it sat. The council was, of course, composed of bishops, and the number of bishops attending varied between sessions but was somewhere between 2,100–2,300. A small number of theologians were also invited to attend, and the Orthodox and Protestant denominations were invited to send observers. There were no female attendees other than 23 women auditors who were not allowed to speak, but nevertheless this council was different to earlier councils such as the Council of Trent and Vatican I in that it had been called to actually look at the church critically and to attempt to bring about reform rather than to make triumphalist declarations.

The council's teaching is contained in sixteen documents comprising four constitutions, nine decrees, and three declarations. These documents addressed the council's relationship with the modern world; instigated a wide variety of reforms; and reversed some of the damaging teachings of the Council of Trent. Throughout the period of the council, it was made clear that its main purpose was to promote a universal call to holiness and a turning away from clericalism toward a new age of the laity.

Vatican II instigated many reforms, including the following: the widespread use of the vernacular languages (instead of Latin) in the Mass; the revision of Eucharistic prayers; the abbreviation of the liturgical calendar; the ability to celebrate Mass with the priest facing the congregation; an emphasis on laypeople as the "people of God"; a new emphasis on biblical theology; a new emphasis on ecumenism; recognition of the rites of Eastern Catholics in communion with Rome to keep their distinct liturgical practices; a new recognition of the apostolate of the laity; a call for the adaptation and renewal of the religious life and a call for priests to become brothers as well as fathers and teachers.

Initially, Vatican II was greeted with enthusiasm by the vast majority of clergy and laypeople, and a new era of hope dawned within the Catholic Church. The minor orders were suppressed and replaced by two new ministries of lector and acolyte that could be assigned to lay Christians, and these were taken up with great enthusiasm. In addition to this, in 1967, Pope St. Paul VI restored the rite of the permanent diaconate for married men. This meant that married men could now be ordained as deacons; but unfortunately, the female diaconate was not restored. This was very disappointing, bearing in mind that women had also been enrolled into the diaconate until the tenth century in some countries. Meanwhile, there was also in the wake of Vatican II a surge in Europe of some of the newer forms of consecrated life, such as Opus Dei and the secular institutes. These forms of consecrated life had actually been founded just before Vatican II, but they began to grow much faster in its wake. In addition to this, the council had requested a revision of the rite of the consecration of virgins, and a revised rite was approved by Pope St. Paul VI and eventually published in 1970. This rite also attracted new members across Europe and in other countries, although not so much in Britain, where this form of consecrated life was not very well promoted. Furthermore, a large number of laypeople also sought to study theology, and in England both Heythrop College and Plater College attracted many students from Britain and Ireland in the 1970s and 1980s. There was a feeling of optimism in the air, and many students studying at these colleges, myself included, would discuss the future of the church. It was believed that the ordination of married priests was imminent, and the inclusion of women in the female diaconate was also expected. Unfortunately, these two anticipated changes have not occurred.

During the 1970s, vocations to the female consecrated life began to decline across Europe. This decline was worse in some European countries than in others. There were a few possible main reasons for the decline. Firstly, a much more wholesome view of human sexuality together with a more positive theology of marriage was developing, and therefore many women no longer found the celibate life attractive or desirable; secondly, many women had often embraced the female consecrated life not only for spiritual reasons but also to receive a good education and career. However, now all women were well educated by the state and did not need the religious orders to educate them. And thirdly, many of the roles of the religious orders in the sphere of education and care had now been taken over by the state. This meant that a lot of the religious congregations had lost their raison d'être and were unable to promote their vocations in the way they had done in previous years. Later, in some countries such as Ireland, the religious congregations were also to lose their credibility due to their involvement in institutional abuse; but this began to be highlighted around the turn of the twentieth century. The initial reasons for the decline in vocations were a declining interest in celibacy and the fact that the state was now the provider of education and care.

Within some countries, such as Britain and Ireland, the decline in the number of vocations to the consecrated life was much more severe than in others. There are a number of possible reasons for this. Firstly, Vatican II seems to have been interpreted differently in Britain and Ireland to other European countries in regards to the role of the laity. When the council had sought to promote and encourage new ministries for the laity, it had not intended these lay vocations to replace vocations to the female consecrated life. The council had envisaged a collaborative ministry. However, unfortunately in Britain and Ireland, many bishops and priests took to promoting the lay vocations at the expense of vocations to the female consecrated life. Lay vocations were now promoted and female consecrated vocations were simply ignored. Secondly, within Britain and Ireland, the active female religious found it very difficult to find a new purpose when their roles in education and care ceased. This did not apply to religious in other countries, such as Italy, where many new roles were open to them, such as working in the various departments of the Vatican and using their convents as accommodation for tourists. Thirdly, in other European countries the new and restored forms of consecrated life were growing, and a sizable number of women were being consecrated as virgins or within secular institutes. Unfortunately, these vocations were not as well promoted in Britain and Ireland. Some bishops and priests harbored a great suspicion in regard to consecrated women living independently within their own homes and would not promote these vocations. This meant that many Catholic women were completely unaware of these new and restored forms of consecrated life, and so these vocations failed to grow and thrive in the United Kingdom and Ireland as they did in other European countries.

The decline in vocations to the female consecrated life was very problematic for women as it began to produce a more unbalanced church than there had ever been before. This was because if there were no consecrated women with influence within the church then there were, in effect, no women at all with any influence in the church. Yes, laywomen now took up lay ministries and were involved in teaching and also in various ministries in their own parishes, such as reader and acolyte, music, and the distribution of the Blessed Sacrament. Yes, these ministries were important locally to the people of God. But what effect could these ministries have on the governance of the Catholic Church in their own dioceses? How did these ministries assist women to be heard? The answer was, of course, that they didn't, because these ministries did not enable women to be an official part of the "ruling caste" of the church. They did not enable women to be decision makers in their own dioceses, and they did not enable women to have a vote on any large church council. The situation was slightly better for married men because they at least could be ordained as permanent deacons, and this official role did enable them to meet ad clerum in their own dioceses with other deacons, priests, and the bishops. However, for women there was no place in such meetings. They were completely excluded from the governance of the church, which produced a state of affairs for Catholic women that was far worse than it had ever been before. As has already been noted, in pre-Reformation Britain women were consulted by bishops, and while it would be true to say that post-Reformation women had lost a great deal of influence, the active female religious orders in their heyday still had a lot more influence than modern Catholic women have today. Some of these religious orders were very large and owned many properties, and this did at least ensure that some bishops took some notice of these women and consulted with them.

While the situation in Britain and Ireland was particularly dire for women, it could be said that in other European countries it was slightly better. This was because in countries such as Italy, France, and Poland, the restored vocation of consecrated virgin was better promoted, as were the vocations to secular institutes. These vocations enabled women to take vows of poverty, chastity, and obedience and live out their vocations independently in their own homes. In addition to this, these countries did not seem to have such a crisis in vocations to the active female religious life as there were in Britain and Ireland. This was probably due to the fact that these vocations were much better supported by the bishops in these countries and were still actively promoted. In addition to this, these women were assisted to find alternative ministries after their roles in education and social care had been taken over by the state. Nevertheless, the influence of women in these countries was still also at a very low ebb. No woman, for example, had acquired the influence of the fourteenth-century saint Catherine of Siena, who had given spiritual advice to two popes, and it was becoming increasingly unlikely that any future woman would ever do so.

While the teachings of the Second Vatican Council had initially been greeted with great enthusiasm by the majority of priests and laity and had also initially attracted many new people to the Catholic Church, this state of affairs was not to last, and there was eventually to be a great hemorrhaging of members from the Catholic Church within the Western world. Millions were to become disappointed with the church and to leave en masse. The main reason why people began to leave the church was almost certainly because Vatican II was never fully implemented and the further reforms that people had expected did not happen. There were five things in particular that disappointed many Catholics post-Council: the publication of the papal encyclical *Humanae Vitae*; the emergence of the Society of St. Pius X and the church's failure to deal with this challenge; the publication of *Ordinatio Sacerdotalis*; the rushed canonization of Pope St. John Paul II; and the involvement of a substantial number of the clergy in sexual abuse.

Humanae Vitae was written by Pope St. Paul VI and was dated July 25, 1968. It was therefore published only three years after the Second Vatican Council. This document reaffirmed earlier Catholic teaching on the procreative and unitive nature of conjugal relations, married love, responsible parenthood, and the rejection of artificial contraception. This teaching had not been expected to be reaffirmed for the following reasons: firstly, the oral contraceptive pill had actually been invented by a devout Catholic and eminent gynecologist, John Rock, and Rock had believed that the contraceptive was in line with Catholic teaching; secondly, the post–Vatican II church had seemed to be so much more positive in regards to sexuality; and finally, members of an earlier commission, the Pontifical Commission on Birth Control, had voted by an overwhelming majority (in 1966) to allow Catholic couples to decide for themselves about birth control. The Pope had therefore, in issuing this encyclical, gone against the findings of his own commission which had comprised of cardinals, bishops, theologians, physicians, and even women.

Humanae Vitae was received with shock, and open dissent from the laity was voiced widely and publicly. There was also a group of dissident theologians led by Rev. Charles Curran that issued a statement that Catholics should decide for themselves about artificial contraception in accordance with their own consciences. The Canadian bishops also opposed this teaching in the "Winnipeg Statement," as did many theologians and several episcopal conferences. This teaching was widely rejected in Europe, America, and Canada and was a factor in many people leaving the church as it clearly demonstrated that despite Vatican II, married people and women still had no say in regards to the teaching of the church. They had been consulted but ignored, and a previous teaching had been reaffirmed by a celibate Pope who, it could be argued, had little idea what it was like to be married and also had no real understanding of human sexuality. This encyclical stated that procreation remained the main purpose of the sexual act and failed to understand the sexual act as a means of bonding and as a means of expressing love and belonging, which is of extreme importance to the psychological well-being of humans.

Humanae Vitae was widely rejected and remains so to this day. It has undermined the credibility of the church, and it is likely that a vast number of Catholics have left due to it. Furthermore, the vast majority of those who have remained in the church have clearly ignored it. This can be evidenced when attending any Mass as it is very rare to find any family with more than three children. Yet the papacy has sadly continued to endorse this encyclical in current times and to ignore the vast majority of its members. Many people would argue that in doing so the hierarchy is treating the laity with contempt. Unfortunately, what the hierarchy are failing to understand is that laypeople will no longer be dictated to by celibate men, and if celibate men continue to make decisions of which the vast majority of laypeople do not approve, then they will continue to cause the current church to hemorrhage in numbers. The early church, the church of Jesus of Nazareth, was not governed by a small band of celibate men, and modern Christians are becoming increasingly reluctant to allow this kind of dictatorship. The failure of the church hierarchy to consult and debate with its members on moral teaching is seen by many as another abuse of power.

The Society of St. Pius X (SSPX) has also proved to be very problematic for the majority of mainstream Catholics. This society was founded in 1970 by Archbishop Marcel Lefebvre. This archbishop referred to himself as a "traditionalist," although he was no such thing. Lefebvre had no time for the teachings of the early church and instead preferred the much later teachings of the Council of Trent. The society he founded stresses the retaining of the non-biblical Tridentine Mass and pre–Vatican II liturgical books in Latin. It is also strongly opposed to all the teaching documents of Vatican II. In addition, the society presents itself as misogynistic not only because it does not support any form of female ordination but also because of the attitudes it promotes in regard to women. It appears to reject the idea of women working, and very few, if any, of its female members work. Moreover, it seeks to meddle in every aspect of women's lives, even prescribing the kind of attire that women should wear. Some of its clerics have stated that women's trousers are an assault on their womanhood and represent a revolt against the order created by God. Neither men nor women are allowed to use artificial contraception within this society, and many women have in excess of eight children. It has also been alleged that some children who are brought up within this society are not allowed to mix with children outside of it and are homeschooled. There have been reports of some of these children being the subject of abusive physical "punishments" if they question the views of their parents. Sadly, this society is way out of touch not only with mainstream Catholicism but also with the majority of people across the globe who see it as completely normal for women today to work in all roles and capacities and to be elected as heads of state. This society bears all the hallmarks of a religious cult, the definition of which is as follows:

> A system of beliefs and rituals based on dogma or religious teachings and characterized by devoted adherents who display a readiness to obey, an unrealistic idealization of the leader, an abandonment of personal ambition and goals, and an eschewing of traditional societal values.

While this society was initially regarded with suspicion by Pope St. John XXIII, it later received increasing recognition from the hierarchical church with a growing recognition of its sacramental and pastoral activities. This increasing recognition of such a cult was disturbing and created even more dismay among many mainstream Catholics. Many Catholics had hoped that this society would be condemned by the papacy, and its increasing recognition led to further numbers of Catholics leaving the church. Recently Pope Francis has placed some restrictions on the Latin Mass, but this will not bring back many former Catholics who do not feel this goes far enough. The hierarchy appear to want to keep this group within the church at all costs despite the overall negative effect it is having on church membership. Sadly, it is likely that if the Catholic Church continues on this course of acceptance of those who adhere to the teachings of the SSPX it could eventually become a cult itself. Within twenty to thirty years all mainstream Catholics in the West could leave the church and a small misogynistic sect may be all that is left of Catholicism. This cult bears all the hallmarks of a spiritually abusive organization and cannot in any way be seen as promoting the good news of Jesus. Rather, it represents a spiritual "elite" who appear to believe that anyone who does not share their minority views is destined to perdition and damnation. Followers of this society have also shown themselves to be extremely aggressive and prepared to use violence to promote their causes. After the election of the last US president, many people who tried to cause an insurrection to overturn the democratic vote declared themselves on social media to be members or followers of the SSPX.

In 1994 Pope St. John Paul II published the apostolic letter *Ordinatio Sacerdotalis,* or "On reserving priestly ordination to men alone." While women had not been ordained as priests since the middle of the fourth century, the subject of female ordination had never before been addressed in any papal document, and this letter was written in the wake of the decision by the Anglican community to ordain women. This document was very unfortunate as it only served to widen the division between progressive Catholics and so-called traditionalists and led to even more lay Catholics leaving the church. In addition to this, it could be argued that it was fundamentally flawed for a number of reasons, as detailed here.

Firstly, one of the reasons given for the Catholic Church's inability to ordain women is the assertion that Jesus chose only men to be apostles. This assertion is simply not true. It was not Jesus who chose only men to be apostles. It was the Catholic Church that decided several hundred years after the death of Jesus that he had chosen only men to be apostles. In reality, Jesus had chosen Mary Magdalene as the first witness of the resurrection and had instructed her to go and tell the disciples that he had risen. Why then is Mary not regarded as an apostle? The church regards St. Paul as an apostle even though he never met Jesus while he was alive. He is regarded as an apostle purely because he had a vision of the risen Lord. Why then is Mary not regarded as an apostle when she was not only the first to see the risen Lord but had also known Jesus during his lifetime and followed him to the cross? Surely her credentials for being regarded as an apostle are just as good or even better than St. Paul's? What reason is there for her not being recognized as an apostle? The only reason for this lack of recognition is that men refused to give her this status purely because she was a woman.

Secondly, this document could be viewed as flawed because it states that the church has constantly imitated Christ in choosing only men to be priests. But this is again simply not true. It is absolutely clear from many sources of evidence that the early church ordained women as deacons, and due to this the Orthodox Church has now begun to restore the female diaconate. Furthermore, there is strong evidence that women were being ordained as priests in the writings of the early church fathers not only at the time of Tertullian, but also at the much later time of the Council of Laodicea in the mid-fourth century. This council, by prohibiting the ordination of the "so-called presbyteresses," makes it very clear that women were still being ordained at that time. This is over three hundred years after the death of Jesus, and women were still being ordained. It is therefore not true to state that the Catholic Church kept up, from the time of Christ, the constant practice of ordaining only men, seeing as women were clearly still being ordained in some places in the fourth century. What clearly happened is that women were initially ordained in the early church and their ordinations were later suppressed by men.

Thirdly, this document states that the Blessed Virgin Mary did not receive the ministerial priesthood, but this theological position was not taken by the Catholic Church until 1913, when the Holy Office forbade the practice of portraying Mary as a priest. Later, in 1926, the Holy Office declared that devotion to Mary as a priest was not approved and was not to be promoted. However, John Wijngaards clearly demonstrates in his 1999 article "The Priesthood of Mary" that up until this time, many theologians had regarded Mary as a priest. He states that in the run-up to the declaration of Mary's immaculate conception, the text of Hebrews 7:26 was often applied to her:

> It is fitting that we should have such a high priest, holy, blameless, unstained, separated from sinners, exalted above the heavens.

He also states that the Benedictine prior Jacques Biroat wrote in 1666 that St. Paul's reasoning in the preceding text is relevant to Christ's mother as she shares in the priesthood of her son and is the origin of our relationship to God. Wijngaards also cites Ferdinand Chirino de Salazar SJ (1575–1646) as stating,

> Christ, "the anointed," poured out the abundance of his anointing on Mary, making her a saint, a queen and a priest forever. Mary obtained a priesthood more eminent and excelling than that possessed by anyone else. For in unison with priests who are performing the sacred mysteries and together with Christ and in the same mystical way as he does, she always offers the Eucharistic sacrifice, just as, at one with him, she offered the sacrifice on Calvary.

Wijngaards then goes on to argue that Mary belonged to a priestly family and was often referred to by the church fathers as "Mary the Sanctuary" or "Mary the Ark of the Covenant" and states that there is a rich and continuous tradition that venerated Mary's priesthood.

Finally, *Ordinatio Sacerdotalis* is written in a style that clearly illustrates that the writer, Pope St. John Paul II, did not really regard women as part of the church because he frequently writes of what "the Church" teaches about women, as if women are not part of the church at all but are instead part of some kind of group or sect. Clearly the writer actually sees only the celibate hierarchy as the church, as can be evidenced from the following quotes from this document:

> The Church does not consider herself authorized to admit women to priestly ordination.

> The Church desires that Christian women should become fully aware of the greatness of their mission.

> I declare that the Church has no authority whatsoever to confer priestly ordination on women and that this judgment is to be definitively held by all the Church's faithful.

Who are "the Church" here in this document? The New Testament tells us that the church is the people of God; however, the Council of Trent changed all that. From the time of that council, the official teaching church became the hierarchy, which was separate from its members. Many people believe that Vatican II reversed this, but actually it didn't. Although Vatican II stressed the importance of the lay apostolate in *Lumen Gentium*, it did not actually change the teaching that the official church is composed of the hierarchy alone. Therefore, in this document the church is clearly seen as the hierarchy. This papal letter alienated many Catholics—and not just women. There were many theologians and many laymen who were very unhappy with it. Many people have left the church due to it, and the writer finds it very unfortunate that this document was written at this time as it caused a further hemorrhage of church members and further divisions.

It would be true to say that within the church today the issue of the ordination of women as priests has become schismatic. Why then did Pope St. John Paul II find it necessary to raise the issue in the late twentieth century? Surely it would have been obvious that this would cause more people to leave the church. Wouldn't it have been better to have put this subject to one side for the time being and instead to have concentrated on the question of the ordination of women to the diaconate? There is clear historical evidence that women were ordained as deacons in the early centuries, and the consideration of restoring the female diaconate would have been nowhere near as divisive as this document and may have prepared the way for the question of the female priesthood to be considered in later years to come. Indeed, the Orthodox Church was certainly not going to take up such a stance and has acknowledged the evidence for the existence of female deacons within the early church. The Greek Orthodox Patriarchate of Alexandria and All Africa restored the female diaconate in 2017. However, unfortunately the Pope went at the issue of female ordination like a bull in a china shop and more and more people left the church as a result of this encyclical. It has to be recognized that in a world where women have now proved themselves to be competent in almost any office, this stance on the female priesthood seems incomprehensible to the vast majority of people, and due to this and other issues the church in the West is continuously hemorrhaging. In addition, the encyclical *Ordinatio Sacerdotalis* itself could be regarded as spiritually abusive as some of its statements are not true and appear to have been written to defend a spiritual place of authority or dogma that is demeaning to women.

Having seen that the papal letter *Ordinatio Sacedotalis* was controversial, it should therefore be no surprise that the canonization of Pope St. John Paul II was also extremely controversial. While many Catholics recognized that this Pope had done many good things in his papacy, such as helping to bring about the 1989 fall of Communism in Europe and transforming the papal travel schedule, some theologians also thought that his stance on contraception and on women's ordination had been schismatic and had led to many people leaving the church. Eleven dissident theologians objected to his beatification, and many laypeople were dismayed by the fast way in which this canonization occurred. This Pope was canonized only nine years after his death, and many women have expressed the view on social media that his canonization may have been rushed through in an attempt to cement his views on women's ordination. In addition to this, it has since been established that many sexual abuse scandals occurred during his papacy, and due to this a significant number of theologians and laypeople have since called for this canonization to be revoked. Needless to say, this canonization has been schismatic and has led to further numbers of people leaving the church.

Finally, this chapter cannot be concluded without mentioning the sexual abuse scandals and the effects that these have had on the Catholic Church. There have been many cases of the sexual abuse of children within the church, mainly by Catholic priests but also by some nuns. Some of these cases of abuse were institutional in that they thrived within a religious order and its institutions. This is clearly demonstrated, for example, in the report into abuse at Ampleforth and Downside by the Independent Inquiry into Child Sexual Abuse (IICSA) in Britain (2018). It is also clearly demonstrated in the many cases of sexual abuse that occurred in the Republic of Ireland. Within that country many institutions were run by the church acting on behalf of the state, and when these cases came to light many people felt completely betrayed by the Catholic Church. Therefore, these sexual abuse scandals in Irish institutions contributed directly to the secularization of Ireland and to the extreme decline of the influence of the Catholic Church within that country.

Cases of sexual abuse within the church first began to receive attention in the late 1980s, and since then there have been many cases all over the world that have attracted a great deal of media attention. From 2001 until 2010 alone the Vatican examined approximately three thousand cases of sexual abuse by priests, some of which dated back many years. While it would be true to say that child sexual abuse has occurred in many other organizations and not just in the Catholic Church, one of the main reasons why sexual abuse was able to thrive within the Catholic Church was the unaccountability of bishops. A diocesan bishop is responsible for the teaching, sanctifying, and governance of the faithful in his own diocese, and until recently it was not possible to bring a complaint against any bishop as he was not accountable to any superior—even the Pope himself. This frequently led to members of the Catholic hierarchy covering up sex abuse allegations and moving priests to other parishes, where the abuse continued. This practice naturally created a climate in which abuse was able to thrive. In recent years, this has been addressed, and all Catholic dioceses today have safeguarding procedures in place. All bishops, however, still remain unaccountable in all other areas, and it is still not possible to bring any complaint against a bishop on any matter other than sex abuse. This means that while sexual abuse has now been addressed, other forms of abuse by bishops, such as spiritual and power abuse, remain unaddressed. Naturally, this is a cause for concern, as there remains a notion that as a bishop has "divine" status due to his so-called descendance from the apostles, he can therefore commit no sin and therefore policies to hold him to account are not needed.

In regard to the cases of sexual abuse within the Catholic Church, these have undeniably brought the church into great disrepute because, although it is acknowledged that abuse can occur in any organization, the majority of people would expect the church to do better. There is therefore no doubt that these cases of sexual abuse have also led to a decline in membership of the Catholic Church. It can also be argued that the failure to include women within the priesthood has led to more cases of sexual abuse within the church than there would have been had there been women priests or deacons. This is because although a small number of women do commit sexual abuse offenses, it is undeniable that these offenses are much lower among women than they are among men. Most statistics state that around 90 percent of sexual abuse is committed by men.

In conclusion to this chapter, the calling of the Second Vatican Council and the promulgation of its teachings represented a great step forward for the Roman Catholic Church as the purpose of the council had clearly been to connect with Christians in the modern world and to reform the church and bring it more in keeping with the church of the New Testament. The council had not been called to promote any triumphalist agenda. The teachings of the council were initially very well received by both priests and laypeople, and there was a great deal of optimism following the closure of this council. Unfortunately, however, many people expected further reforms to follow on from this council, and some of the hoped-for reforms, such as the ordination of women as deacons, did not materialize. In addition to this, some encyclicals issued after the Second Vatican Council, such as *Humanae Vitae* and *Ordinatio Sacerdotalis*, have not been very well received by mainstream Catholics and have led to a hemorrhaging of people from the Catholic Church. The failure of the church to take any real action against the schismatic Society of St. Pius X and its increasing acceptance by the hierarchy in recent years has also been of great concern to modern Catholics and has further contributed to the exodus from the church. This exodus has also been heightened by the fast-tracking of the canonization of Pope St. John Paul II and by the recent sexual abuse scandals within the church.

In regard to the position of women, vocations to the female consecrated life have declined in recent years mainly due to the fact that celibacy is no longer considered a healthy way of living by most people in modern society. Unfortunately, no alternative ministry such as the female diaconate has been offered to women, and due to this the influence of women in the church is now at its lowest ebb in history. This means that, unless there is a change, there is likely to be very few women in the church in the West within twenty or thirty years. As women represent half of the human race, the church could therefore be reduced to the status of a small minor religious cult in years to come.

CHAPTER SEVEN

The Hierarchy of the Catholic Church

This chapter examines the hierarchy of the Catholic Church. First, the current hierarchical model will be examined, and the particular offices of deacon, priest, bishop, archbishop, cardinal, and Pope will be discussed. The concept of *apostolic succession* will then be examined. After this, I will describe the organization of the church at the time of the New Testament and in early and later church history. Finally, I will look at what the current hierarchical model of the church means for the half of the human race that is excluded from church governance, namely women. The question as to whether this state of affairs could be changed without there being a schism will also be discussed.

The Catholic Church uses the term *hierarchy* to mean, in the ecclesiological sense, the "holy ordering" of the church. In canonical and general usage, it refers to those who exercise authority within the church. The current hierarchical model of the Catholic Church is always presented as a pyramid, as illustrated in the following figure.

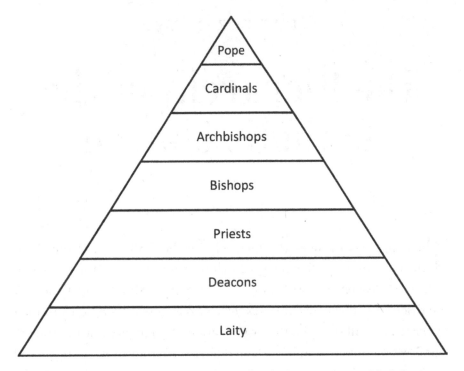

The hierarchy of the Roman Catholic Church. Source: Susan Littleford

At the bottom of the pyramid are the laity, who have no real say in the governance of the church. The laity consists of all church members who are not deacons, priests, bishops, archbishops, cardinals, or Pope. It also technically includes all consecrated women, as these women are not part of the clergy and therefore are not members of the hierarchy of the church and have no powers of governance. All female members of the church are therefore technically lay and only lay, as they cannot go on to exercise any authority within the church of today.

Just above the laity are the deacons. Within the current hierarchical structure of the church deacons must be male, although it is beyond dispute that female deacons did exist in the early church. Male deacons can be either transitional or permanent. The term *transitional deacon* refers to a usually celibate man who is in formation for the priesthood and is ordained as a deacon as a kind of internship. He will serve in a parish or in some other capacity for practical experience while continuing with his final studies before ordination to the priesthood.

The term *permanent deacon* refers to a man who is ordained as a deacon in a permanent state of life and will not go on to the priesthood. This man can be either married or single at the time of his ordination to the diaconate, but if he is single at this time he cannot later go on to marry. Also, if a married deacon is later widowed, he is not permitted to remarry. All deacons, whether they are transitional or permanent, may perform baptisms; witness the exchange of vows and bless marriages; distribute Holy Communion; impart benediction with the Blessed Sacrament; bring viaticum to the dying; read the Gospel in church; preach; officiate at funerals and burials; and administer the sacramentals. Unlike priests, they cannot absolve sins in the sacrament of reconciliation; offer the Mass; anoint the sick; or administer the sacrament of confirmation. All ordained deacons are accountable to their diocesan bishops and may attend diocesan meetings with their bishop and other clergy.

The Catholic priesthood consists of men who are ordained by bishops through the sacrament of holy orders. Technically, deacons are in a priestly order as well, but the term *priest* only refers to those men who have already been a deacon and have gone on to be ordained a priest by the bishop through the rite of ordination. The Catholic Church consists of the Latin Church and the Eastern Catholic Church, but there are different rules of selection for the priesthood in these two branches. Notably, priests in the Latin Church must take a vow of celibacy, whereas within the Eastern Catholic Church married men can be ordained. Celibacy did not become mandatory in the Latin Church until the time of the First Lateran Council in 1122. However, even in the Latin Church there are some exemptions to the celibate rule. For example, if a married priest from another Christian denomination converts to Catholicism, he is allowed to be ordained as a married man. Obviously, there have been many debates around these differences in selection procedures, with many priests in the Western (Latin) rite naturally thinking it is unfair that they are not allowed to be ordained as married men whereas men in the Eastern-Rite Catholic Church are.

All Catholic priests carry out the functions listed for deacons as stipulated previously as well as the additional functions of consecrating the Eucharist, absolving sins, and performing the anointing of the sick. Catholic priests may also be responsible for the administration of at least one parish and attend to the spiritual needs of Catholics who are members of those parishes. However, not all priests are involved in the administration of a parish. This is because there are two types of priests: the diocesan clergy and the regular clergy. Diocesan priests are accountable to their diocesan bishop and usually always manage at least one parish. Regular clergy are members of religious orders, and while some of them may very well manage a parish, others may be involved in other ministries, perhaps as missionaries or in academia. They are ultimately accountable to the provincial of their order, but they may also be accountable to their diocesan bishop as well if they do run a parish on behalf of the bishop.

The Catholic Church teaches that when a man participates in the priesthood, he acts *in persona Christi capitis*, or "in the person of Christ." This phrase distinguishes the priest, who acts on the part of Christ, from the layperson, who is a member of the church. This way of thinking divides the church into two castes, the clergy and the laity, of which only the clergy are officially "the Church" in the sense that only they have the power of governance and only they can act in the person of Christ.

The Orthodox Church does not concur with this teaching, stating that it comes from a mistranslation of 2 Corinthians 2:10 that ought to read "in the presence of Christ." It states that nobody at all can stand in Christ's place or act in his person and that the clergy are meant to be living icons of Christ rather than standing in his place. In the Mass, according to the Orthodox, priests perform the visible counterparts of what Christ himself is doing invisibly, and when the priest prays it is the Holy Spirit that consecrates the bread and wine, not the priest. They state that the degree of fullness by which Christ is present in a person depends on a person's heart and not on his ordination. Therefore, a layperson can be just as spiritual or more spiritual than a priest. The Orthodox do not ordain women as priests but state that this is purely due to tradition. In addition to this, some branches of the Orthodox Church have recently restored the female diaconate, as there is clear historical evidence that women were ordained as deacons in earlier centuries. Married men are also not barred from ordination within the

Orthodox Church, and it is normal for married men to be ordained. But, due to the fact that the Orthodox Church does not teach *in persona Christi capitis*, Orthodox priests do not appear to have acquired the kind of cultish status within Orthodoxy that they have acquired within Catholicism, and women are also much better respected. Women are also much less likely to be spiritually abused within Orthodoxy because one of the main levers that a spiritual abuser will use is the suggestion that he has a divine position of authority. Orthodox priests are not able to use this lever as it has no basis in their theology.

Bishops within the current model of the church are theologically alleged to possess the fullness of both priesthood and diaconate and are considered the successors of the apostles. They are the teachers of sacred doctrine, the priests of sacred worship, and the ministers of governance. They are said to "represent the Church." The Pope himself is a bishop whose title is also "the bishop of Rome." The role of a bishop is to provide pastoral governance for a diocese, and bishops who fulfill this function are known as diocesan ordinaries. Sometimes other bishops may be appointed to assist ordinaries, such as auxiliary bishops. Bishops today are usually ordained to the episcopy by at least three other bishops, although for validity only one bishop is needed together with a mandatum from the Holy See. However, this was not always the case, as it is clear from the writings of the early church fathers that originally the bishop was directly elected by the people, as seen here:

> Elect for yourselves, therefore, bishops and deacons worthy of the Lord; humble men and not lovers of money; truthful and proven; for they also serve you in the ministry of the prophets and teachers . . . (Didache, AD 140)

> Let the bishop be ordained after he has been chosen by all the people. When someone pleasing to all has been named, let the people assemble on the Lord's Day with the presbyters and such bishops as may be present. All giving assent, the bishops shall then impose hands on him and the presbytery shall stand in silence. (The Apostolic Tradition AD 215—St. Hippolytus of Rome)

These writings of the early church fathers are clear evidence that the selection of bishops in the early church actually rested with the people, and the model of the early church was therefore much more horizontal than vertical.

On ordination a bishop is believed to be a successor of the apostles, and ordination to the episcopate is considered to be the completion of the sacrament of holy orders. This means that even when a bishop retires, he remains a bishop, as it is alleged that the ontological effect of holy orders is permanent.

Unfortunately, the almost divine status that is attributed to bishops in the Catholic Church today (due to teachings of certain councils), such as the "indelible character" that was alleged to have been placed on their souls at ordination into the priesthood, and their positions as supreme governors of their dioceses, has resulted in many abuses taking place. For many years it was believed that no complaint process was needed for bishops as they were the ultimate authority in the church and could do no wrong. Therefore, many cases of sexual abuse against children, young men (who were often seminarians), and women were not investigated, as there was no place to take these cases, and often if they were taken to the bishop they were covered up. Today this has been rectified, and safeguarding procedures are in place in all dioceses to protect people from sexual abuse. However, it is still not possible (at the diocesan level) to make a complaint against any bishop for any misuse of his power or governance. There are no independent panels in any diocese to which one can complain about a bishop, and the only way to complain is to either write to the Pope himself or to his nuncio, a process that could take years. This means that the spiritual and political power abuse of individuals within the Catholic Church is still possible and still remains as there is no local accountability. The Orthodox Church does not have these problems to the same degree as although Orthodox bishops are considered to be the successors of the apostles, no bishop in orthodoxy is considered infallible. No Orthodox bishop has any authority over and apart from his priests, deacons, and people. They simply have the responsibility of maintaining the unity of the Orthodox Church throughout the world. Bishops are not seen as representatives of

Christ within Christian Orthodoxy and therefore do not have the elite and cultish status that they have acquired within Catholicism.

The title of archbishop is given to bishops who head metropolitan sees and also to those who head archdioceses that are not metropolitan sees. These bishops are overseeing a larger or more heavily populated area, but generally speaking their responsibilities are no different to those of ordinary bishops. Titular archbishops are those who have been given archdioceses that are no longer residential and are regarded as titular sees; for example, as in the case of papal nuncios.

Cardinals are princes of the Catholic Church appointed by the Pope. The cardinalate is not an integral part of the theological structure of the Catholic Church, and the term *cardinal* was originally an honorary title bestowed by the Pope. Originally it was not necessary to be a deacon, priest, or bishop in order to receive this honor, and laypeople were also made cardinals. The original cardinals were friends or counselors of the bishop of Rome, and while some were originally deacons or priests, others were not. Sadly, in 1917, due to increased clericalism, the Code of Canon Law was changed and it was decreed that from then onward only those who were priests or bishops could be chosen as cardinals. However, this decree could be reversed, as there is historical precedent for the existence of lay cardinals. It is believed that in 1968 Pope St. Paul VI was considering changing this law as he proposed the philosopher Jacques Maritain as a lay cardinal. However, Maritain refused this honor.

Cardinals often head departments of the Roman Curia or important episcopal sees throughout the world. As a whole, the cardinals form a College of Cardinals that advises the Pope. Cardinals are also responsible for electing any new Pope, although they must be under eighty to vote in the consistory. It has been suggested (Flint, 2021) that as cardinals did not have to be ordained priests in the past, women could be made lay cardinals today. This would enable women to vote in important councils of the church and may be a way to give women more influence without ordaining them, seeing as the ordination of women could be schismatic in present times.

The Pope is the bishop of Rome and by virtue of that office he is also known as vicar of Jesus Christ, successor of the Prince of the Apostles, supreme pontiff of the Universal Church, patriarch of the Latin Church, primate of Italy, archbishop and metropolitan of the Roman Province, sovereign of the Vatican City State, and servant of the servants of God. The Pope resides in Vatican City, which is an independent state within the city of Rome, and as the sovereign of this state he exercises absolute civil authority. The Pope is at the pinnacle of the hierarchical model of the church.

The term *apostolic succession* refers to a belief that the ministry of the Christian Church is derived from the apostles by a continuous succession through a series of bishops. This in effect means that each bishop has been consecrated by another bishop, who was consecrated by a previous bishop, in a continuous line of succession going back to the apostles. In Catholic theology the apostolic tradition, which includes teaching, preaching, and authority, is handed down from the college of apostles to the college of bishops by the laying on of hands. The apostolic succession, given to the consecrated priest by the bishop when he lays on his hands, gives this priest the power and authority to administer all the sacraments except for baptism and marriage. In regards to baptism, it is taught by the church that while the priest usually does this, anyone can actually baptize. In regards to marriage, the church teaches that the priest is merely a witness while the couple give the sacrament to each other. Both the Catholic and the Orthodox churches accept the doctrine of apostolic succession and recognize each other's orders as valid. The Anglican Church claims apostolic succession, but the Catholic Church does not recognize the validity of Anglican orders, stating that the line of succession was broken in England under the reign of King Edward VI. Although the Catholic and Orthodox churches recognize each other's orders as valid, there are differences in the way they perceive apostolic succession. The Orthodox Church does not teach that ordination confers an indelible mark on the soul, and it has also commenced the restoration of the female diaconate, which it recognizes as a minor order. The Catholic Church has not restored this diaconate.

Some Christian denominations deny the doctrine of apostolic succession and state that it is not taught in scripture and is also not necessary for Christian life, teaching, and practice. They state that to be apostolic is simply to submit to the teachings of the twelve apostles. Other theologians such as Michael Ramsey, a former Anglican archbishop of Canterbury, have stated that the concept of grace being transmitted by each generation of bishops through the imposition of hands has been controversial. He stated that this doctrine is not found explicitly before the time of St. Augustine of Hippo. However, some early church fathers, such as St. Hippolytus of Rome, referred to this doctrine inexplicitly, in the sense that Hippolytus wrote that after the bishop had been selected by the people, he was to receive the laying on of hands by a current bishop. Nevertheless, Hippolytus does not actually link the laying on of hands to a direct succession from the apostles.

While it is highly likely that the apostolic succession was conveyed by the laying on of hands, this obviously cannot be proved definitively. There is also the question, as has been noted in earlier chapters, as to why Mary Magdalene was not declared an apostle when she met all the requirements needed to be declared as such. In regard to the apostolic succession's having been passed on from the twelve other apostles (excluding Mary) to the bishops of today, the reasons why some theologians believe this is difficult to prove are detailed very briefly here.

As has been noted in an earlier chapter, the early Christian Church was made up of different Christian communities that were widely dispersed around the eastern Mediterranean. These communities were often very isolated from each other and initially developed different traditions that may have been around the teaching of a central Christian figure. The oral tradition was the main means of communication, and not all of these communities possessed the same Christian literature. It has actually been suggested by some theologians that 85 percent of early Christian literature has been lost.

Due to the fact that early Christian communities developed independently, there was, in the early church, a wide range of different perspectives on Christian belief and practice. This led to many controversies, and most early Christian documents give examples of these controversies. For example, the letters of St. Paul illustrate that there were many differences of opinion on issues of Jewish Law, such as circumcision and food rules. This was because the earliest followers of

Jesus had been a sect of apocalyptic Jewish Christians within the realm of Second Temple Judaism. When Saul of Tarsus (St. Paul) converted he started his mission to the gentiles, which led to many discussions about Jewish issues that needed to be resolved. However, there were also differences of practice among the Jewish Christian people just before the conversion of St. Paul due to the isolation of different Jewish Christian groups from each other. The writings of the early church fathers also give examples of controversies, and in the First Epistle of Clement, Pope Clement calls on the Christians of Corinth to maintain harmony and order. Due to these differences and controversies, it is difficult to state definitively that all early bishops would have been consecrated by the laying on of hands. This does not mean that this did not happen. It just means that it is difficult to prove.

In regard to Christian ministry and the development of a definitive church structure, it would seem that a church hierarchy emerged very slowly and at different times in different places. Most of the information that we have about ministry in the very early church comes from the Acts of the Apostles and the letters of St. Paul. Within the New Testament there are three main ministries described: *episkopei* (επίσκοποι, overseers); *presbyteroi* (πρεσβύτεροι, elders/presbyters, known today as priests); and *diakonoi* (διάκονοι, servants/deacons).

It is clear from the New Testament and from later evidence (such as the writings of the early church fathers, other Roman writings, and archaeological finds) that the overseers were usually male; presbyters were usually male, but there were some females in some areas; and deacons were male or female. However, what seems to have happened is that there was never any universal consensus on women being admitted to the presbyterate, and by the third and fourth centuries the practice of admitting women to the presbyterate was suppressed. There was, however, universal agreement that women could be admitted to a form of the diaconate, and the practice of ordaining women as deacons did not cease until much later. It also seems to have fallen out of practice rather than to have been suppressed.

The idea of one single man leading a church of elders and deacons does not seem to have appeared until the second century. Initially, the roles of the overseer and the presbyter was interchangeable, and the first century saint Clement in his epistle to Corinthians certainly saw these roles in this way. But later, in the very early second century, St. Ignatius of Antioch writes about three degrees of ministry and urges all church members to follow their bishop:

> See that you all follow the bishop, even as Jesus Christ does the Father, and the presbytery as you would the apostles; and reverence the deacons, as being the institution of God. Let no man do anything connected with the Church without the bishop.

However, Ramsey argues that this reference in St. Ignatius's Epistle to the Smyrnaeans does not necessarily mean that St. Ignatius believed in an apostolic succession passed on by the laying on of hands. It could just mean that he believed that the bishops and presbyters were teaching the true faith of the apostles. The teaching of apostolic succession as Catholics will understand it today, a lineage from the apostles that is passed on by hands from the time of the apostles to a succession of priests, is inexplicitly referred to by St. Hippolytus of Rome, who mentions the laying on of hands at ordination, although he does not actually speak of a direct lineage from the apostles. This concept does not seem to have been explicitly recognized until the time of St. Augustine of Hippo, who refers to it when writing *Against the Epistle of Manichaeus, Called Fundamental.* Nevertheless, even if there are no earlier direct references to this succession, this does not necessarily mean that it was not actually passed on by the laying of hands. It could have been, and many Christian churches claim lineage to an apostle. For example, the see of Rome says it was founded by St. Peter and St. Paul; the Ecumenical Patriarchate of Constantinople says St. Andrew was its founder; the Orthodox Church of Cyprus says it was founded by St. Paul and St. Barnabas; the Eastern Orthodox Patriarchate of Jerusalem says it was founded by James the Just; and the Patriarch of Alexandria says it was founded by St. Mark the Evangelist. The Old Catholic Church of the Netherlands also claims apostolic succession through St. Peter and St. Paul. This church rejected papal infallibility but continued to claim the line of succession from

Rome and other churches such as the Open Episcopal Church have claimed apostolic succession through this line.

Claiming a line of succession to the apostles is all very well and good, but what has really been the problem within Catholicism has been the way this apostolic succession has been used to promote an elite and cultish priesthood that is far removed from the people and excludes many from ordination. As has already been noted, the bishops were originally elected by the people themselves, and married men are today excluded from the priesthood in the Catholic Latin rite. Women are excluded from both the priesthood and the diaconate in all Catholic rites, and while it may be possible to argue from history that the ordination of women as priests in the early church was never universal, it is not possible to argue this about the female diaconate. The female diaconate was universal, and women had specific roles in it, such as baptizing other women and keeping the church gates. The Orthodox Church has recognized this and has begun to restore the female diaconate. There is no reason why the baptismal function cannot be restored to women. They also could preside over the exchange of wedding vows, which does not require a priest to be present. The Orthodox Church is clearly moving against any kind of discrimination for which there is no historical precedent in order to bring its current church in line with the early church. As has been noted, the Orthodox Church has always ordained married men and is thus far more inclusive than the Catholic Church.

Since the time of the schism with the Orthodox in 1054 right up until Vatican II, the Catholic hierarchy seems to have used a series of ecumenical councils to promote an initially white European (but now more racially diverse) male celibate elite and to stifle all theological debates.

Many of the Catholic ecumenical councils were concerned with condemning so-called heresies and also with creating some kind of priestly caste that would keep all power and influence in the hands of the celibate few. This is usually, however, done under some kind of pretext. For example, the First and Second Councils of the Lateran supposedly denied priests their rights to be in a married sexual relationship due to the fact that some priests were having affairs. It supposedly wished to promote celibacy as a "higher path." However, many have opined that the council's real reason for banning the marriage of priests was so that the church could keep control of property and secure it in the hands of the celibate few. This is much more likely, seeing as the priestly celibate state probably results in more priests having illicit affairs than the married state does. In addition to this, the Second Council of the Lateran named Anacletus II as the antipope due to his Jewish origins. He was deposed on the same grounds. How far away from the historical Jesus was that? There is also no record of Jesus ever promoting celibacy. He does make a reference to eunuchs in Matthew 19:11–12, but this is in response to a question on adultery and divorce, and verse 12 has been mistranslated from the original Greek in many western New Testaments. What Jesus is usually translated as saying in verse 12, which follows his comments on eunuchs, is *the one who can accept this should accept this*. But what he actually says in the original Greek is ὁ δυνάμενος χωρεῖν χωρείτω, which actually means *the one being able to receive this I also receive*. This is rather different to the usual translation, as there is no instruction to be celibate at all but rather just an affirmation that is fine to be celibate. This verse has probably been deliberately mistranslated by so-called scholars in the West in order to promote celibacy.

The later declarations of the Council of Trent in 1563 clearly had the purpose of condemning Protestantism and keeping power in the hands of the celibate few. While the council did make some small reforms in regard to indulgences and the morality of the religious life, the main thrust of its decrees was to make the clergy a separate and elitist cult with almost divine status. The council stated that Christ had given his priests sacerdotal power and that ordination imprinted an indelible character on their souls. The Latin Vulgate became the official translation of the scriptures, and only the church (i.e., celibate men) could interpret scripture. Jesus had been removed from the worlds of married men (in the Latin Church) and women. They could not access him in the scriptures and neither could they access the indelible imprint that he could place on a priest's soul. This Jesus was very far away from the Jesus in St. Mark's Gospel (the earliest Gospel), who repeatedly condemns clericalism. Some examples follow:

Beware of the scribes who like to walk about in long robes, to be greeted respectfully in the market squares; to take the front seats in the synagogues and the places of honor at banquets: these are the men who devour the properties of widows and for show offer long prayers. The more severe will be the sentence they receive. (Mark 12:38–40)

Does not scripture say: My house will be called a house of prayer for all peoples? But you have turned it into a bandit's den. (Mark 11:17)

So, he sat down, called the twelve to him and said, "if anyone wants to be first, he must make himself last of all and servant of all." He then took a little child whom he set among them and said to them, "anyone who welcomes a little child such as this welcomes me . . ." (Mark 9:35–36)

He answered, how rightly Isaiah prophesized about you hypocrites in the passage of scripture; This people honor me only with lip-service, while their hearts are far from me. Their reverence of me is worthless: The lessons they teach are nothing but human commandments. (Mark 7:6–7)

In conclusion, Jesus condemned the pharisaical religion of his day, with its cumbersome laws and elitist clericalism, and instead proclaimed a new religion, a religion of the heart that anyone could access. However, today the hierarchy has created another cumbersome religion full of rules and laws and presided over by the elitist, celibate few. The people have no influence in this church. They cannot even elect their own bishops. Vatican II did not change the hierarchy of the church. Although it did bring about some reforms, such as the offering of the Mass in the vernacular and the creation of a new lay apostolate, it left the power and influence within the church where it had always been for hundreds of years: with the celibate few.

The Catholic Church is a hierarchical pyramid with laypeople on the bottom and the celibate few on the top. Decision-making does not rest with the people of God but with the celibate few, and often this results in a stifling suppression of the Holy Spirit. New ideas coming from the laity or from women are often killed off by the priest or bishop in charge. There is often no possibility for new initiatives in the church unless the priest or the bishop gives his rubber stamp. Of course, there are some good priests and bishops who do encourage spiritual growth, but sadly there are others who stamp on any new suggestion. I know of one young woman who wanted to set up a young person's prayer group in a parish in her diocese, but the priest would not allow it. In the end, she moved a hundred miles away and managed to set up a prayer group in another diocese where the clergy were more welcoming. New initiatives like this are stamped on all the time, and it takes a very special person to keep going with them after the hierarchy has closed its patriarchal door. Other examples of this include women who have sought consecration as a virgin by their bishop only to be told by that particular bishop that even though these vocations are legitimate vocations of the church, he will not consecrate them because he does not "like" these vocations and does not "agree with them." Some women have moved over a hundred miles away to another diocese in order to be consecrated. Other women have simply given up.

The current hierarchical model of the Catholic Church is abusive. Now, when I say it is abusive, I do not mean that all bishops are abusive. Of course, I am aware that there are many good and caring bishops. What I actually mean is that an organizational system has been set up with rules of governance that can lead to and cause abuse. As we saw in earlier chapters, when an organization has policies that can sanction abuse this is termed organizational abuse.

Firstly, the hierarchical model is abusive because it denies all women and some married men the right to enter into the holy orders that were accessible to them in the early church. It also forces priestly celibacy onto most of its priests, which is not only abusive but a denial of human rights.

Secondly, it is abusive because it tries to deny the vast majority of the people of God, the laypeople, any say not only in the decisions of the church to which they are supposed to belong but also in their own personal lives. It is a controlling, stifling organization in which celibate men issue encyclicals telling married people and others how to live their lives. This can be seen, for example, in *Humanae Vitae*, where laypeople are told how to live out their sex lives. Another example of a controlling, abusive practice is the obligation to attend Sunday Mass. This rule uses fear to force people to attend Mass, stating that it is a serious sin not to attend. What kind of organization tries to force people to attend Mass using fear as a lever? Isn't it the spirit of God that moves a person to want to attend Mass? What happens if a person would rather attend Mass on a Monday than a Sunday for personal reasons? Shouldn't a person go to Mass when their heart tells them they want an encounter with Jesus? Who are these celibate men to order people to attend church? These kinds of rules are an insult to all adults. Adults do not need to be told when they should attend church. Grown-ups will decide for themselves when they will attend. This rule is an example of the hierarchy attempting to treat people like children. How can many bishops really think that people will be ordered about like this anymore? People will no longer buy the fear ticket. They do not believe that a loving God will punish them if they decide to attend Mass on a Monday rather than on a Sunday. Unfortunately, many members of the hierarchy seem to have lost all touch with reality to such a degree that they cannot even see that people today value their autonomy and their rights to make personal choices. Hardly anybody in the modern Western world wishes to listen to the bishops anymore due to their being so out of touch. People will no longer be controlled in this dictatorial way and so they simply walk away. These rules do not encourage people to attend church as the hierarchy think they will do. Instead, they turn people off the church because it is seen as a dated, controlling institution. The message of Christ no longer reaches the people, and all of this is a great pity.

Finally, the hierarchy of the Catholic Church is abusive because bishops are not accountable. There is no group or body in any diocese to which any person can go if they have a complaint against a bishop. What happens if a woman goes to a bishop and asks him to consecrate her as a virgin and he says that he will not consecrate her because he does not like this particular vocation? This vocation is a legal vocation of the church written into Canon Law, but if a bishop refuses to carry out consecrations there is no way that any complaint can be made against him. Another member of the hierarchy, such as an archbishop, will simply say he has no jurisdiction over another bishop. Each bishop is his own boss in his own diocese and is accountable to no one. It is as simple and as abusive as that. A bishop can do whatever he wants. So, the woman seeking consecration will be forced to move house or give up the idea of consecration. There is sadly no room for the Holy Spirit there.

The current hierarchy is not a vehicle for the Holy Spirit but a vehicle of control. Can it ever be changed? Some people state that it is not possible to change it, because any change will lead to a schism. However, a failure to change it will ultimately lead to an end of the Catholic Church in the West within twenty or thirty years. Most laypeople will leave, and those who remain will simply be the members of the Society of St. Pius X and other so-called traditionalists. This will mean that the church will become an insignificant cult. Only the hierarchy can decide whether the church will change, because they currently hold all the power and influence. They can either share that power or follow the path of death. Therefore, only the hierarchy can save the Catholic Church; otherwise it will die with them.

CHAPTER EIGHT

Current Vocations
and Women

This chapter will examine most of the full-time vocations that are open to women within the Catholic Church today and will also discuss how relevant these vocations are in the modern world. Do these vocations that are open to women today enable them to fully respond to God's call? Do they enable women to pass on to others the original good news of Jesus Christ? Do they enable women to further build the Kingdom of God? Are all of these vocations supported by the church hierarchy? Have certain vocations currently open to women been suppressed by bishops in some areas of the world? This chapter will also examine other vocations that could be, from a purely historical perspective, open to women but are not actually open to women today. Are some women called to ministries that they are currently denied? Is the current hierarchy of the church hearing the call of the Holy Spirit to women, or is it suppressing the call of the Spirit for reasons of preservation of power and the legacy of misogynism? Will misogynism ultimately destroy the Latin Church? I will argue that there can be no future for the Catholic Church of today unless it takes on board the perspectives of half of its members, the perspectives of women. The hierarchy of this church has moved, through a historical process, very far away from the ministries that were open to women in earlier centuries.

Some of the main ministries that are open to women today are consecration as an enclosed religious, consecration as an active religious, consecration as a virgin, consecration as a widow, consecration as a hermit, consecration as a member of a secular institute, profession as a member of a third order, membership of a personal prelature, teaching roles, and other lay theological roles. Ministries that are currently not open to women but could be open in the future are the diaconate, the priesthood, and the cardinalate. All of these ministries will now be examined.

The enclosed religious life is often thought to be the oldest form of female consecrated life but, in fact, it is not. The oldest forms of female consecrated life are the order of consecrated widow and the order of consecrated virgin, and women were originally enrolled individually into one or the other of these two orders. The enclosed religious life developed at a later date, and the first religious communities are believed to have been established by St. Pachomius, who was an Egyptian who converted to Christianity. In AD 320 he established a religious community in Tabennisi under the authority of the bishop of Tentyra. This community was male, but St. Pachomius almost certainly established the first female religious community as well. At the time of his death in AD 346 he left two nunneries as well as the nine monasteries which he founded for men. Later in the sixth century the Order of St. Benedict was established by St. Benedict of Nursia, and the Rule of St. Benedict spread around the world. The first enclosed religious women in Britain were almost certainly Benedictine, but this was probably not the case in Ireland. In that country, monasticism was first established by St. Finnian of Clonard who had studied in Gaul. The first form of enclosed religious life for women in Ireland was established by St. Brigid of Kildare. St. Brigid is believed to have converted to Christianity, and she established a double monastery that was rather like the double monasteries in Anglo-Saxon England and probably preceded them. This abbey was in Kildare, and St. Brigid was the abbess and ranked above both the monks and the nuns living there.

Women living in the enclosed religious orders of the Catholic Church are the only women who, under Canon Law, are actually entitled to call themselves nuns. This is because enclosed nuns are the only women to take solemn vows. All other women take simple vows, and technically, according to Canon Law, only those who take solemn vows are nuns. Those who take simple vows are sisters or consecrated women.

Enclosed religious women live separately from the world as members of a religious community in a house within enclosed grounds. Generally, an enclosed nun will not leave her enclosure unless she requires medical treatment. Some outsiders are, however, permitted to enter parts of the enclosure for a variety of reasons. The rules regarding outsiders vary from community to community, depending on the constitution of each particular religious order. For example, in some communities laypeople may be allowed to enter the chapel just for Mass and on these occasions will sit separately from the nuns. However, other communities may run retreat houses. In this case, visitors will be allowed into various parts of the enclosure as paying guests. The visitors will live with the nuns for a few days and join in with their worship. The nuns may even cook meals for the visitors and perhaps join them for a meal. Nuns such as this run a self-funding community, and the retreat center provides them with a substantial amount of income. These nuns do, however, remain enclosed, and the people come to them rather than the other way around. Many of these communities may also produce their own food, keep animals, grow their own fruit and vegetables, or keep bees or hens. Anything they cannot produce will be delivered to the community so that the nuns do not have to go out shopping.

While enclosed nuns may engage in some business activities in order to fund their community, they do, overall, live a life of prayer. Their lives revolve around the Divine Office, or Liturgy of the Hours. This is the Catholic Church's official set of prayers, which marks the hours of each day and sanctifies the day with prayer. Enclosed nuns are expected to pray seven times within twenty-four hours together with their religious communities, but, generally speaking, they are well able to combine this with any holistic business venture they may be involved in. Most of these communities are self-sufficient, and the nuns may be involved in a variety of occupations within their enclosure, such as painting icons, making hosts for communion, making religious cards or rosaries, and producing wild honey or jams.

Although vocations to the active religious life have declined in recent years, vocations to the enclosed religious life have managed to hold their own in Britain and Ireland with some nuns, such as the Dominican

Monastery of St. Catherine of Siena in Drogheda, Ireland, doing particularly well. This is perhaps because it can be argued that there will always be a small number of women who seek to live an enclosed and contemplative life.

In regard to the active religious sisters, this form of consecrated life is generally in a state of decline across the whole of Europe and also in Canada, America, and all other parts of the Western world. In some countries, the decline is much worse than in others, and it is probably fair to say that the decline is worse in Britain and Ireland than other Western countries for different reasons. Generally speaking, one of the main reasons for the decline of this form of religious life in Europe and America is that originally most of these active religious orders were set up to provide teaching to those who were not receiving an education and also to provide social care to poorer families. Obviously, the various secular states have now taken over these functions and so there is no need for active religious to provide education and care in the West anymore. In some European countries, active religious have managed to find other missions, but in both Britain and Ireland they have struggled to do so. In addition to this, vocations to this kind of religious life have been affected, in Ireland in particular, by abuse scandals. Some religious orders in Ireland ran children's homes and mother and baby homes on behalf of the state, and many of these homes have since been found to have delivered very poor care and to also have been abusive. In some mother and baby homes it was found that one baby died every two weeks, and many babies were buried in unmarked graves en masse. In some orphanages the sisters also covered up the sexual abuse of children that was being carried out by priests, and some sisters even sexually abused children themselves. One religious congregation, the Sisters of Mercy, had at least twenty-six industrial schools in Ireland, and some sisters at this school were found to have been emotionally abusive to children and to have overused corporal punishment. Due to all these scandals this form of religious life lost a lot of credibility in Ireland, and there are now very few vocations to the active religious life there. In Britain, vocations to this form of religious life have also declined drastically, although for different reasons. There have not been as many scandals involving female religious congregations in Britain, but vocations to this form of consecrated life have not been well supported or promoted by the clergy for some years. In addition to this, many British congregations have lost their raison d'être, as they were originally involved in education and care, both of which are now provided by the state. This has meant that often the sisters themselves have not promoted their way of life with the fervor they may have done in the past.

One of the main problems with the active religious life is that, generally speaking, it simply does not appeal to the modern woman of today no matter how religious or spiritual she may be. This is mainly due to the fact that the community religious life is not seen to be attractive or desirable to women in the modern secular world. Women today are generally much more autonomous than women in earlier centuries, and they have no desire to live in a convent. Modern spiritual women are also often involved in careers that do not sit well with the community religious life. For example, they may be working in the religious media or in academia. The vow of obedience also does not appeal to many women, and this has in the past often led to spiritual abuse, which will be examined in more depth in a later chapter. Some women have found themselves with superiors who have abused them both emotionally and spiritually, and they have not been able to get out of this situation due to the vow of obedience. These women have been placed in very difficult positions, having to answer to tyrannical superiors who have felt they must be obeyed at all costs. Naturally, today, when there is a much greater awareness of this kind of abuse, women are not going to put themselves into this kind of vulnerable position. However, although most active religious communities are generally in decline in Europe (and in Britain and Ireland in particular), there are a small number of communities that have bucked the trend—usually because they have modeled themselves in a different way to the declining religious communities.

One such example is the Community of Our Lady of Walsingham, which is an ecclesial family of consecrated life rather than a religious congregation. This is a community of consecrated sisters, lay associates, and priest associates. The community is based in Walsingham, England, near the National Shrine of Our Lady. Its mission is "to hasten the coming of God's Kingdom by living in the joy of Mary's Fiat in the Divine Will." These sisters offer accommodation to visitors at the Walsingham shrine as well as spiritual direction and vocational accompaniment. They also give talks for young people in schools and host retreats and conferences. While these sisters do not wear secular dress, they do wear a habit, which is both practical and attractive and gives them a very positive image.

The attire of active religious women is of interest because it can be argued that presentation is very important if modern religious women want to present themselves as being in touch with the modern world and display their way of life as appealing. This is because in the past the attire of religious women was often associated with a dire sexuality, and one of the purposes of that attire was seen as preventing a woman's looking attractive, so as to repel men. This attitude was very damaging to the self-esteem of women and also presented their vocations in a very poor way. If women could only keep their vows by making themselves unattractive, what did this say about the strength of their vocations? Surely if a woman really has a strong and well-rounded vocation to the religious life and feels a definite call to celibacy then she will not need to make herself unattractive in order to keep her vows. There is a very strong argument that says that women who have a healthy view of sexuality and are happy in their own skin make the best celibates. In addition to this, the traditional habit does have, for some, strong mental associations with repression and abuse, and it may be that due to those associations it is better avoided by the active religious congregations that really wish to grow. The same does not apply to the contemplative enclosed orders, which set themselves apart from the world and are not active within it. For them, a distinctive habit is probably more appropriate.

It is good that some active religious communities have bucked the decline of this form of consecrated life in the West. Religious communities that have not been too badly hit by the decline in vocations are those involved in the media or those in Italy, where many religious women have been able to work in the various administrative departments of the Vatican. However, it is unlikely that there will ever be a great revival of the active religious life, simply because it does not fit with the needs of society today. Most forms of consecrated life have arisen as a response to needs within society. Even the Anglo-Saxon monasteries were serving the needs of their own society by providing education for the ruling classes and overseeing the formation of priests. The active religious orders do still attract a large number of vocations in the less affluent countries where they continue to provide education and care, but as these countries become wealthier and the state begins to take over the provision of education and care, there could also be a decline of these congregations.

The order of consecrated virgins is one of the oldest forms of consecrated life in the history of the Christian Church. It is mentioned by St. Paul in 1 Corinthians, where he suggests a special role for unmarried women in the church. In the New Testament, chastity is often praised as a Christian virtue, and some form of consecrated rite for virgins is believed to have existed since the time of the apostles. The first known formal rite of consecration is that of St. Marcellina (AD 335). Initially, consecrated virgins lived independently, but this did not continue for very long, because these women did not have the means to be self-funding in the world unless their parents supported them. Therefore, this form of independent consecrated life gradually died out and was eventually replaced by the enclosed religious life. During the medieval period, women were still consecrated as virgins, but by that time the consecration of virgins was maintained by nuns in religious orders. This consecration was then usually done concurrently with the profession of solemn vows. It was later completely eradicated and wiped out during the Reformation.

The rite of consecrated virgin remained lost until the early twentieth century, when a return to this ancient practice began to be supported by some bishops. One bishop, the bishop of Montpelier, encouraged a young woman called Anne Leflaive to seek consecration, and she was consecrated on January 6, 1924, by the bishop of Autun. After this event, more women began to seek consecration, and the local bishops sought clarification from the Congregation for Institutes of Consecrated Life and Societies of Apostolic Life as to whether they could proceed with more consecrations. Unfortunately, the congregation forbade this type of consecration, stating that it had long since fallen out of use. Leflaive, however, would not give up, and in 1939 she founded the secular Missionaries of Catholic Action, which was an institute of celibate women living in the world. But this institute was also eventually suppressed by the hierarchy. After this, it just happened that Leflaive began to form a friendship with one Angelo Roncalli, who would become the future Pope St. John XXIII. This cleric was very receptive to her ideas. During the 1950s, Leflaive began to visit Rome every year in order to lobby for the reinstatement of the rite of consecrated virgins. She also wrote a book about the vocation called *Espouse du Christ*. In 1953, Pope Pius XII issued *Sponsa Christi* and there was a revival of the rite of consecration for virgins, but the Pope had decreed that only enclosed nuns could receive this rite. However, in 1963, which was actually thirty-nine years after the original "unofficial" consecration of Leflaive, the Second Vatican Council requested a revision of the consecration of virgins. This revised rite was approved by Pope St. Paul VI and was published in 1970. This consecration could now be bestowed on women living in the world as well as in convents. It had taken Anne forty-six years of perseverance to achieve her goal, and she went on to live until 1987, when she died at the age of eighty-eight.

Today, the rite of consecrated virgin has spread all over the world and has also been written into Canon Law. In 2018, the Vatican published "Ecclesiae Sponsae Imago," which details the norms for this way of life. Consecrated virgins live in their own homes and are financially self-sufficient. They are accountable to their diocesan bishops. Like all consecrated women, consecrated virgins are expected to pray the Divine Office at least in the morning, evening, and night. However, these women are also women of action living within the secular world. They are contemplatives in action. Many of them work, and while a lot of them work in the religious sphere, others may work in a completely secular job. Others may be involved in some form of social action, such as fighting for the cessation of the death penalty in the United States. On some occasions, these women might, perhaps, see no need to declare their consecrated status to others and might act as a hidden leaven in the world. This vocation is very flexible, and it is up to each woman to find her own personal way of living it out. Also, while it is officially referred to as the rite of consecrated virgins, there is no longer any insistence on virginity. The sexual history of any woman would not be a barrier to her seeking consecration as long as she was willing to take a vow of chastity pertaining to the rest of her life. For this reason, these women today are often referred to as "consecrated women."

While the rite of consecrated virgin has spread across the world, some countries have embraced it much more than others, which has of course been due to the level of support the vocation has received from the hierarchy in different countries. In Britain and Ireland this vocation has grown very slowly, although there are now over two hundred consecrated virgins in Britain. However, there are only four known consecrated virgins in Scotland, where the hierarchy has been very reluctant to promote this vocation. I was advised by two women that one bishop had been particularly hostile. A certain number of bishops in nearly all countries have actually refused to consecrate women as virgins on occasions, stating that they "do not like this vocation." What this usually means is that they do not like the idea of women living out their vocations independently and believe any woman with a vocation should be herded into a convent. Some women who feel called to this way of life have been forced to move house in order to find a bishop who will consecrate them. This is yet another example of spiritual abuse. These vocations are now official vocations of the church, and bishops should not be allowed to refuse to consecrate women in this manner. This is another reason why complaint procedures against bishops are desperately needed. Of course, there are many good bishops who have supported these vocations, but others have acted like autocratic despots and refused to have consecrated virgins in their dioceses. It is completely wrong that they are allowed to act like this, as they are suppressing the work of the Holy Spirit and denying the callings of many women.

Another very early form of consecrated life was that of the consecrated widow. This vocation also existed in the very early church and is referred to in the New Testament (1 Timothy 5:3–5). At that time, in order to be enrolled into the order of consecrated widows, a woman had to be at least sixty years of age, have been married only once, and have lived a life of prayer and service to others following the death of her husband. This order became very well established within the early church and is mentioned by several of the early church fathers, including St. Polycarp, St. Hippolytus, and St. Jerome. Consecrated widows were mature women of faith who took part in the Eucharist; prayed with psalms, hymns, and meditations; and were also known for their intercessory power. They lived in their own homes. In the Mediterranean world of the early centuries, legal and social norms granted women property rights and substantial authority within their households and communities. While some widows were disadvantaged, others experienced only a very slight drop in their economic and social status after being widowed, or no change at all. Many widows who were Roman citizens owned a substantial amount of property under Roman law, and evidence would also suggest that Jewish widows were not that different to Roman widows and also owned their own houses. Therefore, these women were usually fairly affluent and chose to use what they owned for the glory of God and the spreading of the Christian message.

The vocation of consecrated widow became particularly popular in Britain from early Christian times until the Reformation. The origins of formalized chastity vows for women in Britain are unknown, but Laura Mary Wood, PhD, states that there are vowing ceremonies for widows in England that date back to the seventh century. These vowing ceremonies continued until the Reformation. The widows who were to be consecrated were known as vowesses, and they took a vow of chastity but did not take vows of poverty and obedience. However, before taking these vows, these women did have to submit a formal request to their bishop and have their lives scrutinized to see if they were suitable. In her 2015 article for *Pastoral Review*, Elizabeth Rees states that the pontifical of the Anglo-Saxon archbishop of York, Egbert, included a consecration of widows during Mass and also a blessing of widows and their habit. The ceremony was later included in at least five eleventh-century pontificals. Usually, during these ceremonies, the vowess was clothed in a mantle and veil and wore a ring that was blessed. After her consecration, she was qualified by vow to refer to herself as a bride of Christ.

Consecrated widows were free to own their own property and live wherever they wanted in their dioceses. Often, of course, they continued to live in the marital homes they had shared with their husbands, and they would become very involved in serving their own communities in a variety of ways. More important, they were free to discern their own spirituality. They could decide whether to be a contemplative in action or a semi-enclosed solitary contemplative living near a monastery. One of them may have founded the original shrine at Walsingham in Britain. We know that this visionary was a widow, but not whether she was consecrated. However, it's very likely that she was, as in the eleventh century it had almost become the norm for well-off widows in England to take vows of chastity and do something for God and the community. This way of life was extremely popular for widows, and these women were very fortunate in that they were very autonomous and had great religious freedom. Writing in c. 1591, Michael Sherbrook stated that the number of consecrated widows, anchorites, and anchoresses far exceeded the number of secular priests in England prior to the Reformation: "all the said Religious Persons, which far passed the Number of Secular Priests, there were many more, yea thousands, as Ancerers, both men and women; and widows that had taken the Mantle and Ring" (Sherbrook, 1591, cited in Wood 2017).

This statement gives us a glimpse of a Christian Church that has been lost to us. In this church, the secular priest is not the head of a parish; there are just as many consecrated widows, anchorites, and anchoresses. We also know, of course, that some of the anchoresses, such as Julian of Norwich, were sought after for their counsel, so we can assume that they had a similar status to that of the priest. Unfortunately, this more horizontal church was completely destroyed by the Reformation, as were many of the records that evidenced it. The order of consecrated widow was also eradicated at this time—not only in England, but everywhere else in the world too.

After the Reformation, it was to be four hundred years before a movement began to restore the vocation of vowess, or consecrated widow. In the late 1940s, in France, some war widows began to take vows. Later, an acknowledgment of the spirituality of widows began under Pope Pius

XII, in 1957, when he addressed young French widows with children at home when attending the Congress of the International Union of the Organizations concerning Family Life. This address was published in *L'Osservatore Romano* later that year. He was succeeded by Pope St. John XXIII, who called the Second Vatican Council. However, little mention of consecrated widows was made at that time. Later, in 1967 and 1977, Pope St. Paul VI addressed widows at Pentecost. By this time, an increasing number of widowed women were again seeking consecration. The Pope who would later do the most to restore the vocation of consecrated widows was Pope St. John Paul II, but unfortunately this vocation has still not been properly restored.

In 1982, during the Hope and Life pilgrimage to Lourdes, Pope St. John Paul II made a special address to widows of faith. He later reaffirmed the consecration of widows in his encyclical *Vita Consecrata,* which was published in 1996. Since then, the vocation of consecrated widow has grown rapidly both in Italy and in France. It has also reemerged in England, where there are now around thirty women who have been consecrated as widows. However, there are definitely not any consecrated widows in Scotland, and I have not heard of any in Wales, Northern Ireland, or the Republic of Ireland. The main problem with this vocation is that the current Pope has not, as yet, approved any universal rite for it. This means that the vocation is not written into Canon Law, and consecrations performed by bishops are by local rite only.

It is a great pity that this vocation has not been fully restored, as I know of many widows who would be interested in being consecrated. It is to be hoped that this vocation has not been overlooked simply because some of the candidates are older women, as that would be highly discriminatory. Their faith matters as much as anyone else's and, as has already been noted, Jesus is presented as being very sympathetic toward widows in the New Testament. In any case, many of the women seeking consecration are not very old, anyway, and younger women have also been consecrated as widows. One can only hope that this vocation will be fully restored soon. To leave the restoration unfinished would be yet another suppression of the Holy Spirit and another holding back of women who feel called to a particular spiritual way of life. This is because while some women are happy to be consecrated by local rite, others would prefer to be consecrated by a universally approved rite. In addition to this, the lack of a universal rite does mean that the consecration of a widow can only happen if a bishop is prepared to do it, and he is under no obligation to consecrate widows at all. This is not the case with the consecration of virgins, where there is an obligation to consecrate, although some bishops still refuse to do so.

Women who are consecrated as widows by local rite today take vows of poverty, chastity, and obedience. The vow of obedience is to the diocesan bishop. The vow of chastity is obviously a vow of celibacy, and the vow of poverty is a commitment to a simple, non-extravagant lifestyle. Consecrated widows are required to be financially independent. They are no longer required to be over sixty years of age, and younger women can seek consecration. They may work full time or live off private and state pensions. Many consecrated widows are involved in ministries within their dioceses or beyond, such as teaching, visiting the sick, reading, and working for justice and peace. The vocation has never been well promoted or well supported by the hierarchy in Britain and Ireland, and this is not helped by the lack of a universal rite, which means that, yet again, women are held back.

Another restored form of consecrated life being practiced today is that of the consecrated hermit. This vocation, unlike that of the consecrated widow, has been fully restored. This is quite a rare vocation today, which again has its roots in the early church. The first Christian hermits experienced a call to leave the world and seek God in solitude, austerity, and prayer. Consecrated hermits are sometimes referred to as anchorites, and there is some similarity between the lives of the current consecrated hermits and the pre-Reformation anchoresses. However, the pre-Reformation anchoresses, while living alone, tended to live in a cell attached to a church, and they were also sought out by the laity for spiritual direction. Modern consecrated hermits usually live completely alone in a very isolated location, although they may very well occasionally engage with the world for a specific purpose, as did Sr. Wendy Beckett when she produced a series of television documentaries on the history of art. Consecrated hermits take vows of poverty, chastity, and obedience. They are consecrated by diocesan bishops according to the Code of Canon Law 1983.

Another relatively new form of female consecrated life is consecration as a member of a secular institute. A secular institute is an organization of consecrated persons who profess the evangelical counsels of chastity, poverty, and obedience but live independently in the world, unlike members of a religious order or congregation who live in a convent. Some secular institutes appear to have been founded in France under persecution, at times when the French secular state was hostile to the active religious life. In France, active religious sisters were driven underground due to state hostility, and this led to groups of women meeting in secret and, eventually, after a period of formation, being consecrated in secret. These consecrated women saw themselves as hidden leaven through serving others and secretly promoting the consecrated life within the world. While their organizations were originally founded under persecution, the idea of an active religious life lived by a group of people who met regularly but lived in their own houses eventually became attractive and began to spread throughout the world. Eventually, restrictions were lifted in France in regard to the active religious life, but the secular institutes continued. These women carried on with the new form of consecrated life that they had created under times of persecution. They continued to take vows of poverty, chastity, and obedience but lived in their own homes and met with their fellow sisters every month for prayer and reflection. They also joined together for annual retreats.

In 1947, secular institutes received formal recognition from Pope Pius XII in the document "Provida Mater Ecclesia." Today, these institutes are recognized either by a bishop (diocesan right) or by the Holy See. Each secular institute is a member of the World Conference of Secular Institutes, and it is estimated that there are sixty thousand members of secular institutes across the world. There are nine secular institutes in the United Kingdom, and these institutes belong to the National Institute of Secular Institutes (NCSI). One of these institutes also has members in the Republic of Ireland. After this form of consecrated life was approved by Pope Pius XII, there was a surge of membership across Europe. However, within the United Kingdom, although secular institutes were created, they never achieved the levels of membership that occurred in other countries, such as France, Italy, Poland, and parts of Africa. This is almost certainly due to the fact that this vocation has not received as much support from the hierarchy in Britain as it has in other countries and has been very poorly promoted. Most United Kingdom members are in England, where there have been some efforts in some areas to promote this vocation. However, there are no known members in Scotland, where once again the clergy have been very reluctant to promote any new or restored form of consecrated life, and the situation is not much better in the Republic of Ireland, where this vocation is virtually unknown. Nevertheless, there are some signs in Ireland that this vocation is now beginning to receive some attention, and it is mentioned on the Vocations Ireland website.

Members of secular institutes usually follow a seven-year formation path that in many ways parallels the formation of the active religious in convents. There is a short period of inquiry or postulancy that generally lasts about six months. After this, the member becomes a novice, and the novitiate can last up to two years. Once this period is completed, the member begins to take annual vows of poverty, chastity, and obedience, and these will be taken for at least five years, and sometimes for longer, until the member is ready to make a final permanent commitment to the institute or decides to leave. Members can leave at any time during formation, but once the final commitment has been made, they can only leave with the permission of their diocesan bishop (if the institute is diocesan) or the Holy See (if the institute is pontifical).

The lifestyle of members of secular institutes is to be fully immersed in the world, and for this reason this form of consecrated life does sit very well with modern society. Members live independently and support themselves financially. They are meant to be contemplatives in action and a hidden leaven within the world. Therefore, they do not necessarily advise others that they are consecrated women, although they may do so depending on the situation or circumstances. These women can be found in a wide variety of occupations, which may be religious or secular. One woman, for example, works in the media. Those who do not work in the religious sphere and have more secular occupations may also have various ministries in their local church. All women are expected to bring Christ to others in whatever way they can, and the vocations are very flexible.

While vocations to a secular institute are flexible, they are not, however, completely freelance, as obviously each woman is a member of a group of women within an institute. Members of a secular institute might be expected to attend at least three residential weekends a year and an annual seven-day retreat. They may also be expected to attend the annual residential conference of secular institutes. If their institute is part of a large religious family (such as the Carmelite family), they might also be expected to attend a residential weekend with other members of that family, such as religious and friars. They may also have to attend chapter meetings of their institute as and when these are arranged. This means that a member might have to spend a considerable amount of time away with the institute. Nevertheless, it is possible for a woman to combine this vocation with a full-time occupation and simply take annual leave to meet these commitments required by the institute. Therefore, overall, these institutes do provide very good settings for modern women who wish to remain single, pursue a career, develop their personal spiritual lives, and pass on the message of the Gospel to others.

It is a great pity that this vocation has not been better promoted within Britain and Ireland and that many women have not heard about it. There has, unfortunately, been some hostility toward this vocation from some members of the clergy and others. Some members of the clergy did not promote this vocation because they saw it as "inferior" to the active religious life, as the women did not live in-community and wear a habit. The idea that all women who wish to be consecrated should be herded into a convent and forced to wear a habit is spiritually abusive. Of course, there are some women who prefer to live in a community, and that is all very well and good. Other women, however, prefer their own space, and there is nothing wrong with that. Every woman is different. What is really important is that the vows that these women take are exactly the same as the vows that active religious sisters take, and any woman who follows this path should be absolutely sure that the celibate single life is for her. If she is sure, then her commitment is just as good as that of any other consecrated woman. This form of consecrated life could be very popular with some women, and it would be good if more effort would be made to make it known.

All of the vocations mentioned here have been full-time vocations to the consecrated life that are available to celibate women, and while there are a number of vocations available, it should be noted that none of them enable these women to have any say in the actual governance of the church. But what of other women in the church? What full-time ministries are available to single women who do not wish to take vows of celibacy, or to married women? Ministries for these women are extremely important because although a few people do genuinely seek to follow a celibate path, the majority of people do not wish to be celibate, and God did not create us to be celibate. For many centuries and for far too long now, the church has not only denied women a voice, but has also denied married people a voice. Within the church there are a celibate few speaking on behalf of the whole of humanity, and people will simply not tolerate this any longer. That is why the church in the West is hemorrhaging, and that is why full-time ministries for women and married people are so important if the church is to survive.

We are considering here only full-time ministries that are currently available to women and not ministries such as reading or distributing communion in Mass, as these ministries, although important, are not ministries that can be taken up as a way of life. The main ministries that non-celibate women can currently take up as a way of life are membership of a third order, membership of a personal prelature, and various full-time occupations—for example, in teaching, academia, lay chaplaincy, or the media.

The term *third order* generally applies to lay members of religious communities who do not live in community but associate themselves with the spirit of a particular religious community while living a secular life. Their aim is usually to strive for Christian perfection in the world under the guidance of that particular community. Originally, third orders were a twelfth-century adaptation of the medieval monastic confraternities. These orders often had a first order, which were the male religious; a second order, which were the female religious; and a third order of laity. So, the term was somewhat hierarchical in its usage, which is why many members today prefer to use the term *secular order.* However, the term *third order* will be used here in order to avoid confusion with the secular institutes, which are something different altogether.

Members of third orders may be male or female and married or single. They usually meet on a monthly basis. They seek to live the charism of the order to which they belong within secular life. This involves seeking the sanctification of a person's work and family life in the midst of the world. Members of third orders do not take vows but instead make promises. These promises may involve obedience to the order and promises of faithfulness (chastity) to a spouse in marriage or in the single life. Third orders are popular among some of the laity who find this way of life enriching and fulfilling. The association with a religious order can also be supportive, and many members of third orders will often link up with members of the first and second orders for residential weekends or away days. However, while this vocation is personally fulfilling, it gives lay people no direct say in the governance of the church. The only way to have any influence indirectly would be to convince the celibate men in the first order of a particular view on a certain issue and hope that they would take this forward.

Another lay path open to all women today is membership of a prelature such as Opus Dei. This organization was founded in 1928 by Josemaría Escrivá and was approved by the church in 1950. It was made a prelature in 1982 by Pope St. John Paul II. The term *prelature* meant that Opus Dei was an organization whose jurisdictions of its own bishop covered all members of Opus Dei everywhere in the world, and these members were thus not subject to bishops in their own dioceses. This arrangement continued until July 2022, when Pope Francis suddenly declared that the leader of Opus Dei would no longer be a bishop and the prelature would fall under the competence of the Vatican Dicastery for the Clergy. This, in effect, removed the independence of Opus Dei and is one of several moves that Pope Francis has made to undermine the religious orders and make them subject to the Vatican. He has also made it impossible for new religious orders to be established without Vatican approval. These seem to be very strange actions coming from a Pope who has often spoken out about clericalism, but it may be that the Pope has had some personal concerns of which it is impossible for us to be aware.

Opus Dei has approximately ninety-five thousand members and the majority of its members are laypeople. It has been estimated that approximately 70 percent of Opus Dei members live in their own homes, leading family lives with secular careers, while around 30 percent of members are celibate. Most celibate members live in Opus Dei centers. The society states that it places a special emphasis on the lives of laypeople who are neither priests nor religious and stresses a universal call to holiness that is available to everyone. It stresses the unification of the spiritual life with the professional, social, and family lives. It is made up of several different types of "the faithful": supernumeraries, numeraries, numerary assistants, associates, the Prelature of Opus Dei clergy, the Priestly Society of the Holy Cross, and the Cooperators of Opus Dei. The largest group of members are the supernumeraries, who make up 70 percent of total membership. These supernumeraries are laypeople with careers and families. The second largest group are the numeraries, and they make up 20 percent of total membership. These are celibate members who give themselves in full availability to the official undertakings of the prelature and are expected to live in special centers run by Opus Dei. One of their main duties is to give doctrinal and ascetical formation to other members. Numeraries can be male or female.

Opus Dei has been criticized for maintaining a high degree of control over its members, and it has been alleged that numeraries have been forbidden to read certain books and have had their outgoing and incoming mail opened by their superiors. The prelature has also been accused of elitism and misogyny. However, in all fairness, women do seem to be very much included within the hierarchical structure of the prelature, and their voices appear to be heard. The head of Opus Dei is the prelate, and he is the primary governing authority for the organization, although he is now no longer a bishop and is therefore technically accountable to the Vatican. He is assisted by two councils—the General Council (made up of men) and the Central Advisory (made up of women). The prelature therefore does appear to consult and treat all of its members equally. But the main problem with this prelature is that it supports the current hierarchical model of the church and promotes the so-called traditional teaching of the church, which has been defined by celibate men and which the majority of laypeople today reject. Therefore, most of its members tend to join the prelature because they espouse the teaching of the Council of Trent, which came about in the sixteenth century. This prelature, therefore, while providing a supportive organization for a small minority, offers no solutions to the current problems facing the church.

Finally, the way in which most women tend to attempt to be involved in full-time ministries in the church today is through full-time secular occupations. Some women may teach in Catholic schools or perhaps be qualified as academics by obtaining a doctorate in theology. Other women may be involved in the media, writing articles in the Catholic press or working for religious broadcasting channels. There are also Catholic women who work as lay chaplains in schools and universities. Obviously, these women cannot consecrate the Eucharist, but they can organize Eucharistic services and take the Eucharist to those they serve. Often, they may offer counseling to those they serve as well. Other women may run retreat centers and offer spiritual direction. All of these ministries are very powerful because they do enable women to exercise some influence at a grassroots level even if the hierarchy does not listen to them. Teachers in schools can encourage discussion on church issues; academics can deliver lectures and write; those involved in the media can encourage thought, discussion, and reflection on important theological issues; lay chaplains can support, encourage, and counsel people; and those who work in retreat centers can promote good adult discussion. The important thing is to try to encourage a spirituality that regains the egalitarianism of the early church and is of relevance to those seeking God today. This brings us to the ministries that are not currently available to women but could be.

As has been noted in earlier chapters, there is very strong evidence that there was a female diaconate within the early Christian church and that this was universally supported by both the apostles and the early church fathers. The role of the female deacon was to keep the Holy Gates and to baptize women. The term *Holy Gates* probably refers to the iconostasis, which was a wall of icons and religious paintings that separated the nave from the sanctuary in the church. The role of the female deacon, therefore, was probably to ensure no one other than the priest entered the sanctuary. The other role of the female deacon, that of baptism, arose in order to meet the needs of the time. This is because during the early centuries many adults converted to Christianity and it was not thought appropriate that men should baptize adult women. The female diaconate was never suppressed but fell into disuse around the tenth century. This is believed to be due to the fact that it was felt that there was no longer any need for women to baptize due to infant baptism.

In 2017, patriarch Theodoros II and the Greek Orthodox Holy Synod of the Patriarch of Alexandria made a decision to reinstate the order of female deacons. The patriarch who covers the area of Alexandria and all Africa consecrated five women to the diaconate after this decision was made, and all the women were African. He stated that their role would be to assist in missionary churches. As Orthodox patriarchs do not answer to a pope or head patriarch, the restoration of the female diaconate applied to his area only, and it is up to other areas under other patriarchs to follow suit. As yet no other areas have done so, but many within the Orthodox Church are discussing the issue. The Greek Orthodox Church has voted to restore the female diaconate, but as yet no one has been ordained. In regards to the Orthodox Church as a whole, there is a small number of people who oppose the restoration of the female diaconate, but the vast majority appear to support it. However, the vast majority of Orthodox do not support women's ordination to the priesthood. This is because their church is very much based on tradition, and they are clear that while the female diaconate was universally accepted within the early church, the female priesthood was not. It is true that some women were ordained as priests up until the fourth century, but there is evidence this was not a universal phenomenon. This is rather different to the diaconate, where there is clear evidence that the ordination of women was universal.

In regard to the Catholic Church, in 2016 the International Union of Superiors General asked the Pope to consider ordaining women deacons when they were having an audience with him. In response to this, the Pope commissioned a study on the possibility of allowing women deacons in the Catholic Church. But when that commission handed in its research to the Pope, he stated that it was inconclusive. In 2019, some members of the Amazon synod requested that the Pope reestablish the 2016 project. The Pope considered this and in April 2020 a new commission was established. This commission comprises of ten members from Europe and the United States and has not, at the time of writing, reached any conclusions.

My view on this matter is as follows. The Catholic Church claims to be a historical church that bases itself on tradition as well as scripture, although some of its current practices have in fact moved very much away from the traditions of the early church. Protestant churches, however, do not base themselves on tradition. They believe that the Bible is the sole source of infallible truth and that salvation is through grace alone. They encourage individual interpretations of the scriptures inspired by the Holy Spirit. Any church can therefore, within Protestantism, be a true manifestation of the body of Christ on Earth, and the Holy Spirit may lead Christians to make changes to meet the needs of the time. So, for most Protestants, female ordination is not a problem, as they do not have to model themselves on tradition. But the Catholic Church has stated it is a historical church that does base itself on tradition. Therefore, the only way forward for this church is to base itself on true tradition. This will mean some reform in order for the church to bring itself in line with the traditions of Christianity in the early centuries. One of these reforms should be the restoration of the female diaconate.

It is clear that within the early church there was a female diaconate and this diaconate had been created to meet the needs of the time. Those needs were the keeping of the Holy Gates and the baptism of women. There is no reason why this diaconate cannot be restored to meet the needs of our time. These needs could again include baptism. We do not have enough priests, and if female deacons could baptize, that would free priests up to concentrate on consecrating the Eucharist, anointing the sick, and hearing confessions. Other things that women deacons could do would be to officiate at weddings and funerals where there are no nuptial or requiem Masses. These services do not require a priest and would take a lot of pressure off the priest. Of course, there are already male deacons who carry out these functions, but there is no reason why there cannot be female deacons too. The church may eventually become a church of many deacons and few priests due to the shortage of vocations. Ordaining women to the female diaconate would also enable women to have a say in the governance of their dioceses, as they would then be present at the regular diocesan meetings that the bishop has with his clergy.

Moving on from here, I would argue that it is not currently in the interests of the church to ordain women to the priesthood, as this would clearly be schismatic. It has been noted that although some women were ordained to the priesthood in the early church, it was not a universal practice. Of course, this can also be challenged by asserting that the ordination of women was clearly suppressed by misogynists in the early church and may therefore not have been the will of God, particularly as Mary Magdalene was also sidelined as an apostle. But would pursuing this argument help the church to grow at the moment? The answer is clearly not. It would almost certainly create a schism. The best way forward, therefore, would be to create a female lay cardinalate, which would not be as controversial.

It cannot be disputed that women had powers of governance within the early Christian Church. They ruled over double monasteries in Anglo-Saxon England and were the superiors of both men and women. In Ireland, St. Brigid of Kildare was the abbess of a double monastery, and there were similar monasteries led by women in France and Germany. In addition to this, it cannot be refuted that both St. Hilda and the abbess Aelffled attended and voted at church synods, where they were highly influential. Surely it is now time to fully restore the female vote and give women a say at church synods? Pope Francis has recently announced that a small number of women religious and some lay women will be allowed a vote at the forthcoming Synod on Synodality. This is a good beginning, but it is not enough. The best way to fully restore the female synodal vote would be to create lay cardinals. As noted in an earlier chapter, these cardinals were men who had not been ordained as a deacon, priest, or bishop. They existed from the sixteenth to the twentieth century, when the hierarchy decided to terminate them in the same way as it has previously changed and terminated so many other earlier traditions. Canon law was changed, and the 1917 Code of Canon Law dispensed with them and decreed that from then on only those who were priests or deacons could be cardinals. This current Code of Canon Law could also be dispensed with, and the church could return to the practice of admitting laypeople to the cardinalate, and there is no reason why it could not admit both non-ordained men and women. The role of lay cardinal would be a way to give both consecrated and laywomen a stronger voice in the church while at the same time being true to church history. The church can take up this opportunity or choose to leave what it sees as "the power" in the hands of the celibate few. But any inaction by the hierarchy in the short term will only mean that the church is likely to bring about its own extinction in the long term. The modern world has developed an understanding of abuse that earlier societies did not have, and no abusive power structure will now survive long term.

CHAPTER NINE

Synod on Synodality

This chapter examines the current Synod on Synodality, which was opened by Pope Francis on October 10, 2021. This synodal process will end in late 2024. Firstly, the Synod on Synodality will be defined. What is it? How has Pope Francis described it, and what does he see it as achieving? Secondly, various reactions to this synodal process will be discussed. In particular, I will look at how various members of the hierarchy have reacted to this process. Finally, the question as to whether this process can make any difference to women and to the problems that the church faces today will also be considered.

Church synods have their roots in the early church, where synodality was a process by which decisions were made through discussion, reflection, and constructive disagreement rather than through the issuing of orders from on high. Indeed, in the early church it was not possible to issue orders from on high due to poor communication methods and a lack of definite structures. At that time and in later centuries, synods were usually convened to decide an issue of doctrine, administration, or application. While bishops always attended synods, it was also not uncommon to find royalty, women, and laypeople in attendance. It has already been noted that two Anglo-Saxon women, St. Hilda and the abbess Aelffled, were very influential at two early synods. Unfortunately, however, in more recent centuries the presence of laypeople or women at either councils of the church or synods has become almost impossible, as women have not had a synodal vote. But, as will be seen later, Pope Francis has made some attempts to change this for the final sitting of the current Synod on Synodality.

In May 1917, the church hierarchy produced the Pio-Benedictine Code. This was the first official comprehensive codification of Latin

Canon Law. It was promulgated by Pope Benedictine XV, and with it the hierarchy took on even more power and the laity and women were further sidelined. It has already been noted how, throughout history, the male celibate hierarchy of the Catholic Church has progressively passed decrees at councils that have increased its power and taken the church further and further away from the people. This new Code of Canon Law was another example of a hierarchical power grab, as it decreed that laypeople could no longer be cardinals. This meant, of course, that there would no longer be any chance of laypeople's having a vote at ecumenical councils. Later, at Vatican II, there was a call for a Synod of Bishops to be established. This was followed in 1966 by an ordo setting out procedures. The first Synod of Bishops was then held in 1967. Following on from this, in 1983 a new Code of Canon Law was produced that situated the Synod of Bishops as part of the hierarchical constitution of the church.

Canon 342 of this new Code of Canon Law states that the Synod of Bishops is a group of bishops selected from different parts of the world who meet together at specified times to promote the close relationship between the Roman pontiff and the bishops. These bishops assist the pontiff in the defense of faith and morals, in the preservation and strengthening of ecclesiastical discipline, and in the consideration of questions concerning the activity of the church in the world. Thus, a new power structure had been created to "be" the church and to tell everyone in the church what to do, and there wasn't a single married layperson or woman included in this structure! The Orthodox Church also has a Synod of Bishops within each of its autonomous churches, but in that church lesser clerics and laypeople are also delegated to attend these synods. Anglican synods consist of elected clergy and lay members and are not just confined to bishops. The Catholic Church, however, has continued over the centuries to place more and more power into the hands of an elite celibate few.

While it is undeniable that the Roman Catholic Church of today is more clericalist than it has ever previously been, there have been some indications that the current Pope at the time of writing (Francis) is aware of this. What we will never know, however, is how much influence he really has and whether he has a license to do as he wants or whether he is held back by others in the Vatican. However, there have been many occasions when he has spoken out about clericalism. For example, at a meeting with the bishops of Chile on January 16, 2018, he stated the following:

> The lack of consciousness of belonging to God's faithful people as servants, and not masters, can lead us to one of the temptations that is the most damaging to the missionary outreach that we are called to promote: clericalism, which ends up as a caricature of the vocation we have received. A failure to realize that the mission belongs to the entire Church, and not to the individual priest or bishop, limits the horizon, and even worse, stifles all the initiatives that the Spirit may be awakening in our midst. Let us be clear about this. The lay persons are not our peons, or our employees. They don't have to parrot back whatever we say. Clericalism, far from giving impetus to various contributions and proposals, gradually extinguishes the prophetic flame to which the entire Church is called to bear witness. Clericalism forgets that the visibility and the sacramentality of the Church belongs to all the faithful people of God (cf. *Lumen Gentium*, 9–14), not only to the few chosen and enlightened.

Pope Francis also mentioned clericalism in the apostolic exhortation *Evangelii Gaudium,* stating that in some churches the laity have not been given room to speak and act due to an excessive clericalism.

It was no doubt with clericalism in mind that Pope Francis decided in 2020 to make synodality the theme of the sixteenth Synod of Bishops, which opened on October 10, 2021. The Pope declared the topic of the synod "a synodal Church," which he stated consists of "communion, participation and mission." He stated that a synodal church was one that walks together, bringing people, priests, and bishops together in an ongoing mission to spread the Gospel. This, he intimated, is an ecclesial model of church that moves Catholicism away from a top-down Rome model and gives a greater voice to laypeople. On opening the synod, the Pope stated the following:

There is no need to create another Church, but to create a different Church. That is the challenge. For a different Church, a Church open to the newness that God wants to suggest, let us with greater fervor and frequency invoke the Holy Spirit and humbly listen to him, journeying together as he, the source of communion and mission, desires: with docility and courage. Keep us from becoming a "museum Church," beautiful but mute, with much past and little future.

While Pope Francis may clearly desire some form of change, there are several things to consider in regard to whether there will actually be any changes achieved: the attitude of some of the hierarchy to this synod, whether the synod is the appropriate vehicle to bring about change, and whether the synodal process will enable the voices of the laity to be heard.

Firstly, in regard to the attitude of some of the hierarchy, there have already been numerous statements from some members of the hierarchy that show that they have felt that their power is threatened by this synodal process and that this has been a major concern for them. For example, Bishop Robert Barron wrote the following in February 2020 in regard to the preliminary text:

> . . . it gave the impression that the Church is a kind of freewheeling democracy, making up its principles and teachings as it goes along. Rather alarmed by this section of the draft, a number of bishops and archbishops, myself included, rose to speak against it. We wondered aloud how to square this language with the teaching authority of the bishops, the binding quality of the Church's dogmatic statements, and the practical process of governing the people of God.

What is particularly to be noted here is his defense of the authority of the celibate bishops in regard to teaching and the practical process of "governing" the people of God. He then went on to write:

> I learned that the German Bishops' Conference was gathering under the rubric of "synodality" and had committed to walk the "synodal path." My attention turned to something closer to alarm when I gathered that they were open to a reconsideration of some

of the most fundamental moral teachings and disciplines of the Church, including the nature of the sexual act, the theology of the priesthood, and the possibility of ordination for women. Further, the bishops of Germany were endeavouring to undertake their deliberations in collaboration with the Central Committee for German Catholics, a lay organization, and they were insisting that the decisions of this joint body would be "binding." To state it bluntly, every fear that I and a number of other bishops had when we first read the open-ended language regarding "synodality" in the preliminary document of the Youth Synod now seemed justified.

So here we have it. The bishop feared that there might be some reconsideration on some of what he describes as "the most fundamental moral teachings . . . of the Church"—namely, the nature of the sexual act, the theology of the priesthood, and the possibility of the ordination of women—and he also feared that the German bishops were going to discuss these issues with a German lay organization! Now let us be clear here. The church does not belong to Bishop Robert Barron and approximately 5,600 celibate bishops across the world. The church is not the hierarchy, even if they wish to teach that it is. The church is the people of God, and we—the people of God—were never consulted on these so-called fundamental moral teachings. They were imposed on us by the elite, privileged, celibate few. It is right that we should be consulted, and if we are not consulted then we should not remain in this church, as it will not have the spiritual hearts of its core members at its center. Will we ever be consulted? The bishop then went on to write that he and others later met with Pope Francis on an ad limina visit and the Pope advised them as follows:

> He told us, in no uncertain terms, that a synod is "not a parliament," and that the synodal process is not simply a matter of canvassing the participants and counting votes. And then he added, with particular emphasis, that the "protagonist" of a synod is not any of the delegates to the gathering, but rather the Holy Spirit. This last observation is of signal importance. The point of a democratic assembly is to discern the will of the people, for in a democratic polity, they are finally sovereign. But in a synod, the point is

discerning, not the will of the people, but the will of the Holy Spirit, for the Spirit in that context is sovereign, or in the language of Pope Francis, the "protagonist."

Bishop Barron was then assured that all would be well and nothing would change. Really? It seems that in this bishop's world only the bishops can discern the will of the Holy Spirit, and therefore nothing will change. The Holy Spirit doesn't speak to laypeople or women in particular, it would seem. It only speaks to bishops. Since when did the New Testament tell us that only an elite celibate few could discern the Holy Spirit?

Sadly, a similar view to that of Bishop Barron's was also articulated in 2020 by Cardinal Gerhard Muller, a former prefect of the Congregation for the Doctrine of the Faith. Also referring to the desire of the German bishops to be more inclusive in their synodal processes, he wrote:

> It can hardly be assumed that a body like the Synodal Path in Germany could claim the Holy Spirit for itself in order to suspend, correct and reinterpret the authority of Holy Scripture, the Apostolic Tradition and the infallible decisions of the Magisterium . . . Nor is it an entity authorised by the Church, nor an academically-recognised authority that can "further develop" dogmas or divine law.

According to this cardinal, the previous decisions of the magisterium are infallible. They cannot be changed. The Holy Spirit has spoken forever. What, then, is the purpose of this Synod on Synodality if the laity will never be listened to? Also, how is it that the Holy Spirit did not decide that the Pope was infallible until 1,870 years after the birth of Christ? Was he asleep for all the years preceding the solemn declaration of papal infallibility, or was this declaration just another example of the distortion of tradition to keep power within the church in the hands of a celibate few? The Eastern Orthodox Church has never made any claims of infallibility, and that church has also existed since the time of Christ.

Another account on the poor attitude of some Catholic bishops toward the Synod on Synodality was printed online in the *National Catholic Reporter* on December 7, 2021. This article, written by Phyllis

Zagano, alleged that many American bishops were ignoring the synod. She stated that only half of the US bishops had even named someone to run the synod project in their dioceses. Half of the US bishops, she alleged, are not interested in what the people of God think.

We would do well, having looked at these examples of the unwillingness of some bishops to contribute to this synodal process or to see any change, to remember the definitions of spiritual abuse that were examined in an earlier chapter, namely "control through the use of sacred texts or teaching" and "the suggestion that the abuser has a divine position." These bishops certainly think they are divinely appointed to ignore the people of God and keep power in their own hands, it would seem. The problem that they have yet failed to recognize is that it is possible that within thirty years there will no longer be any laypeople within the Western church for them to control.

Despite the doubts some members of the hierarchy have in regard to this synod, it has now gone ahead, albeit with some bishops allegedly not participating. But what processes are being followed during this synod? Will they make any difference for women or in any way address the problems that the church currently faces?

The Synod on Synodality consists of three phases, detailed in an official handbook produced by the Vatican known as a vademecum: the diocesan phase, lasting from October 2021 to April 2022; the second continental phase, from September 2022 to March 2023; and the final universal phase, from October 2023 to October 2024. This third stage is actually the XVI Ordinary General Assembly of the Synod of Bishops dedicated to the theme "For a Synodal Church: Communion, Participation and Mission."

It was during the first phase of this process that the people of God were meant to be consulted. The official handbook suggested discussions among parishes, lay movements, schools and universities, religious congregations, neighborhood Christian communities, social action, and ecumenical and inter-religious movements. It stated that bishops should initiate this process, and all involvement should be coordinated through the regular communication channels of the diocesan bishop. I sampled the processes that were being used to consult the people by visiting the websites of various dioceses in the UK and Ireland. Many dioceses had online surveys, but most of the ones I saw avoided any difficult topics. There was more willingness to discuss difficult subjects in the Republic of Ireland than in the United Kingdom. Some bishops were suggesting a theme to be discussed every week, and, needless to say, none of these themes were in conflict with current church teaching. I also saw a few themes that were new and innovative but not necessarily in conflict with current church teaching. For example, the restoration of the female diaconate has not, as yet, been ruled to be in conflict with current church teaching, but I saw no evidence that it was being discussed anywhere in the United Kingdom, although there was some evidence it was being discussed in Ireland. There already seemed to be a degree of control being exercised in regard to what was being discussed, with difficult subjects being carefully avoided.

The process was meant to be that after having consulted with the laity in their various dioceses across the world, the bishops would then feed back all the information they had gathered from the laity into a diocesan pre-synodal meeting and synthesis. This synthesis would then form the basis of an *instrumentum laboris* that would be used at the Assembly of the Synod of Bishops in October 2023. There would also be seven international meetings in Africa, Oceania, the Middle East, Asia, Latin America, Europe, and North America. These meetings would in turn also produce seven final documents that would serve as the basis for a second instrumentum laboris to be used at the same assembly. The bishops would then, according to the official handbook, discern at a universal level the voice of the Holy Spirit, who has been speaking throughout the church. The official handbook states the following:

> Synodality does not exist without the pastoral authority of the College of Bishops, under the primacy of the Successor of Peter, as well as the pastoral authority of each diocesan Bishop in the diocese entrusted to his care. The ministry of Bishops is to be pastors, teachers, and priests of sacred worship. Their charism of discernment calls them to be authentic guardians, interpreters, and witnesses to the faith of the Church.

However, since the production of this handbook, Pope Francis has made some significant change as he has now given five religious sisters and 70 lay people (of which half will be women) the synodal vote at this particular synod. While this restoration of the synodal vote to laypeople is significant, I am of the view that it will be difficult for this synod to make any great changes for several reasons.

Firstly, laypeople and women have not, in all dioceses, been allowed to discuss the subjects that concern them during the first stage of this synod, and the topics of discussion were often largely decided for them. This means that many of the areas of Catholic teaching on which a large number of the people of God dissent were off the agenda in a significant number of areas. A church that really involved the people of God should have insisted that the people of God set the agenda. Unfortunately, this has not been the case in all dioceses, and due to this many parishioners did not participate—and the millions who have left the church did not come back to join in these discussions. They had realized that these diocesan meetings might not enable them to express their views and might be nothing more than social talking shops.

Secondly, this synodal process gave all power to diocesan bishops. After the laypeople had been consulted, it was the bishops, perhaps in consultation with the clergy, who decided what to feed back at the diocesan pre-synodal meeting, and if there was anything they did not like or did not want to discuss, they had the power to ignore it. It is also the bishops who will in the main, at the last stage of this synod, discern at a universal level the voice of the Holy Spirit, who has been speaking throughout the church. It is true that five religious sisters and 70 laypeople will now be voting at the synod. However, these people will be a small minority in comparison to the number of bishops. The best one can hope for is that the very presence of these laypeople at this synod might change its culture, but that remains to be seen.

Thirdly, while it is clear that the Pope is serious about involving women and other laypeople in this synod of the church (through giving them a synodal vote), it is unclear if any future synods after this one will also be composed of both bishops and laypeople as happened in the synods of the early church and as happens in both the Orthodox and Anglican communions today. It is simply not Christian nor in line with true tradition to have a small number of celibate men deciding what being a church means for around one billion church members across the world. The Synod of Bishops is a fairly recent creation within the Catholic Church, and it is an unfortunate creation in its current state. There needs to be some further commitment to the involvement of laypeople in all future synods of the church.

Finally, once again in this synodal process despite all the welcome efforts of Pope Francis, we still see the status of the bishops being lifted to that of demigods. Ultimately, despite the presence of a small number of lay people, it is still the bishops, who are in the main, discerning the workings of the Holy Spirit. Apparently, the Holy Spirit speaks to virtually no one other than these few celibate men. The problem with this placing of so much power in the hands of an elitist few is that it has caused much abuse and suffering in the church. Bishops, who were sole governors of their dioceses and thus accountable to no one, protected priests who had abused children by moving them from place to place. For example, in the Roman Catholic Diocese of Galloway in Scotland, one priest, Paul Moore, confessed to abusing boys to the then bishop of Galloway (Maurice Taylor) in 1996. However, the bishop elected not to go to the police and instead sent Moore to a clinic for child sex offenders in Canada. It is alleged that he withheld this information from his parishioners and said the priest had gone on sabbatical. On his return, Paul Moore was sent to Fort Augustus Abbey, which was run by Benedictine monks. He lived there with another self-confessed pedophile. The priest was eventually arrested and was jailed for nine years in 2018. These kinds of cover-ups happened across the world, with bishops protecting many abusers. They were able to do this because they had so much power and were subject to no scrutiny, being answerable to no one but themselves. While today there are child protection procedures in place in dioceses to prevent child abuse, the status of a bishop within the church has not changed in any other way. They continue to be seen as almost divine. They continue to be seen as the only vehicles for the Holy Spirit, and they continue to rule their dioceses autonomously. One has to ask, how on earth does the Catholic hierarchy have the gall to claim divine authority for this group of men when so many of them have covered up nasty cases of child abuse and others, such as the laicized Cardinal McCarrick, have actually committed these abuses themselves? Have they no shame? How can they not see that this celibate institution has become cultish and elitist and that married laity and women are permanently needed on synods to break up the corrupt stranglehold on power that they have become so used to having?

While of course there are some very good bishops, the autocratic power and status that each bishop has ensures that if a bishop wishes to be spiritually or politically abusive, he can be so. Sadly, it is unlikely that the bishops will ever invite laypeople or women to share in their power in any real and meaningful sense. What organization usually gives up its power? As noted earlier in this chapter, some bishops are concerned with holding on to their power at all costs. The real problem here is that the governance of the church is in the hands of a Synod of Bishops rather than in the hands of a permanent synod or assembly comprising both bishops and lay people. Until this happens, the governance of the church remains with a small number of male celibate men, and the only way that this will finally end, it seems, could be when there are no laypeople left within the church for the bishops to govern. This is likely to happen much sooner in Europe than in other continents. In the meantime, the current Synod on Synodality continues to proceed to its conclusion, and while it may herald some small changes it seems unlikely that it will herald any major ones.

CHAPTER TEN

Disturbing
Misogynistic Trends

This chapter examines disturbing trends in relationships between the Catholic clergy and women within the Latin Church. Firstly, I will examine relationships between the clergy and women in parishes, raising the question as to whether women in parishes are treated differently than men by the clergy, and if so, why? Secondly, the question of friendships between women and members of the clergy will be discussed. Famous historical friendships between women and members of the clergy will be examined, and I will then consider friendships and relationships between women and the clergy today. Issues to be discussed will include whether nonsexual friendships between the clergy and women are frowned upon, and if so, why? Surely it would be misogynistic to allow a priest to be able to enjoy nonsexual friendships with men but not with women? When are such friendships with either sex appropriate? What constitutes an inappropriate relationship between a member of the clergy and a woman? Are inappropriate relationships between the clergy and women dealt with differently than inappropriate relationships between the clergy and men? The issue of illicit sexual relationships between members of the clergy and women will also be discussed.

Every spiritual woman who chooses to belong to a Catholic parish will not only be seeking God but also community. A Catholic community is a place where Christians can feel a quality of togetherness with others who share their own beliefs and practices and, in particular, meet to participate in the Eucharist. Many women who are part of such a community will be seeking to love and serve each other, to grow and develop their knowledge of the faith, and to support each other in times of difficulty. Unfortunately, in Catholic parishes today, many priests are thought to have an elevated status due to the fact that they administer the sacraments. This was not the case in the pre-Reformation church, where ministries such as teaching and spiritual direction were also regarded to be of great importance. This elevated status, as has been noted, came about due to the Council of Trent's teaching that ordination placed an indelible mark on the soul of the priest, and also due to later teaching that a priest acts in the person of Christ when pronouncing words that form part of a sacramental rite—e.g., as in the Words of Institution at the Eucharistic consecration. The Orthodox reject this teaching. Nevertheless, it is this teaching that has resulted in priests' having a high status in parishes and being perceived as different and slightly apart from others. Naturally, this high status only serves to make the attention of a priest highly desirable for any parishioner, and probably more desirable than it should be in a healthy church. Therefore, any lack of such priestly attention can be felt as a slight. In addition to this, there are often occasions when the advice of a priest on theological or moral matters can be very valuable to laypeople. Priests will generally have a better knowledge of theology than most of their parishioners as they will have studied the subject for many years. Some of them will also (despite the official teaching on morals, which has never been agreed on by the universal lay church) be able to offer very good advice on morals due to all the experience they will have gained listening to others in the confessional. On those occasions, the counsel of a priest can be very important to a parishioner, and any parishioner who does not feel able to access this counsel in the same way as others will feel to some degree a sense of discrimination. Sadly, there seem to be a significant number of women who feel this way.

I am not aware of any independent research that has been done on the feelings of female parishioners with regard to their interactions with their parish priests, and such research would also be very difficult to carry out. Most parish priests would not take too kindly to someone surveying their parishioners in regard to their feelings about them. However, I myself have done some limited research both in person and online, and what I have generally found is that although married women do not seem to have any issues with their relationship with their parish priests, some single women do feel that they are discriminated against precisely because they are female and single. One woman stated the following:

> It always seems to me that my priest is strained and distant with me and different towards me to the way he is with married women. For example, I have often seen him hug married women who have been distressed due to bereavements or other events in their lives but I am sure that if I was distressed, I would not be hugged. Not that I want a hug in any case. Of course, I don't care about that. That is not the issue. It's just the feeling I have that my priest sees me as a threat due to the fact I am a single woman and therefore I am treated differently to other parishioners. I don't like it. I think it's all probably because he has issues with sexuality which he hasn't addressed, and I don't like being a victim of his issues.

Another single woman had this experience:

> I have often seen the priest looking very relaxed and engaged in friendly banter with other single men but he never engaged with me in that way. He always seemed very wary when I approached him. I would have liked to have gone to him for some advice about a personal problem as I would have liked a religious slant on it. But I just knew from the way he behaved with me that he wouldn't be comfortable in a face-to-face meeting with me discussing my personal problems. In the end I went to a professional counsellor but obviously my counsellor didn't really understand how important my faith is in my life in the way that a priest might have.

These are just a couple examples of comments I received from single women in regard to their relationship with their parish priest. A significant number of them felt that they were treated differently purely because they were both female and single. Most of them felt that the priest perceived them to be a threat. It should be noted that this state of affairs is not universal in all parishes, and of course there are some parishes where single women feel that their needs are well met because they have a very good and emotionally well-rounded priest. But a significant number of women I spoke to did feel that they are discriminated against due to their sex and single status.

Most single women who feel that their priests discriminate against them due to their sex and marital status also feel that this is due to their priests' having issues with sexuality, and this will almost certainly be true in most cases. However, even then, this discrimination is hard to fully understand unless there is also an element of entrenched misogyny here. This is due to the fact that a priest could just as easily break his vows with a single man as with a single woman; so why is only the female treated as if she were a threat to his chastity? Due to the fact that the Vatican is not open and transparent, there is no data available that would indicate whether priests break their vows more often with men than with women. The Vatican will not put these figures in the public domain because it still wishes to try to preserve the myth of priest as demigod, a myth that has long since lost credibility. However, statistics regarding sexual abuse are in the public domain and show that most of the victims of sexual abuse are generally male. It is therefore reasonable to assume that priests in mutually consensual sexual relationships have probably broken their vows more often with men than with women. If that assumption is correct, this victimization of single women in parishes as persons to be avoided is likely due to deeply entrenched misogyny just as much as it is due to priestly issues with sexuality.

Sadly, all incidents of discrimination against women in parishes, be they due to issues with sexuality or misogynism, will have their roots in enforced celibacy. Voluntary celibacy, which is taken up by a well-rounded person who fully understands what he is giving up and wants to live the single life and give more of his time to God and others, can be a beautiful gift. But enforced celibacy is destroying the church and its reputation because it causes so many problems and scandals: forcing a man to give up his sexuality before he has fully grown to understand it—when this happens, he will later encounter difficulties when he experiences a sexual awakening; creating a celibate culture due to the fact that all the people a priest works with are celibate—this can lead to a failure to understand those who live a different lifestyle; creating a select elitist minority group—this can lead to delusions of superiority and grandeur; causing loneliness and depression in those who would not naturally have chosen to be celibate and single—this affects the lives and ministries of priests; causing sexual frustration in those who again would not naturally have chosen to be celibate—this can lead to sexual scandals; creating conditions in which misogyny can thrive due to an absence of women—this can lead to women's being sidelined in all areas of Christian life and ministry; creating conditions where it will be easier for sexual abuse to thrive due to a lack of scrutiny from others who live a different lifestyle—this decimates the reputation of the clergy and is unfair to those priests who have never been involved in these scandals; creating great suffering in some priests due to the high expectations placed upon them, particularly when they fail to meet these expectations—this again affects the ministries and lives of priests; creating a hidden church lacking in transparency due to the need to cover up sexual lapses; and, finally, creating suffering in women for a variety of reasons, such as discrimination, misogyny, and, of course, illicit sexual relationships.

Having illustrated how single women feel that they can be sidelined in parishes due to issues a priest may have with his sexuality or misogynistic attitudes, I will now move on to discuss the question of friendships between women and the clergy.

While the society of today tends to picture all relationships in sexual terms, there have been many great spiritual nonsexual relationships between members of the clergy and women in the past, and there is no reason why there should not always be so. The key to a good nonsexual friendship is, of course, the maturity of both individuals and what they see as the aim of their friendship. If it is a mutual mission or mutual prayer and support, then it can and will work. Some great historical examples of good friendships between members of the clergy and women include St. Catherine of Siena and Bl. Raymond of Capua, Queen Catherine of Aragon and Fr. John Forest, and St. Teresa of Avila and St. John of the Cross.

St. Catherine of Siena was born in 1347 and decided at a very young age that she wanted to give her life to God. She grew up near the

Dominican church in Siena and joined the lay Dominicans when she was about sixteen. Catherine became well known for her kindness in visiting those who were sick as well as those in prison. On one occasion, she stayed with a prisoner throughout his execution, praying for him and whispering words of encouragement. She found herself drawn into the political life of her day and gained a great reputation as an unofficial spiritual counselor; her influence on Pope Gregory XI played a role in his decision to leave Avignon for Rome. Later, she was sent by him to negotiate peace with Florence. After his death came the Great Schism of the West, and she sent numerous letters to princes and cardinals to promote obedience to Pope Urban VI. In addition to these letters, Catherine also dictated many others to a great number of people, and these are considered one of the great works of early Tuscan literature. She also dictated a famous work known as the "Dialogue of Divine Providence" and composed twenty-six poems. St. Catherine of Siena was declared a doctor of the church in October 1970 by Pope St. Paul VI.

Catherine first met Raymond of Capua in 1347 when he was appointed by the Dominican Order as her theological guide and confessor. Over the years he became her closest friend, and they supported and helped each other in a friendship of equals. It is clear from her letters to him that they had a relationship in which they were able to be perfectly open with each other. While praising his virtues on many occasions she was also not afraid to challenge him when she thought that he may not have behaved correctly in any matter. After her death, Raymond of Capua wrote St. Catherine's biography. Following are some extracts of the letter that she dictated to him shortly before she passed:

> I beg you that you pardon me every disobedience, irreverence and ingratitude which I showed to you or committed against you, and all pain and bitterness which I may have caused you; and the slight zeal which I have had for our salvation . . .
>
> Pardon me, that I have written you words of bitterness. I do not write them, however, to cause you bitterness, but because I am in doubt and do not know what the goodness of God will do with me. I wish to have done my duty. And do not regret that we are separated one from the other in the body; although you would have been the

very greatest consolation to me, greater are my consolation and gladness to see the fruit that you are bearing in Holy Church. And now I beg you to labor yet more zealously, for she never had so great a need. . . .

It had been a very close friendship between two people who shared a similar spirituality, and it lasted until St. Catherine's death.

Another close and truly amazing nonsexual relationship between a woman and a priest was the friendship between Catherine of Aragon, Queen of England, and Blessed John Forest. Forest was an English Franciscan friar who became the provincial of his order. He was the confessor of the queen and became spiritually close to her before King Henry VIII ended his marriage with her. At the time of the Reformation, Forest refused to acknowledge King Henry VIII as head of the church in England and also declared his allegiance both to his queen and to the Catholic faith. He was held at Newgate Prison and eventually burned at the stake. The following are extracts of a letter the queen sent to him during his imprisonment before his death. During this letter, she attempts to support and counsel the priest in a similar way to the way he had supported and counseled her in the past through the confessional:

> My Reverend Father,
>
> Since you have ever been want in dubious cases to give good counsel to others, you will necessarily know all the better what is needed for yourself, being called to combat for the love of Christ and the truth of the Catholic faith. If you will bear up under these few and short pains of your torments which are prepared for you, you will receive, as you well know, eternal reward. . . .
>
> But woe to me, your poor and wretched daughter, who, in the time of this my solitude and the extreme anguish of my soul shall be deprived of such a corrector and father so loved by me in the bowels of Christ. And truly, if it were lawful for me freely to confess what is my most ardent desire in reverence to this, to your paternity, to whom I have always revealed (as was my duty) all the secrets of my heart and conscience, I confess to you that I am consumed by a very great desire to be able to die, either together with you or before you. . . .

But perhaps I have spoken as a foolish woman. Therefore, since it appears that God has thus ordained, go you, my father, first with joy and fortitude, and by your prayers plead with Jesus Christ for me, that I may speedily and intrepidly follow you through the same wearisome and difficult journey. . . .

Farewell, my Reverend Father, and on earth and in heaven always have me in remembrance before God.

Your very sad and afflicted daughter, Katharine.

Apparently, the priest replied that in justification of her cause he was content to suffer all things and that he had no fear of death, having worn the habit of the glorious St. Francis for forty years. This was a very passionate friendship, but it was not sexual. Spiritual friendships can also be passionate. Catherine, in fact, never stopped loving her husband, King Henry VIII, despite all his transgressions against her. Indeed, she wrote to him on her deathbed, stating that she pardoned him of all things and prayed that God would pardon him also. Her last written words to her husband were "mine eyes desire you above all things." So, she had continued to love her husband all her life, and her friendship with Fr. John Forest was one of spiritual affinity from which both gained inspiration and support. Moving on from here, I will now describe another similar, powerful, and spiritual friendship—the spiritual relationship between St. Teresa of Avila and St. John of the Cross.

St. Teresa of Avila was born in 1515. She became a major figure in what is known as the Counter-Reformation. The Counter-Reformation was a period of Catholic resurgence that occurred in response to the Protestant Reformation. St. Teresa was a reformer, and she reformed the Carmelite Order. The movement that she initiated was later joined by the younger Spanish Carmelite friar and mystic St. John of the Cross. This movement led eventually to the establishment of a new reformed Carmelite Order known as the Discalced Carmelites.

St. Teresa and St. John of the Cross first met when Teresa was fifty-two years and John was twenty-five. Both were dissatisfied with their current forms of religious life. They initially agreed to create a reformed priory together and later went on to found a new religious order. Out of this grew a deep and lasting friendship that has always been recognized by the Carmelites across the world. For example, the Carmelite Sisters of Los Angeles state that this was a very "well balanced friendship of spiritual depth" that expressed the need for human companionship and support. They state:

> Since no one person possesses all gifts, each must have gifts to offer the other and the capacity to receive from the other. Thus, each makes up to some extent what is lacking in oneself. This source of mutual help must be rooted in one's love of God. Thomas Merton expressed this well when he said, "We will see that we are human, like everyone else, that we all have weaknesses and deficiencies, and that these limitations of ours play a most important part in all our lives. It is because of them that we need others and others need us. We are not all weak in the same spots, and so we supplement and complete one another, each one making up in himself for the lack in another."

They then go on to state:

> John recognized in Teresa's reform what he had so ardently been seeking and acknowledged her leadership and guidance. Teresa appreciated in this new acquaintance the richness of his deep interior life and soon selected him as her spiritual director and later requested him as the confessor for the Incarnation Convent. Their likenesses advanced them toward the same goal while their differences enhanced the spirit that would permeate the reform . . . the test of a holy friendship, therefore, is our desire for the other to be totally immersed in God.

This friendship between these two, therefore, was a great spiritual friendship where the two had a natural affinity and, due to this, were able to achieve great things for God. They were able to make a difference to the church through being friends with each other. They were able to keep the church alight. The same also applies to the other two spiritual friendships that have also been discussed. But what of today? Does the church of today recognize the value of chaste friendships between clergy and women? Does it realize that these friendships could enable the church in the modern world to grow? Or does the church stamp on such friendships? I am concerned that the current church may stamp on such friendships and thus, yet again, suppress the workings of the Holy Spirit. However, before reaching this conclusion, I must first examine the question of friendship between members of the clergy and women in modern times and when these friendships might be appropriate.

I myself have had several good friendships with priests, and I had one particular friendship that lasted over twenty years. While this friendship was never on the level of the friendships that are described above due to the fact that it did not ever change the world, it was still a valid and wonderful friendship due to the fact that we prayed for each other and gave each other mutual support. Sadly, this priest is now deceased. I first met him when on a retreat in a location away from the parish in which I lived. He was never my parish priest and so there was never any reason why we could not be friends. There was no conflict of interest. The two of us felt a spiritual affinity and therefore became friends. At the time I was a married woman (I was widowed toward the end of our friendship), and I certainly did not feel any physical attraction toward this man. My attraction to him was purely spiritual. Sometimes my husband and I disagreed on spiritual matters, and I felt I could discuss my spirituality with this man and he would always understand where I was coming from. He, in turn, would also discuss with me the difficulties he had sometimes experienced within the priesthood. I never at any time went to confession with him because he was my friend and not "my priest." Our friendship consisted of mainly email and phone contact and meetings for dinner once or twice a year when we would discuss modern theology, our spirituality, our issues, and difficulties with the spiritual life and where we were at. We were able to be spiritually close and honest with each other when we met. Later, when we parted, we would give each other a hug as a sign of our spiritual closeness. There was never anything sexually inappropriate in our friendship. We were simply great buddies. Friends hug each other, don't they? I always hug my other friends; why shouldn't I have hugged a friend who was a priest? This priest was also actually quite a senior priest for six years of our friendship. He was provincial of his order. However, this office never made any difference to our friendship. Our friendship sadly ended with his death.

During the course of my open and genuine friendship with this man who was a priest, and a very senior priest for part of that time, he often discussed with me the difficulties he experienced as a priest due to celibacy. He told me that the majority of priests were actually homosexual and that there were more homosexual than heterosexual priests within the church. He also told me that for him nonsexual friendships with women were extremely important. He stated that he would actually have liked to have married but gave up the idea of marriage in order to become a priest. He stated that he had an important psychological need for the company and friendship of women, and the only way he could survive the celibate priesthood was to have strong nonsexual attachments with women who would support him in friendship. This priest was a very mature man who understood his sexuality, and I was not his only close female friend. He had several others. This meant that he had people outside of the priesthood to whom he could talk, people who did not expect him to be a demigod, and, perhaps partly due to the support of these people, he was able to sustain his vocation.

Due to my own personal experience above, I think that I can state that some members of the celibate clergy definitely need spiritual friendships with women on similar lines to the historical friendships that have existed between members of the clergy and women in the past. Also, some of these friendships could potentially lead to very great things. Ours did not lead to very great things, but it was still important to us and it gave us essential support through difficulties. But are these kind of friendships between members of the clergy and women frowned on today? Also, in what circumstances are these friendships permissible?

Firstly, friendship is a normal human need, and it would be absolutely barbaric to try to deny a priest a friendship with a woman. Priests are already, as we know, denied the right to marry if they would wish to do so, and that denial is a denial of a fundamental human right. Also, if priests are allowed friendships with men, then they should be allowed friendships with women as well. To allow a priest to be friends with men but not with women would be misogynistic, and why would the hierarchy wish to deny the clergy friendships with women only? There is no greater risk of a priest breaking his vows with a woman than there is with a man. He can break his vows with either if he so desires, depending on his sexual orientation. Most priests are not seeking to break their vows, however; they are simply seeking a spiritual connection or companionship.

When would a friendship between a priest and a person, either male or female, be appropriate? My view is that these friendships are only appropriate if there are no professional links between the two people. So, the priest should not enter into a friendship with a parishioner or with any person with whom he has a professional relationship. However, a friendship that starts in a neutral place, such as at a retreat center, as mine did, should be perfectly acceptable, as should any friendship that starts after any professional ties have been severed. For example, if a priest and a woman get to know each other in a parish setting and the priest later leaves that parish, there should surely be no reason why the two could not develop a friendship at that point, seeing as they would no longer have any professional connection.

What constitutes an appropriate friendship between a member of the clergy and a woman? An appropriate friendship would be a friendship in which the two prayed for each other and helped and supported each other. It would be a relationship of trust, a relationship in which the two could be open with each other and discuss any difficulties they might experience in life. It would be a relationship where two people created a space where they felt safe with each other and where they could let off steam. Of course, an appropriate friendship would not be sexual, as the priest has taken vows, but there is no reason why the friends could not hug each other. Human beings need human contact, and hugs communicate friendship, warmth, and appreciation. Hugs are pervasive throughout the whole animal kingdom, not just among human beings, and they generally leave both parties better through the experience.

There are disturbing misogynistic trends within the church today that would seek to prevent appropriate friendships between the clergy and women. There is also often a quiet assumption that a member of the clergy will not include women among his friends. Friendships between priests and laymen are considered to be a great blessing, but if a priest is friends with a woman, then eyebrows begin to rise. This attitude is completely unacceptable. If a priest can be friends with a man, then he should also be able to be friends with a woman. The risk of a priest breaking his vows is no higher with a woman than with a man. In fact, it is probably lower, as it is likely that more priests are homosexual than heterosexual. This attitude is just another form of misogyny and should be stamped out.

Toward the end of 2021, a very disturbing incident occurred in regard to Pope Francis and his dealings with the then archbishop of Paris, Michel Aupetit. This archbishop resigned mainly, it appears, due to a previous relationship he'd had with a woman ten years before. Apparently, the woman may have been his secretary. The archbishop denied that the relationship was ever sexual and explained further:

> My behaviour towards her may have been ambiguous, thus suggesting the existence between us of an intimate relationship and sexual relations, which I strongly refute. . . . I decided not to see her again, and I informed her.

The archbishop had ended the relationship ten years previously. Now, if this woman was indeed his secretary, it would be true to state that this relationship was inappropriate; but, as the archbishop had denied that this was ever a sexual relationship, the fact that the Pope had accepted his resignation for this seemed well over the top, particularly when the relationship was historic. The respected female theologian Anne Soupa had this take:

> For a disciplinary problem of a liaison with a woman, an archbishop resigns in three days. And for crimes committed against children, no bishop has resigned in France.

Moreover, what was particularly disturbing was the news conference that Pope Francis gave on a flight on his way back from Greece where he discussed this issue. The Pope made it perfectly clear that he believed that the archbishop had not had an affair and stated that he had accepted his resignation because he had lost his reputation. He then went on to state that people were used to having bishops whom they perceived to be saints, and due to his liaison with a woman this bishop was no longer perceived to be a saint. He stated that gossip had grown, and although this gossip was an injustice, he felt he should accept this resignation. He stated that the archbishop had given the woman "small caresses." What were these small caresses? we may wonder. A hug? A kiss on the cheek?

The Pope's acceptance of this resignation was misogynistic because had the archbishop been friends with a man, and had he hugged or kissed a man on the cheek, there would never have been calls for his resignation. But the church appears to see women as so poisonous that any cleric must step down if he has ever dared to touch one—even if the incident was only a minor expression of affection. Now, I do not deny that the archbishop should not have become friends with his secretary (if, indeed, the woman concerned was his secretary—there have been contradictory reports); but the Pope had no need to react like this. He could have advised the world that he would not accept the resignation because there had never been any affair between the two and, in any case, the relationship was historic. He could have stated to the world that the resignation of the archbishop would not have been sought if he had been inappropriately friendly with a man, and therefore, he was not allowing him to resign for an inappropriate nonsexual relationship with a woman. Instead, he chose to accept the archbishop's resignation and send a message out to the world that no cleric must ever go anywhere near a woman! We are the untouchables. Moreover, the Pope's actions in regard to this resignation were not only very unfortunate for women in that they reinforced misogynism; they were also unfortunate for clerics. We already have a religion that denies Catholic clerics the right to marry. Now it seems that it is also prepared to deny them the right even to hug a woman or kiss her on the cheek. This is not Christianity. This is a cruel and inhuman denial of a person's God-given humanity. Every person has a fundamental need for human affection.

It was very disappointing that Pope Francis, who has so often showed sympathy for homosexual men, could, on this occasion, not show the same sympathy for women and could not perceive the effect his words might have on the perception of women within the church. In addition to this, his use of the idea that people like to pretend that a bishop is a saint as an excuse to accept this resignation showed how shockingly out of touch he is with the real world. The fact is that bishops are not saints, they are human beings; and if the church accepted this, rather than trying to pretend otherwise, it would do better with people. A defense of the bishop as a human being would have better served the church. The Catholic Church must rid itself of misogyny if it is ever to be a light to the world. Jesus was not a misogynist. As we have seen in earlier chapters, throughout his ministry, he had encounters with women that others thought were inappropriate. However, they were not inappropriate. These encounters showed Jesus as a caring human being who was happy to connect with other, female, human beings.

Finally, having discussed the question of friendships between the clergy and women, the issue of illicit sexual relationships will now be briefly examined. When examining this issue, I must stress· that I am only briefly looking at sexual relationships that are consensual here. I am well aware that there are and have been many occasions when women have been sexually abused by priests; but this is not a book about sexual abuse. It is about spiritual abuse and organizational power abuse.

Firstly, it is not possible to state how many priests may have broken their vows with women, as the Vatican will not release any information on this matter; and also, in any case, the Vatican itself will not accurately know how many priests have had affairs with women. This is because the Vatican will only record details of priests who have actually been caught out or confessed to having had an affair with a woman. There will, of course, be many others who have never been caught out and are not known to have broken their vows. However, no matter how many priests may have broken their vows with women, it is actually likely that more priests will have broken their vows with men. This is due to the fact that it is very likely that more priests are homosexual than heterosexual and also because, as has already been noted, relationships between priests and men do not draw the same attention as relationships between priests and women. They are therefore easier to hide. In fact, most known cases of sexual affairs between priests and women only come to light either because they have resulted in a pregnancy or because the priest has decided to seek laicization, or because the woman has actually made a complaint against the priest. Some women who have engaged in sexual relationships with priests have later complained that they have been taken advantage of and abused because the relationship started when the priest was in a position of power over them, perhaps as their parish priest. In these cases, there is, of course, a record of those incidents. However, any records that the Vatican may have in regard to the number of clergy who have been involved in sexual relationships with women will always be way below the true number. Many priests will be involved in sexual relationships with women that have never been revealed to others, some of which may have gone on for many years.

Some women who are involved in sexual relationships with priests have discussed these relationships and the pain that has been involved while they are actually in the relationship, but these women are very few and far between due to the need to keep the relationship secret. I knew one woman who was involved with a priest for five years. Eventually, this person ended the relationship with the priest because she felt it was going nowhere. This woman knew the priest would never leave the priesthood, and she did not want to live a double life indefinitely.

One woman who was in a sexual relationship with a priest actually went to the *Irish Times* and discussed it anonymously after securing an agreement that her identity would be kept secret. She stated that she had been in a sexual relationship with a priest for twenty-five years. She stated that he lived abroad and so she only saw him sporadically. She did not want him to leave the priesthood because she knew he loved his job and, also, she thought that he would not be happy if he did this—so the two just met off and on as and when they could. She stated that she did not see it as second best and valued the relationship that she had.

Some priests in sexual relationships do, of course, leave the priesthood to be with the woman concerned, as was the case with one Swiss woman who had formed a relationship with a priest while working as his pastoral assistant in a parish. This woman stated that they had a relationship for five years before eventually coming out into the open, as they just did not feel they could live a double life. This woman went on to found Zöfra, which is a support group in Switzerland for women in relationships with priests.

Since the time, in the twelfth century, when celibacy was made compulsory in the Latin Church, many priests have fathered children with women. For many centuries until very recently, these relationships that had led to the birth of a child were covered up by the church. Often, the priest would simply be moved, and the woman would be left to fend for herself and her child alone. In more recent times, however, the church has acknowledged that these relationships exist and has worked with the priests concerned to reach a resolution. This has been largely due to the efforts of Vincent Doyle, who set up a support group for the children of Catholic priests in Ireland known as Coping International.

Doyle was the son of a Catholic priest and had a relationship with his father until he died; however, he did not know that this priest was actually his father. He had believed him to be his godfather and only found out the truth on the death of the priest involved. He was very shocked and upset when he found out, and as a result of this he set up Coping International in 2014. Since then, approximately fifty thousand people have approached the organization. This gives an idea of the numbers of liaisons between priests and women that have resulted in pregnancy. The Catholic Church has recognized the work of this organization and has begun to cooperate with it, but even so, the church still retains its official stance that, generally speaking, in all cases where the priest is under the age of forty, the best thing for him to do is to resign. Only if the paternity is discovered when the child has grown up does the Vatican acknowledge that it might be possible for the priest to remain in ministry. This is highly unsatisfactory because the church's position is not universal. As has already been noted, compulsory celibacy does not apply to priests of the Eastern rite. It also does not apply to married priests of a different denomination who convert to Catholicism. They are allowed to be ordained as married priests and to continue to be with their wives and children. It simply cannot be right that the majority of priests have celibacy forced upon them while others are allowed to remain married. There is no justification for this church discipline, which has caused huge amounts of suffering not only for women but also for priests and the children of priests. The Greek Orthodox Church has always had a married priesthood and has functioned very well with it. There have been far fewer sexual scandals in the Orthodox Church than in the Latin one, and there are also far fewer sexual scandals in the Eastern rite of the Catholic Church.

In conclusion, this chapter has examined some disturbing misogynistic trends in the relationships between the clergy and women in the Latin Church. Firstly, some women in parishes feel that they are treated differently by their priests purely on account of their gender and marital status. No female parishioner should experience this kind of discrimination in any church. Secondly, there are disturbing signs that friendships between women and the clergy are frowned upon today, while male friendships are encouraged. This situation is worryingly misogynistic and should not be tolerated. It is unfair both to women and to the clergy, and it could also lead to the suppression of some healthy spiritual friendships that could bear great fruits. It is yet again a suppression of the Holy Spirit within the Catholic Church. Thirdly, an archbishop who had an inappropriate nonsexual friendship with a woman who may have been his secretary was treated in a different manner to the way he would have been had his inappropriate friendship been with a man. This case was highly concerning because it yet again reinforced the idea that women, who are half of the human race, should be avoided by the clergy. Finally, priests in the Latin Church who father children are still forced to leave the priesthood. This is discriminatory against both the priests and the women concerned because the same rule does not apply to priests in the Eastern rite or to convert priests who are allowed to function as married priests. This practice can also cause great suffering to women and children because it forces the father, if he leaves the priesthood, to give up his job and find another occupation. There is no reason why a parish cannot support a married priest and children. Parishes do so in the Eastern-Rite Catholic Church. In every relationship between women and the clergy within the Latin Church, the church is blatantly discriminatory. The church cannot survive if it continues to be discriminatory, and neither should it. Women represent half of the church's membership, and in all aspects of their relationships with the clergy they should be afforded the same dignity and respect that is given to men.

CHAPTER ELEVEN

Spiritual Power Abuse and Female Victims

This chapter details some examples of spiritual power abuse that have been directed against women by the hierarchy of the church during the last forty years. However, before I consider these cases of spiritual power abuse against women, I would like to look at the case of one eminent layman who used his gifts to strive for better lives for women and was sadly ignored and knocked back by the Vatican. That man was John Rock. Unfortunately, Rock left the church due to the appalling way in which his work was pushed aside by the Catholic hierarchy, who seem to believe that only they, the celibate few, could discern the will of God and the movement of the Holy Spirit. Having briefly examined Rock and his work, I will then consider various cases of female spiritual power abuse. While many people may think of spiritual abuse as emotional or psychological pain, it must be stressed that it is usually much more than this. Spiritual abuse targets a person's whole being. It questions their *raison d'être,* lifestyle, and core principles. Spiritual abuse can therefore be soul crushing. It can often destroy a person's economic security and cause great disruption in their lives. Spiritual abuse usually happens to more consecrated women than laywomen. This is because consecrated women are often dependent on the church for their home and livelihoods, which makes them very vulnerable. Spiritual abuse is emotionally violent, callous, cruel, and unchristian. It should have no place in any Christian community.

John Rock was a highly regarded obstetrician and gynecologist. He was born in 1890 in Marlborough, Massachusetts, and graduated from

Harvard Medical School in 1918. He was also a devout Catholic who attended Mass daily and kept a crucifix on the wall above his office desk. However, despite his devout Catholicism, Rock believed his conscience was paramount, a belief he had acquired from a Catholic priest who had told him as a child, "John, always stick to your conscience. Never let anyone keep it for you."

John Rock was one of the inventors of the oral contraceptive pill. In the course of his practice of medicine he had witnessed the suffering of many women. He had seen how much women were brought down by collapsed wombs, premature aging, and desperation brought about by the fact that there were too many mouths to feed. In 1936, the celibate hierarchy of the Catholic Church approved the rhythm method of birth control, and Rock was the first doctor to open a rhythm clinic in Boston. In 1949, Rock coauthored a book called *Voluntary Parenthood* explaining birth control methods for the general reader and later, in the early 1950s, Rock began trials of the contraceptive pill. Rock thought that the Vatican would approve of the pill because he saw the pill as a more precise way of following the rhythm method. He believed that the hierarchy of the church should consider it a natural and acceptable form of birth control because it contained the same hormones already present in every woman's reproductive system and just extended the safe period a woman would have every month.

John Rock received a lot of publicity for his cause, and he was featured in *Time* magazine and on the cover of *Newsweek*. However, the Catholic hierarchy—a group of celibate men who had never studied gynecology nor seen the devastating effects that the lack of birth control had on married women—paid no attention whatsoever to this eminent gynecologist and in 1968 published *Humanae Vitae*. The publication of this document was particularly sad because it saw women as purely productive machines and failed to recognize that there could be a beauty women could enjoy in the unitive sexual act that did not always lead to pain and suffering. It also failed to recognize that women might have other intellectual and spiritual desires that could fulfill them apart from motherhood. *Humanae Vitae* was clearly heralding back to St. Thomas Aquinas, who had stated that women were subhuman and the only purpose in their creation had been ensuring the continuation of the human race. Due to the suffering that this encyclical continues to perpetuate, there can be made a very strong argument that it is actually abusive.

Because the hierarchy would not consult or listen to eminent lay experts such as himself who were actually specialists in their own fields, John Rock lost his faith in the institution of the church and ceased to attend daily Mass. Sadly, this kind of story is a very common one. The hierarchy has driven out millions of intelligent and often eminent laypeople, both male and female, from the church. This is because they have refused to take on board the specialisms of lay experts on many matters and remained firm in their blind, ignorant beliefs that celibate men always know best. However, despite the hierarchy's refusal to listen to Rock, his achievements alleviated the suffering of many women, and the vast majority of the people of God decided that they approved of birth control and ignored the hierarchy.

This case sadly illustrates how blind the hierarchy is, not only to the pain of women, but also to the knowledge of many lay specialists in many fields of expertise and how this blindness, this disconnectedness from reality, destroys the church. The Catholic celibate hierarchy decided that it could pronounce on birth control when there wasn't a gynecologist in its midst. In the past, Catholic celibate clerics have pronounced on many things of which they knew very little, contrary to the advice of eminent lay experts. I recall the teachings of Copernicus and Galileo that the Earth revolves around the sun. One has to wonder how, after so many failures, this hierarchy continues to believe that its discernments are divine, but having examined this issue, I will now move on to consider some cases of direct spiritual or power abuse by the hierarchy against women.

Lavinia Byrne was born in Birmingham in 1947 to Catholic parents. She had a very strong faith and lived a devout Catholic childhood, and this led to her joining a religious order, the Institute of the Blessed Virgin Mary, at the age of seventeen. Ironically, this religious order was founded by Mary Ward who, as has already been noted, was a reformer who tried to found an active form of religious life during her lifetime. Mary had suffered great persecution for her attempts to do this, and she, too, was a victim of spiritual abuse. The order that she had founded was not officially recognized until 232 years after her death.

Lavinia read modern languages at London University and obtained a Post-Graduate Certificate of Education from Cambridge University in 1971. She later obtained a Westminster diploma in theology and a postgraduate certificate in information studies. Lavinia was happy as a religious sister within the Roman Catholic Church. She worked across all churches speaking on behalf of women and was also involved in the training of men and women for service in the Anglican Church.

In 1992, the Church of England approved the ordination of women priests. Lavinia had followed the debate about the ordination of women in the Anglican Church very closely, and, as a result of this, she wrote her book, *Woman at the Altar.* This book advocated the ordination of women within the Catholic Church and was published in 1994. Lavinia stated that the book was never meant to be destructive. She said that it was "a genuine piece of journalism looking at the arguments that surrounded the debate around the ordination of women."

However, the Vatican decided that her book was incorrect. They then went on to decide that not only was it incorrect, but no one should discuss this issue anymore. As has been noted in previous chapters, when the Vatican does not like something, it does not allow the issue to continue to be discussed but simply stamps on it and becomes spiritually abusive. That is exactly what they did to Lavinia.

The then prefect of the Congregation for the Doctrine of the Faith, Joseph Ratzinger, demanded that Lavinia recant her work and make a public statement supporting the Vatican's ban on women priests. While communicating with Lavinia, the Vatican did not contact her directly but only contacted her superior. They also put the existence of Lavinia's religious order under threat and so Lavinia felt that she had no option but to resign. Ratzinger then ordered that the book be burned and her publishers duly burned thirteen hundred copies.

Lavinia left her order, which had been the heart of her life for thirty-five years. One would assume that she would not have had any personal finances of her own when she left her order. She would have actually had to make great sacrifices in order to protect her personal conscience and her right to speak out on theological matters. Lavinia said, "It seemed to me that it was not proper to try to control what was in someone's head."

Lavinia stated that this was not an easy time for her. In fact, I am sure that it would have been deeply traumatic. For over thirty-five years, she had given her whole life to a religious order. That order was her life, but the Vatican had no concern about this. They simply wanted to destroy her and her book. Time and time again, the hierarchy has shown that it will stop at nothing to destroy the core of someone's very being in order to maintain their control on dogma. Whenever they do this, they are replicating the exact sins that Jesus condemned in the Pharisees, an obsession with the law that takes precedence over loving God and one's neighbor as oneself. Lavinia herself fought this appalling spiritual abuse with great dignity. She stated:

> While I continued to work at the Theological College in Cambridge, training both men and women into the church, I had been a nun since I was 17 and the order had been my life. My whole life had been based around that conviction. It was through that conviction that I left and I had to re-invent myself. Lots of women have to do this, after divorce, separation, when the kids leave home so I was no different in that sense. It was a very interesting process. (We Are The 51, n.d.)

Lavinia managed to resurrect herself, and she went on to write more books and give interviews. She also, at one point in her life, worked as a tour guide in the Middle East. Her ability to overcome this spiritual abuse shows her to be an honest woman of strong conviction and a person of great faith. However, this case remains an example of appalling spiritual abuse. I refer the reader to our definition at the beginning of this study:

> Spiritual abuse is a form of emotional and psychological abuse. It is characterized by a systematic pattern of coercive and controlling behaviour in a religious context. Spiritual abuse can have a deeply damaging impact on those who experience it.
>
> This abuse may include manipulation and exploitation, enforced accountability, censorship of decision-making, the requirement of secrecy and silence, coercion to conform, control through the use of sacred texts or teaching, the requirement of obedience to the abuser,

the suggestion that the abuser has a "divine" position, isolation as a means of punishment, and superiority and elitism.

Sadly, the case of Lavinia Byrne was a classic example of this form of abuse.

The preceding case is an example of spiritual abuse carried out by the church hierarchy on one individual woman within an order due to her views. However, there are others ways in which spiritual abuse can occur within an order, and on occasion this abuse can run alongside sexual abuse. One woman, Doris Reisinger, who is a former member of a religious order and a survivor of spiritual and sexual abuse, has written two books about her experiences.

Doris was born in 1983 and joined the Catholic religious community Familia Spiritualis Opus in 2002 at age nineteen. Doris left her religious order in 2011. After leaving this order, Doris wrote a book called *Nicht mehr ich: Die wahre Geschichte einer jungen Ordensfrau* [Not Me Anymore: The Story of a Young Nun]. Within this work, Doris alleged that she had been raped by a priest shortly after taking her final vows. She also stated that she was solicited for sex in the confessional by another priest who held a position with the Congregation for the Doctrine of the Faith. This priest, Fr. Hermann Geissler, denied the incident but left the CDF in January 2019 after the allegations were made public. A Vatican tribunal acquitted him in May 2019 without taking oral testimony from Doris, although she was allowed to submit a written testimony. A criminal investigation into her alleged rapist did not result in his prosecution because he claimed that the relationship was consensual; however, Doris claimed that it was not consensual because she had been coerced and spiritually abused. She stated that the hierarchies of many religious and faith communities subordinate individuals and often create the perfect conditions for assault by men higher up in the ranks.

She explains more in the following account:

> I was a very idealistic, pious young woman. I joined at the age of 19, I believed in my calling, and in the idea that one progresses in spiritual life through selflessness and self-abandonment—as well as by doing things that one could not immediately grasp.

At a certain point—it happened so quickly that I hadn't even noticed—I couldn't even say "I" anymore and certainly not "I want" and "I do not want." Thus, I was the perfect victim for a priest who could use this system for sexual assault. And this is true of many nuns . . .

The moment he did it, I knew: "That's not right." I also told him: "You can't do that." But I was incapable of defending myself at that moment. Afterward, I was still unable to understand what had really happened. I was so crushed by the situation that I was completely incapacitated. I first had to restore my inner-self again: "I am someone, I still have a life, and no one has the right to do that to me." Only then could I confront my superiors with these deeds and then, at a later point, quit the community and make it public.

Doris has stated that cases like hers are widespread among religious women and has called for more independent research into this. She has also said that there have been sisters who have been raped and forced into abortions. She has drawn attention to the fact that many women offer their lives enthusiastically to serve the church and then encounter one or more of the following: sexual interference, psychological force, or spiritual abuse. Like all victims of any kind of abuse within the Catholic Church, Doris found that it was very difficult to get anyone to listen to her, as there were no proper complaint procedures in place. She shares this account in her testimony that follows:

The cruellest thing about abuse is the powerlessness and loneliness. Perpetrators have an easy game when their victim is defenceless. Through the act they make them even more defenceless. Through the act the perpetrator conveys to the victim: You don't count. Now nobody can help you. Nobody would believe you. I can do what I like with you. You are completely alone. God-forsaken. All on your own . . .

There is no parliament in our Church. There are no open debates, and no genuinely free theological research, there are no transparent proceedings and law-making processes, there is no independent judge or ecclesiastical lawyer, there is no committee of inquiry, there is no controlling authority and no procedure for removal from office.

We want to give a testimony against abuse. We want to make it clear that we are not in agreement with the way in which the Church wants to deal with perpetrators, with those who cover up, and with those who are affected. That proceedings take place, as before, in the dark, under obligations to secrecy, without either people in general in the Church or even those concerned having a right to examine the records. That laws and measures for dealing with abuse should be negotiated in small, anonymous, ecclesiastical back rooms and announced from on high, without debates within the Church or discoveries by independent experts being considered. That the majority of the accused do not take responsibility for their guilt. That bishops, religious superiors and their assistants, who have systematically covered up for decades, do not have to answer to any Church court, and continue in office as if they had done nothing wrong.

Doris was describing the powerlessness she felt as a member of a religious order in a church that was entirely dominated by a "celibate" all-male hierarchy. As has previously been noted in this book, bishops in particular are all-powerful, and it is very difficult to bring a complaint against them. There are no official complaint procedures in place to enable a person to raise an issue about any bishop with any independent body. Also, if the person tries to raise an issue with a bishop about a member of his clergy, bishops are able to cover this up—and once they cover this up, there is nowhere this complaint can go, as bishops are solely responsible within their area of particular jurisdiction for teaching doctrine, governing Catholics, and representing the church. On many occasions in the past, they have colluded with religious superiors and other members of the clergy to cover up complaints. While there are now some sexual abuse procedures in place in most dioceses, these procedures do not go anywhere near far enough in tackling abuse, particularly as not all abuse is sexual and there are no procedures in place for any other form of complaint. Also, many cases of sexual abuse pertaining to women often involve members of religious orders with whom the bishops may be very chummy.

Interestingly, although Doris left her religious order, she stated that she does believe that there is a future for the female consecrated life—but not in religious communities. She believes that women within these communities often find themselves subject to very strict traditions that require subordination and thus limit a person's ability to think freely and deny them the right to have a voice. She has stated that vows could be developed and interpreted in such a way as to enable people to live self-determined and mentally free lives. Of course, as noted in a previous chapter, this is precisely what the vocations of consecrated virgin, consecrated widow, and member of a secular institute try to achieve, as individuals who follow these paths do live independently in their own homes. They also work and are financially independent. Unfortunately, however, despite living alone and having a certain degree of independence, consecrated virgins and widows are still subject to their diocesan bishop. Every consecrated person must have a religious superior, and being subject to a diocesan bishop would be all very well and good if it were possible to make a complaint against him in any situation of concern. But as has been noted, it is not possible for any person to make any complaint against any diocesan bishop unless it is one of sexual abuse. There are no complaint procedures for any other matters, and this makes both consecrated widows and consecrated virgins very vulnerable. This will be discussed further in the next chapter, when I will share the spiritual abuse I myself experienced while trying to follow this path.

An older, but very similar, version of the story of spiritual and sexual abuse told by Doris Reisinger is the story of Karen Armstrong, which is detailed in her 1981 book, *Through the Narrow Gate: A Memoir of Spiritual Discovery.*

Karen was born in Worcestershire and educated in Bromsgrove and Birmingham, UK. Like Doris, Karen grew up in a Catholic family and joined a religious congregation at a very young age. She was only seventeen when she joined the teaching congregation of the Society of the Holy Child Jesus. Within her book, Karen describes how she suffered physical, sexual, and psychological abuse at the convent. Karen was indoctrinated and subordinated and no longer allowed to think freely for herself. She was taught to mortify her flesh with whips and wear a spiked chain around her arm. Karen implies that these forms of mortification were actually used as a perverse form of sexual gratification. Karen also describes how she was sexually assaulted by a priest who was a regular visitor to the convent. When she once tried to argue with her superior, Karen describes how she was made to "sew" at a sewing machine with no needle for two weeks. This book, although published forty years ago, is very well worth reading, as it gives a good account of the processes of subordination and indoctrination. It would also be true to say that it is Karen who led the way in exposing these issues, and for this she deserves great credit.

While she was still a religious sister, Karen was accepted at St. Anne's College in Oxford to study English. It was this experience that helped her to free herself from the religious congregation, and she left in 1969 while still a student at Oxford. Karen went on to teach English while writing her memoir, which received excellent reviews. She became a well-known independent writer and broadcasting presenter and developed a more mystical and independent Christian faith. She now states that religion is not about believing things but about what a person does. She has written over twenty books in which she has strongly attacked both religious fundamentalism and atheism and advocated a balanced and mystical spiritual path that encompasses individual thought and freedom. Sadly, Karen is another highly gifted person that the church lost.

Another more recent example of spiritual indoctrination, subordination, and abuse has come to light within a lay consecrated society of apostolic life known as the Servants of the Plan of God. This society, along with two others, was founded by Luis Fernando Figari in 1998. The servants wear the traditional habit and state that their mission is to evangelize youth, culture, and family and to give special attention to fragile, sick, and poor people. However, members have left this society and accused Figari of various forms of physical, spiritual, and sexual abuse, as well as abuse of power, authority, and conscience. They have complained of a toxic culture in which members were routinely criticized and publicly humiliated.

Between July 2016 and July 2021, thirty female members left the society and complained to ecclesial authorities in Peru, Chile, and the Vatican. Some of those who left stated that within the society there was a great emphasis on excessive physical exercise, diet, and personal appearance. They have alleged that only the prettiest girls were presented when Figari visited their communities and curvier women were put on strict diets. Others have alleged that the process of their discernment was manipulative and they were told that voicing doubts about their vocation was to give in to the temptations of the devil. They also alleged that they did not have healthy relationships of mutual respect with their superiors and that they were treated like personal servants.

On this occasion the Vatican has taken some action, and Figari was sanctioned and is barred from having any contact with the communities he founded. Vatican delegates are also involved in redrafting the constitutions of those communities. However, former members of the society have stated that Figari is still revered within the community and that there are still members of the old guard within its current leadership. They believe that this society should be completely disbanded. The Vatican Dicastery for Institutes of Consecrated Life and Societies of Apostolic Life has refused to comment on the society's current status.

Although only a small number of cases of abuse have been examined here, what is already very clear is that most cases of spiritual and other abuses of women usually happen due to three factors: the fact that women are not included in the hierarchy of the church; the vow of obedience taken by consecrated women; and the refusal of the church hierarchy to allow not only female members but all members of the church freedom of conscience and freedom of debate.

The noninclusion of women within the hierarchy of the church has created a misogynistic culture that is very ingrained. This culture leads to women's being completely powerless. If they try to speak out, their voices are not usually heard and they are just pushed aside. They do not matter. They are just women. They have no power or influence. Being on the right side of a woman is of no consequence. They can easily be dismissed without any due processes. They are not important. Often, it feels as if women are not part of the human race and are somehow subhuman, and, indeed, that is what was taught by the church in the Middle Ages. St. Thomas Aquinas, a medieval Dominican philosopher and doctor of the church, poses the following in his *Summa Theologica*:

The question under consideration there is whether the female, because of her inherent imperfection, should not have been part of the original creation.

He then goes on to answer:

Woman should have been produced in the Eden, since she is necessary for the generation of the species.

He cites with approval Aristotle's infamous affirmation that "the female is a misbegotten male."

It is views like these that have pervaded Catholic culture for centuries. The hierarchy, of course, would argue that they don't agree with this statement anymore and that they respect women today. Really? Why, then, is St. Thomas Aquinas still a doctor of the church? Why are we revering him as a saint? Doctors of the church and saints are meant to be role models, aren't they? Of course, it is true to say that St. Thomas did not have the knowledge of human psychology and anthropology that we have today. Perhaps it could therefore be argued that he was a saint in his own time and did the best he could within the limitations of that time. That would be fair enough, but his status as doctor of the church should definitely be removed. This status implies that his teachings should be revered when, in fact, many of them are actually flawed. It is because the church does not tackle past wrong decisions like this that its misogynistic culture continues to prevail. How can women ever be respected in the church when an iconic status is given to a person who wrote statements such as the above? This is just one example of how much misogyny is deeply ingrained within Catholic culture. Another example is the fact that male orders are referred to as "first orders" while female orders are referred to as "second orders." Surely a church that really respected women as human beings would abandon these kinds of sexist terms. Other examples of culturally pervasive misogynism include things that we have already touched upon, such as the fact that friendships between members of the clergy and women do not appear to be deemed as appropriate as friendships between members of the clergy and men. There are endless examples of a misogynistic culture that could be given here, but I think I have made my point. There needs to be a complete overhaul of church history and practices if the church is to eliminate spiritual abuse and misogynism. It will not disappear through mere tinkering on the surface.

Moving on now to the vow of obedience. The use of this word is highly unfortunate because it implies that a religious woman should always do whatever her superiors ask, and thus gives the superiors complete authority and power over her. Now, of course, it is recognized in any organization that there has to be some form of hierarchical structure wherein some people must lead. But no one would expect to have to sell their soul in order to comply with the demands of a person in authority, because it is generally recognized by most organizations that these persons can abuse their authority. Therefore, most organizations have policies in place that can be used when that authority is abused. These policies protect individuals from abuse. The Catholic Church has no such policies other than for sexual abuse, and therefore individuals are not protected from spiritual and organizational power abuse by a superior or member of the hierarchy. If they have also taken vows of obedience to that person in authority, then there is no place for them to go when they are abused. They are powerless to end this abuse. This is why vows of obedience should no longer be used in the religious life, because sometimes in order to bring about justice one cannot be obedient to an abuser.

A more appropriate and healthier vow that could be taken would be a vow of respect. Everyone recognizes that some people must lead and enforce rules, but leaders have to earn and win respect. A vow of respect would acknowledge that one should respect a leader, but the rules of an organization would also give any religious woman the right to complain against her superior or leader were they to be abusive. Therefore, I feel that if the consecrated life is to survive, the vow of obedience must be ended and replaced. Many people today often lament about the fall in religious vocations and pray for more vocations, as if the power of prayer will suddenly produce a string of new religious hopefuls. However, what they are failing to understand is that most people today would never take a vow of obedience to another person. They would see such a step as undermining their own personal conscience. Therefore, unless the church reforms practices such as the vow of obedience, vocations will never recover.

Finally, the denial of all members of the church to have the rights of freedom of conscience and freedom of debate is highly coercive and spiritually abusive. Freedom of thought, conscience, and religion is a fundamental human right that no organization should ever deny. This does not mean that the church hierarchy should not proclaim teachings on faith and morals that have been agreed between the members of its ruling body (although membership of that body should be overhauled). What is does mean is that these doctrinal teachings can be proclaimed, but members of the church should be allowed to discuss and disagree with them without being threatened and coerced into submission. Unfortunately, throughout its later history in particular, the Catholic Church has frequently bullied and coerced people into submission.

In ages gone by, when everyone in Europe was Catholic, the majority of people, whether lay or religious, were bullied into submission. For example, the Roman Inquisition was established by the Holy See during the second half of the sixteenth century. Its role was to prosecute any individual of any crimes relating to alternative religious doctrines or beliefs. At the same time, the Spanish Inquisition was established by the Catholic monarchs in Spain for a similar purpose. These inquisitions would target anyone, be they lay or consecrated, who was believed to have undermined the faith, and some great pioneers were subject to them, such as Copernicus and Galileo, who stated that the Earth revolved around the sun. They were declared heretics and their works were placed on the Index of Forbidden Books.

Today, the people who suffer most in regard to the church's denial of freedom of conscience and debate are usually Catholic priests and consecrated women. This is because these individuals depend on the church for their livelihoods and the church thus has a coercive lever over them. It can threaten them with, in the case of priests, laicization, and in the case of consecrated women, expulsion from their order, if they do not comply. This in effect means that if they do not comply, they will lose everything. They will not only lose their status but also their homes and their livelihoods. For this reason, many members of the clergy and many consecrated women who do not agree with various church teachings, such as the suppression of the debate on the ordination of women, feel unable to speak out.

A startling example of how members of the clergy are coerced into accepting the hierarchy's ban on female ordination was seen in Ireland in June 2021. A new bishop was appointed to the Roman Catholic Diocese of Ferns on June 11, 2021. His name was Gerard Nash. Shortly after his appointment, he gave an interview with the press. When asked about whether he agreed with allowing women priests, Nash told Dan Danaher at the *Clare Champion* that the lack of women priests had been a bone of contention for many people in the diocese for decades. He then went on to state that the full ministry of the church should be open to all baptized people:

> When is that going to happen, I don't know. I am in favour of this. Most of the Irish Bishops are on record as striving to make ministry as inclusive as it should be. I think the idea of ministry and governance of the church being entirely male is completely wrong. I will be advocating for change. We must move forward.

However, a few days later, on June 24, 2021, another article appeared in the *Irish Catholic* in which the new bishop-elect did a complete about-turn of his previous views. This article stated that he completely agreed with the rulings of Pope St. John Paul II and Pope Francis that the church has no authority to introduce ordination of women:

> It's way outside my area of competence all together, I suppose what I was coming at there, the work I've done over the past few years is supporting women in ministry. You know, those roles—to get roles for men and women, to develop a whole sense of room for women to minister within the Church. Ordination is a separate issue which is not in our Church and I fully accept that.

This incident is extremely disturbing, because it clearly illustrates that within a few days of becoming the bishop-elect of the Roman Catholic Diocese of the Ferns, Gerard Nash was coerced to change his view on the ordination of women. Clearly, he must have been told that if he did not change his view, his consecration as a bishop would not go ahead. Why else would he revise his statement?

During my life I have known many priests and consecrated women, and only one has ever told me that they disagree with the ordination of women. However, the church hierarchy has not even approved the ordination of women deacons and, in addition to this, has banned the ordination of women priests. I believe that it is highly likely that the vast majority of priests and consecrated women support the ordination of women but are afraid to say so because if they do, they will lose the jobs they love, their homes, and their livelihoods. We have already noted what happened to Sr. Lavinia Byrne. The silencing of people in such a manner is both inhumane and highly abusive. In no way is it Christian, as Jesus coerced nobody. He respected an individual's free will. Fortunately, today, the state no longer requires people to be Catholic, and there is no inquisition. Therefore, laypeople like myself who do not depend on the church for our livelihoods cannot be silenced. The only possible weapon that can be used against someone like me is one of excommunication. But would this bother me? No, it would not, because my conscience is more important to me than belonging to a body that seeks to suppress it; and, in fact, I have already decided to leave the Roman Catholic Church and practice in another Christian denomination that has apostolic succession through the Old Catholic Church. This is because I sadly cannot remain in a misogynistic organization that currently bears no resemblance to the church that Jesus originally founded.

The question that has to be raised today is this: Is the Catholic Church of today really a church at all anymore, or is it just an organization controlled by a few celibate men? The church is meant to be the people of God, and yet the teaching of the Catholic Church today does not represent the views of the people of God. They have never been consulted on this teaching. This teaching represents the views of a few powerful celibate men. Should the people of God remain in an organization that gives them no voice and suppresses the Holy Spirit? Sadly, if there is no reform, perhaps everyone should now be seeking new ways of being in a church outside of Catholicism. However, within Catholicism, the only way forward is actually a way backward. If the church is to survive, it has to go back to the egalitarianism of the early New Testament church.

CHAPTER TWELVE

No Place for a Woman: A Personal Experience

This chapter examines the spiritual abuse I experienced and the effect that this had on my life. As previously stated, spiritual abuse is not just about psychological pain; it usually attacks a person's inner core and their mode of being. It seeks to destroy their *raison d'être*. It causes extreme disruption in a person's life and can cause economic instability. I am very saddened that a cleric of the church decided to treat me in this way because, prior to this experience, my encounters with the clergy had always been extremely positive. I was a post–Vatican II convert to the Catholic Church. Vatican II had begun a process of reform, but this process was later halted. The post–Vatican II church had the potential to change the world by being in touch with the people, evangelizing through love, and serving the dispossessed. This vision has been thwarted, and we are now returning to a cruel and harsh church that does not respect women or represent its members. I see my own experience as symptomatic of that. However, I suppose that if I had not had this particular experience, I would never have come to see the church in its current light and would never have understood the need for reform. Perhaps, from that side of things, this experience can be seen as positive.

I came from a mixed family background. When I say that my family background was mixed, I am referring to functionality. Some members of my family were outstanding role models while others were somewhat dysfunctional. Both of my parents were inadequately functioning as parents, although they loved me in their own way, and I do not think that they deliberately intended to be so. Meanwhile, my grandparents on both sides, but particularly on the maternal side, were exceptional people. In addition, I also had an exceptional uncle who looked out for me, and so, although my childhood was dysfunctional in some ways, in other ways it was highly blessed.

I was only three years of age when my parents separated and divorced, and yet, despite the fact that I was so very young, I can still remember their final argument. I can clearly remember waking up in the middle of the night and hearing my parents quarreling. I then heard my mother shouting that she would go and break all my grandparents' windows. Then I heard a door slamming. I was scared and called my dad, who then arrived in my bedroom and reassured me.

Shortly after this my parents separated, and my mother and I moved onto the land of my maternal grandparents. My grandad owned a nursery. He was a market gardener and dahlia specialist. He ran his business with the assistance of my uncle, who was only eighteen years older than me. They became famous for their propagation of new varieties of the dahlia flower, and they won a lot of gold medals in shows across the country. My mother and I did not live in my grandparents' house but moved onto their land, as the house was not really big enough. We were given an expensive caravan that was situated there.

My early childhood with my grandparents and uncle was extremely happy. My grandparents owned a lot of land, and I used to love being on it. Although my mother was also living with my grandparents and uncle at this time, I have very few memories of being with her. My main memories are of enjoying my life on the land, climbing trees, and trying to imitate and copy my uncle, who was my hero. I used to follow him everywhere and saw him as a big brother rather than an uncle. We had fields of flowers, and he would pick these flowers and put them in bunches either to sell to the public or to sell at market. I was only a little girl, but I, like my uncle, had my own small penknife. I would follow him and pick my own flowers. I would put them into bunches and try to make sure my bunches of flowers were as good as his were. He was my role model, and throughout my childhood he taught me many different things, some of which were to do with our horticultural business and some of which were not, such as how to sterilize and fertilize the ordinary soil to ensure plants would grow in it; how to nurture and grow plants but also how to do a jigsaw; how to play Monopoly and other board games; how to ride a bike; and how to play tennis.

When I was about ten years of age, my mother decided to move off my grandparents' land and into a council flat, a type of public housing. I was devastated and did not want to go with her. However, in those days it was assumed a child was always better off with one or other of the parents, and so off I went. I was not very happy. I suddenly found myself in a little flat on a rundown housing estate, and I was used to being on lots of land. I was moved to a new school on the same housing estate, and all of the kids seemed to sense that I had come from somewhere "posh." I was bullied relentlessly. In addition to that, I was often left alone at night while my mother went out dancing in the hope that she would find the man of her dreams. However, there were still some very bright lights in my life. I visited my grandparents and uncle every weekend, and I passed my eleven-plus and went to a grammar school. That school took me out of an underprivileged area to somewhere brighter.

When I was at the grammar school, I started to become interested in religion. I had been baptized Anglican, but in reality, none of my family were very much interested in religion. They were all agnostics. I started to attend Student Christian Meetings (known as SCM), and I also acquired a Catholic best friend named Lorraine. She would tell me all about her faith, and I was fascinated. I had some kind of conversion experience and became a believer in God.

I enjoyed school and completed and passed eight O levels with flying colors when I was fifteen years of age. In fact, I had passed my English O level when I was fourteen, as I had been put in for it early. I was always very good at English. But I did not stay on at school to do my A levels, and that was because something big had happened in my life. My mother and I had been on holiday to Greece, and she had met and married a Greek. I became fascinated with Greece.

At the age of sixteen, I managed to obtain a job as an au pair in Greece, and I went to work with a family in Athens. The father of the children was an airplane pilot and was not around very often. Unfortunately, I did not get on very well with his wife, and so after a year I found another job and went to work in a hotel. By then my Greek was already very good, as I had a natural flair for languages. I used a "Teach Yourself" book to learn to write the language, and I still have that book.

At the age of eighteen years, I went home to England, and I managed to do my English A level in a year at night school while working in a pub. But Greece still pulled me, and so I decided to return. I got a job as a holiday representative and worked in Greece for another four years. By that time, I was fluent in oral and written Greek. My mastery of the Greek language and my knowledge of the Greek culture are the two things for which I am very grateful to my mother, as it was her remarriage outside her own culture that led to me acquiring these skills.

I finally returned to the United Kingdom for good when I was twenty-three. I had seriously considered staying in Greece, as I had a Greek boyfriend who wanted to marry me, but I just knew it wouldn't work out. His family was well off and owned a cotton farm and a large hotel. He wanted a wife to assist him in running the family businesses, but I was not ready to settle down. By now I was sure I wanted to study. I had traveled and seen a different culture, but it felt like it was time to go home.

On my return to the United Kingdom, I went to work for my uncle in the nursery while trying to decide what to do. My interest in religion had remained during all my time in Greece, and I had often attended the Greek Orthodox Church. I thought that the Catholic Church was probably not that much different to the Orthodox one (I was wrong in this), and there were many more Catholic churches in Britain than Orthodox ones. In addition to that, I had very good memories of my childhood Catholic best friend. For these reasons, I decided to convert to Catholicism.

I turned up on the doorstep of a presbytery in Birmingham and told the Irish priest that I wanted to become a Catholic. He was somewhat surprised but invited me in. He arranged to teach me the catechism, and from then onward I met him every week for several months. Of course, this would never happen today, as there are not enough priests to carry out personal instruction; but back then things were very different. We were living in post–Vatican II times, and since the council there had been a huge influx of modern hopeful seminarians who had turned into trendy priests. The church was full of young priests of vision who dressed in jeans and treated the laity as equals. In addition to this, there were many laypeople who wanted to study theology, and almost every practicing Catholic expected further reforms.

I was one of those laypeople who decided they wanted to study theology, but there was a problem. I only had one A level, and I didn't really want to wait another year while I obtained one or two more in order to study for a degree. Fortunately, I managed to find a college in Oxford that offered an Oxford University diploma in theology. This qualification was higher than two or three A levels but was officially not quite as high as a degree. However, bearing in mind it was an Oxford University qualification, it was quite prestigious, and probably higher than some degrees from other universities. I found out that I could get a grant to study for it and decided to apply.

At this time, I was friends with a Catholic priest called Fr. Brian. He was the first of several priests whom I befriended or who befriended me during my lifetime. Fr. Brian was a pacifist, and he often visited Greenham Common. He had taken me with him on two occasions, and we had also visited some of his relatives who lived near there. We had a very good relationship, and so I asked him if he would support me in my application to study theology. He agreed to do so, and the application was successful. I was so grateful to Fr. Brian for all of his support. He was one of several members of the clergy who had a very positive effect on my life, and I kept in touch with him for many years. After my marriage, he baptized my daughter. Having friends such as Fr. Brian made it even more shocking and difficult when I later encountered a cleric who tried to undermine me and do the very opposite.

At the time that I went up to Oxford to study theology, I think I was probably more of a "traditional" Catholic. After all, I was not from a Catholic background, and all I knew about Catholicism really was the penny catechism I had gone through with a priest. I just assumed that all the statements in the catechism were true, and it never occurred to me to question things like priestly celibacy. I thought that celibacy was simply the way Catholics did things, and as I had very little understanding of sexuality at the time, I couldn't see very much wrong with it. However, studying in Oxford was to change all that.

Although theology was the major subject of my course, I was meant to choose a second subject to study alongside it. I chose philosophy, and my tutor for that subject was a Dominican priest named Nicholas. This man and the subject that he taught had a major effect on my life. Nicholas was an existentialist and a radical, and he had personally studied under Jean-Paul Sartre and had also known Simone de Beauvoir. He had got into a lot of trouble with the church in his earlier years due to his love of existentialist books, which had been placed on the church's Index of Forbidden Books. However, post–Vatican II, the church had become kinder, and Nicholas had been rehabilitated. He was no longer silenced.

Nicholas liked to shock people in order to wake them up from their acceptance of any black-and-white, "a priori" givens. I can always remember his first lecture on Martin Heidegger when he stated that men and women were "beings towards death." I suddenly realized that I was mortal, and this was very shocking to me as a young woman in her midtwenties. But Nicholas was an expert at jolting people out of their personal delusions. He taught me to think for myself; he taught me never to accept any "a priori" givens and to question everything. We studied the history of philosophy together, and I found that, like him, I was drawn to the existentialists. I loved Søren Kierkegaard, Sartre, and Heidegger because they stressed the importance of being authentic. These philosophers taught that creating one's own values and being true to oneself were the most important existential things for every human being to take on board, and I came to believe this. I was never the same person again.

Nicholas was true to himself, and he was like no other priest I had ever known. He had a lady friend named Mary with whom he was very close. Mary would often visit him, and everyone accepted their friendship. He told people that he and Mary had never had a sexual relationship because he had taken vows and also because he would never wish to take away her freedom. He said he thought the sexual act was possessive. Because everyone seemed to accept their friendship, Nicholas and Mary were never the subject of gossip. There was no question that their relationship had ever been or would ever be sexual.

Nicholas radiated honesty and was completely authentic. We remained friends long after I left the college. In fact, I kept in touch with both him and Mary until his death.

During the first year of my studies, I often wondered if I might follow a consecrated path. I had heard about the secular institutes through a woman who worked at Campion Hall. She was a consecrated woman and had told me all about her vocation. The idea of taking vows but living independently in my own home appealed to me, and I was seriously considering it. But then I met Bill.

Bill came into my life at the start of my second year. He was just over twenty years older than me and also divorced. We didn't really click at first, but somehow or other we eventually became friends, and as we got to know each other we became closer. I never really noticed it happening, but gradually we moved from friendship into love, and that was when I had to make my first existential decision, because there was a problem: the fact that Bill was divorced. The Catholic Church, of course, does not recognize divorce. It only recognizes its own system of annulment.

Bill asked me to marry him, and I was caught in a dilemma. Part of me said that the teaching of the church did not matter and only our love and commitment mattered, but another part of me wanted a church wedding and wanted to be in line with the church's teaching. I had not been a Catholic for very long, and I really did not want to be a dissenter already. In the end, I told Bill that I would marry him, but he had to apply for an annulment. I said that I was happy to get married in the registry office at first as long as we could get married in the church later, and that was, in fact, what actually happened.

An annulment is not actually a divorce, as the hierarchy of the Catholic Church does not recognize that any true marriage can end. An annulment is a declaration that a union that was contracted in a church and that to all intents and purposes looked like a marriage was not, in fact, a marriage after all. The most common reason for annulling a marriage is lack of due consent. What this actually means is that one or both parties who entered into the marriage did not really want to get married at all but did so due to some external pressure. Bill believed he could argue the case for this, as neither he nor his first wife had really wanted to get married. They had only done so because she had become pregnant. We took advice from a Jesuit priest at Campion Hall, and Bill began the annulment process.

Bill and I stayed at the college in Oxford until the completion of the diploma. It was a very exciting time to be studying theology at a Catholic college because the church seemed to have really opened up since Vatican II. All issues were up for debate, and everybody was expecting further reforms. In my own circle, most of us felt absolutely certain that it wouldn't be long before married priests and female deacons were ushered in. Sadly, we were all wrong.

Bill and I married in the registry office shortly after leaving the college. I had no problem with initially marrying outside the church, as for some reason I always had an inner feeling that he would eventually obtain an annulment. It did take a while for the annulment to come through, but about four years later we married in the church. We lived in the South West of England and were married for twenty-nine years. We had one daughter. I did not ever use my diploma in theology during our marriage. I trained as a nurse and later obtained a bachelor of science in health and various postgraduate qualifications. I worked in health care for all of my married life, and most of my work was around safeguarding children and vulnerable adults. I took early retirement from health care when I lost my much-loved uncle at fifty-three years of age. He had left his estate to me, and this enabled me to rethink my possibilities and change direction.

Bill and I were happily married overall, although we did have some very difficult and tough times as well as good times. He died suddenly a few days after I reached fifty-four years of age, and his death was a tremendous shock to I was. My birthday meal had been our last meal. Of course, I had always known that it was likely that he would predecease me as he was much older than me, but I had not expected to lose him then. He died of an internal hemorrhage, and my life was thrown into turmoil. However, my faith, family, and friends pulled me through.

As I was only in my early fifties when Bill died, I was still relatively young. I was also very fit and healthy and usually passed for much younger than my actual age. Although I missed Bill very much, I realized that I still had quite a lot of living left to do and began to think very seriously about what I would do next. I knew that I could never marry again, as I just could not see the purpose in any future live-in relationship. I was too old to have any more children, and I did not think that any future relationship could ever compare with what I had experienced over the last twenty-nine years of my life with Bill. Yes, we had gone through some very difficult times as well as good ones, but we had been together for a very long time, and the fact that our relationship had survived some very strong tests only served to make it special at the end. In addition to this, I just did not feel that I wanted to share my roof with anyone else again. I did not want to go through all the trials of getting to know someone again and learning to accept their weaknesses while they learned to accept mine; neither did I want to always have to negotiate with someone on a joint direction of travel. I just felt that now, at this point in my life, I wanted to be independent and to lead an autonomous life and to be accountable only to God and myself.

During the later years of my marriage with Bill I had not been a particularly devout Catholic, as there was a vague sense that I had already begun to think about some of the issues discussed here, although I, myself, had never encountered any personal difficulties with Catholicism. My attendance at Mass had been mainly at the religious festivals, and I had also attended services at other Christian churches. I had remained a very spiritual person but did not particularly think of myself as a very devout Catholic. However, Bill's death was a very great shock to me, and the religious community to which he had belonged was also highly supportive of me during my bereavement. I began to again see the value of belonging to a particular religious community, and so I threw myself into membership of that particular church to which he had belonged. It was a very loving community, and I soon found a place there where I could heal from my sudden bereavement. This led to my searching for a new purpose and direction, and about nine months after Bill's death, I was thinking again about the female consecrated life. I knew I could never live in a convent, as I am a fearlessly independent and strong-minded individual. So, I thought again of the secular institutes that I had considered before I met Bill.

Perhaps it wasn't back then that I was meant to be consecrated in an institute, I thought. *Perhaps it is now.*

Having spent all of my married life working in health care and bringing up my daughter, I was now very drawn to a life where I would have more time for God and more space. I went to meet with the leader of one of the secular institutes in the United Kingdom who I will call Lucy so as to protect her privacy. Lucy was very pleased to meet with me, and we agreed that I would begin to attend their meetings to explore whether the institute could be a place for me. At the time that I started to attend those meetings I would, of course, have never considered myself a so-called traditional Catholic. However, I did not consider myself to be progressive, either. I was somewhere in the middle.

The institute did not have many members, which was probably because their way of life has never been properly promoted within the United Kingdom. There were a small number of consecrated ladies, one of whom was Lucy, who were all very advanced in years. In addition to this, there were two new recruits. I threw myself into institute life with great dedication and enthusiasm and was very happy in the main, although there were some upsets. However, I learned a lot from the consecrated ladies and enjoyed our time together. We used to meet four or five times a year for residential study weekends, and in addition to this we would also meet for an annual seven-day retreat. We all lived at different locations within the United Kingdom and so would meet at various places to ensure that everyone had a meeting near their home at some time and no one was traveling farther than anyone else overall. Lucy was very good at setting us interesting topics to study prior to our meetings, and all of our meetings contained a lot of prayer, intellectual discussion, and theological reflection. The purpose of our meetings was to bond us together as a group and also to enable us to reflect on our own personal lifestyles and our mission. We saw our mission as being a hidden leaven within the secular world. We wanted to bring Christ to others in a quiet and ordinary way, and so we did not proclaim to the world in any exterior way that we would be consecrated women. We just sought to serve our own parish communities in areas where there were particular needs and only revealed our identity as consecrated women to others on an individual basis as and when we felt it appropriate.

After about two years in the institute, I decided to leave England and move to another country within the United Kingdom. I had often visited that country for holidays when Bill was alive and had been very taken with it. I thought it would be nice to have a completely new start and chose a location that appealed to me. I researched who the local bishop was and wrote to him stating that I was on the path to consecration and offered my help in the diocese. I sent him my résumé so that he could see my extensive experience in health care and safeguarding. The bishop replied and said he was very interested in using my skills in the diocese, and we met shortly after my move. He stated that he was keen to have a female on the chaplaincy team, and it was agreed that I would assist the chaplain in five parishes. This involved visiting sick people in care homes, hospitals, and their own homes and bringing them communion. I agreed to do the work as a volunteer alongside a paid part-time job that I had already negotiated. However, initially I encountered some difficulties in taking up this role, as the bishop had not made clear to the cathedral parish priest what my position was or what my areas of responsibility were. The cathedral parish priest was opposed to my being given the title of assistant chaplain because I was a woman and insisted that this be clarified. However, when it was established that I would not be given this title, the parish priest did become more supportive and my ministry was established and began to grow. It may be that I should have been more concerned that the parish priest had initially objected to my being given the title of assistant chaplain, but, as he later became supportive of me after this issue had been resolved, I never gave it much thought afterward. It is also highly probable that the Catholic Church in the country to which I had moved was not as dynamic as the church in England, and perhaps what later happened to me may not have happened in England. However, what later happened to me in the country to which I moved should never happen to any woman anywhere.

I fell in love with the church communities to which I belonged, and I loved visiting sick, disabled, and elderly people and bringing communion to them. My ministry thrived and grew, and it was never a one-way process. I learned so much from the people I visited and admired their many great qualities. These included the elderly gentleman who had been a famous musician and told me all about his interesting life; the man who had been severely disabled from birth but had never let his disability stop him from doing anything; and another elderly man who had spent his life running hotels and restaurants. I spent about two and a half days a week visiting the sick and taking communion to them, and I worked part-time in the civil service for the other days.

After about two years in my new home and four years in the institute, I became a well-established institute member in temporary vows. This meant that each year I would be asked if I wished to take temporary vows of poverty, chastity, and obedience. These vows would last for a year, and I would then be asked if I wished to renew them again at the same time the following year. These temporary vows had to be taken for at least four years in a row, after which the option would arise to make them permanent lifetime vows. However, when I was about halfway through, I began to wonder if I should consider leaving the institute and asking the bishop to consecrate me as a widow instead. There were a number of reasons for this. Firstly, there was a large age gap of twenty years or more between myself and professed institute members, and sometimes I found this difficult. I had wanted to promote the institute a bit more, but the older members seemed rather reluctant. Secondly, I had reconnected with an old acquaintance whom I will call Lyn. Lyn was a consecrated virgin, and she led a group of consecrated virgins and widows. She was very keen for me to cross over and join them and very insistent that I would be much better suited to their form of consecrated life. She said that their group was much bigger and much more diverse. Lastly, I really loved the communities in the diocese to which I now belonged, and it just seemed to make sense to be consecrated there in my own community rather than in some far-off place over three hundred miles away. The institute consecrations usually took place in Oxford, and of course all our retreats and meetings could take place in any part of the United Kingdom. This involved a considerable amount of travel. Also, as the institute was an international community, there was additional overseas travel for meetings. For example, the chapter meetings were usually in France or Poland. Due to all these reasons I decided to explore the possibility of transferring over.

I first discussed transferring over with my parish priest. He was actually in charge of three parishes, as there is a chronic shortage of priests in that diocese. He had also been the one who had initially opposed me being given the title of assistant chaplain within the area; but by this time this did not appear to be relevant, as he now seemed to be very supportive of me. He was very keen on the idea and stated that he would support me in whatever I wanted to do. As he seemed so keen on the idea, I decided to tell the institute members I was considering leaving. At the time I did not really talk about following a different path with them but more about whether the institute was the right place for me. We did not really come to any conclusion. Lucy knew I had some doubts about whether I should continue in the institute and was happy for me to stay another year and see how it went. Then I would have the opportunity to decide whether to renew my vows again or to move on. She would also have the opportunity to consider, in a year's time, whether I was in the right place. She wanted to give it more time before either of us made a definitive judgment, and she acted in a fair manner. However, in the end, I decided to move on from the institute. This may have been a mistake, but I made my mistake based on my situation at the time.

I came to the conclusion that it would probably be better to transfer over to the diocese. Apart from the organizational structure and the travel, there wasn't really a great deal of difference between consecrated life in an institute and consecrated life in a diocese as a consecrated widow. In both cases the consecrated woman lived at home and lived out her consecrated life independently. In both cases there was an emphasis on the individual finding her own spiritual path. In both cases there was also an emphasis on prayer and daily Mass. However, I just thought that it would be more fitting to be consecrated in the large spiritual community that I had come to love. This was the place where I worked and worshipped. These were the people I knew and tried to serve. These were also the people who knew, valued, and supported me. Of course, institute members tried to support me too, but the group was much smaller and I didn't live in the midst of it. I also found the generation gap difficult. I therefore came to the conclusion that being consecrated in the midst of my home community would be the better path to follow.

I made an appointment to see the bishop and ask him if he would consecrate me. I felt very nervous about this meeting. The bishop knew I was with an institute. How would he react to me transferring over? Would he want me? In the event, the bishop seemed very enthusiastic. There were no consecrated widows in this particular UK country; I would be the first one. He seemed really interested in the vocation and very keen to promote it. He stated that if I transferred over, I would not need to start again and could still be consecrated in eighteen months to two years, as would have happened with the institute. We agreed that Lyn would be my spiritual director and she would contact the bishop regularly about my progress. I would carry on with my chaplaincy ministry and would also commence a course in spiritual accompaniment. This would enable me to accompany anyone else who decided they might wish to follow the path of consecrated widow. We thought that there might be quite a few people in the parishes who would be interested in the vocation when they heard about it.

I left the institute and transferred over to the diocese. Later, I often wondered whether I did the right thing, seeing as everything was to go so very wrong; but actually, I still believe that I had a genuine vocation to serve God and my community as a consecrated widow, rather than within an institute. What I had perhaps overlooked, however, was the fact that the vocation of consecrated widow was not written into Catholic Canon Law. This means that a woman can only be consecrated as a widow by local rite. This lack of a formal rite also makes her more vulnerable and more at risk of spiritual abuse. This is due to the fact that in the event of any malpractice, there is no law she can appeal to and no one she can go to other than her own bishop. I did not consider any of this at all. Perhaps if I had done so, I might have been more cautious. Many people are called, but not many vocations last. The question is, why do they not last? Is it because these individuals were unsuitable or because their vocations were suppressed?

A year or so passed and everything was going really well with my vocation. By this time, I had been following the consecrated path for five years. I had commenced the Ignatian course in spiritual conversation and was really enjoying it. It enabled me to reflect on and improve my spiritual communication and to understand the great importance of listening to every human being in a nonjudgmental way in order to understand their own individual needs and the stage they were at in their individual lives. In addition to this, my ministry with the sick was proving very valuable both to parishioners and to myself, and the community valued the work that I did. I was also regularly in touch with the group in England that was led by Lyn. I had been on a retreat with them and met lots of people. Lyn was very pleased I had transferred over, and she was sending very positive reports about me to the bishop. She always sent me a copy of these reports.

The bishop was happy to set a date for my consecration and he, myself, and the parish priest met early in 2020 to discuss this matter. Lyn was very pleased and stressed with me that I should ensure a ring was used as a symbol of ministry in the consecration rite, as widows had worn these since the time of the early church.

We discussed and agreed the rite as there is, as yet, no universal rite and consecration is by local rite. I had a copy of a rite that had been used in other dioceses. We discussed the symbol of ministry and I said I would like to use my engagement ring, as that seemed to link my previous vocation of marriage with this vocation. However, the bishop was not keen to use this at all and insisted we use a pyx to symbolize my work with the sick people of the parish. I was a little disappointed, as I felt my vocation was more than my ministry to the sick. It was a whole way of life; and I was already serving in other areas as well in that I was training in spiritual accompaniment. However, I was very happy that I was to be consecrated and so I did not push this issue about the symbol of ministry with the bishop and accepted his decision. Looking back at this now, I see that incident as an indication that the bishop did not really take the vocation as seriously as that of a consecrated active religious, but at the time I did not think much about it. We set a date for my consecration. It was to be May 3, 2020.

My consecration was officially approved, and I was absolutely certain now that it was going to go ahead, as no bishop ever cancels a consecration after it has been officially approved unless, of course, a person does something terribly wrong. I had no intention of blotting my copybook, and so I had no doubt now that I would be consecrated. I was very happy. I loved my life. I loved praying the Divine Office every day and attending daily Mass; I loved serving the sick; and I was really enjoying the course I was doing in spiritual conversation. I was really pleased with my current life and felt very much fulfilled and part of a wonderful community.

My consecration was announced to the diocese in a newsletter on February 16, 2020:

> Debra, a parishioner known to many of you and especially well known to many of the sick and housebound in our parishes whom she visits regularly, has been given approval by Bishop [X] in her vocation and will be consecrated a widow at the 9.30 am Mass in [X] Cathedral on Sunday 3 May—the World Day of Prayer for Vocations. Please keep Debra in your prayers and over the next few months we will include in the newsletter some explanations of the vocation of a "consecrated widow."

I was very pleased that everyone now knew about my forthcoming consecration and would never have dreamed in a million years that anything could possibly go wrong. I went to see my parish priest for confession around this time, and after the sacrament I asked him how he thought I was doing in my vocation. He told me that I was doing fine and I was "a lovely person." Around this time, I also began to train as a cathedral sacristan. I thought that my life was filled to the brim and felt very fulfilled.

Early in March 2020, COVID-19 began to appear in the United Kingdom, and later that month the nation locked down. At that time no one knew anything about COVID-19 at all and the concept of a lockdown was completely novel to all of us. I was told that I could no longer visit the sick, and I was worried because people in care homes had been told that they were not allowed to have any visitors at all. I emailed the bishop about this and he replied and said that he agreed and thought there should be one designated visitor. I don't know if he ever followed this through with the government, but what I do know is that no one in the cathedral parish officially visited the sick in hospitals during the pandemic, and in March 2022 (two years after the commencement of the first lockdown), I was told by a parishioner that visits to the sick people I had visited had still not been resumed. I was not happy about the way that diocese dealt with sick people during that first lockdown period. I believed that someone should have taken communion to the sick wearing full personal protective equipment (PPE), but no one seemed prepared to fight for this. The other thing that concerned me was the fact that some people who were not computer savvy might lose contact with the community during this lockdown, as they would be unable to access any online Masses. I emailed the bishop about this and suggested that we phone these people and said I was happy to do so. He replied and said that he did not have a list of parishioners. He suggested I contact my parish priest about this, but when I did so, I received no reply.

The first lockdown was a very strange time, and I don't think anyone really knew what was the best thing to do in those novel circumstances. My ministry of visiting the sick ended, although I would actually have been happy to go on with it had I been provided with full PPE, but I was not given that option. In the meantime, my spiritual conversation course continued online, and I also decided to concentrate on a book I was writing about the female consecrated life. I told the bishop via email about this book, as I felt I had a duty to do so, seeing as he was going to be my superior in the consecrated life. He said it sounded interesting and expressed no objection to it, and so I assumed he was quite happy about it. In any case, there was nothing in that particular book that in any way contradicted official church teaching.

By the middle of April 2020, the bishop realized that it was very unlikely that my consecration would go ahead, as there were no signs of the lockdown being lifted. He emailed me and stated that it would have to be postponed. He expressed disappointment about the postponement and stated that he would set a new date as soon as this was possible; i.e., when restrictions were lifted. The postponement of my consecration was announced to the diocese on April 26, 2020, via the newsletter as follows:

> As you are aware Debra was to have been consecrated a widow in [X] Cathedral by Bishop [X] on Sunday 3 May, the World Day of

Prayer for Vocations but, due to the coronavirus restrictions, this has now been postponed to a later date. Please keep Debra in your prayers during this difficult time.

Naturally, I was very disappointed; but there was nothing anyone could do about it, as the situation was beyond our control. However, not long after this, I began to get very sick, and so it turned out that I would not have been fit enough to be consecrated on that date anyway. I had taken an antibiotic for a tick bite and unfortunately was allergic to that antibiotic and developed inflammation of the liver. This was not the first time I had suffered from inflammation of the liver. I had experienced this condition once before, although not as badly, but at the time it was not realized that it was due to medication allergies. My spiritual director also fell ill at the same time. She was sadly diagnosed with cancer of the womb.

I was extremely ill with inflammation of the liver. My liver had almost completely stopped functioning, and my liver function tests went through the roof. I had continuous sickness and nausea and could eat nothing other than bread, fruit, and vegetables, and could drink only water. I also developed jaundice. My doctor was very concerned and wanted to hospitalize me, but I could see no point. There is no cure for a malfunctioning liver. Either it will recover itself or the person will need a transplant. It can take some months for a liver to recover, and I just had to wait and see what happened. In the meantime, my family physician arranged for several tests and I was referred to a consultant. This was to check out whether the problem really was due to the antibiotic allergy or something else. I was very ill and really thought that I might never recover and would need a transplant or die. My family physician also thought the same thing.

I was very worried that due to my illness my consecration might never take place and that I would die without being consecrated. I knew a couple of women who belonged to religious orders whose ceremonies had taken place during the lockdown. These women had taken vows in a private ceremony with no one present other than themselves and the celebrant and with social distancing and face masks in place.

Their superiors had arranged these ceremonies so the women were not disappointed during the lockdown. I wrote to the bishop and asked him if my consecration might be able to take place along these or other lines. I think I came up with two or three suggestions as to how it might happen. I thought that as I was going to be consecrated by the bishop and would technically report to him following this event, there would be no legal problem with going ahead with the ceremony if various safety measures were in place. After all, I was a member of the diocesan team and I knew that the bishop still met with his priest and deacon on occasion with social distancing in place. Why, then, should he not meet with me as a one-off in extraordinary circumstances when he met with other team members? It seemed very logical to me, but it turned out that it did not seem so logical to the bishop. Perhaps he did not see me as a member of the diocesan team at all; indeed, that is what I later came to think.

I received a very sharp reply back from the bishop on the lines that I was not special and there would be no special service just for me. I was simply stunned, as I had never in any way implied that I was special, and I was very upset. I realized, however, that I had not told the bishop that I was seriously ill, as I have never been a person to make a fuss about myself. That was why I was still at home against my doctor's wishes. Anyone else with my condition would have probably gone into hospital. My reasons for staying at home were due to the fact that there was no cure for my condition. Either the liver would eventually recover itself or I would need a transplant. Therefore, hospitalization seemed pointless to me. I was sure that if I had told the bishop that I was very ill he would not have written to me so harshly.

I wrote to the bishop again and explained that I was very seriously ill. I can't remember if I brought up the subject of the consecration again, but I don't think that I did. The bishop replied and stated he was sorry that I was ill and would remember me in his prayers. I wrote to my parish priest and also advised him that I was seriously ill.

In actual fact, I was extremely ill for seven months. My liver function tests remained sky-high during that period, and it was arranged for me to have a liver biopsy. As it happened, this biopsy never took place, as I finally made a full recovery in November 2020, just before I was due to be admitted for it. But right up until that time, I had been thinking that I might never recover and honestly believed that I would either need a liver transplant or die. This illness brought me much nearer to death than I had ever been before.

After I advised both the bishop and the parish priest that I was seriously ill I never heard from either of them again in regards to this. I myself am a nurse and had worked in senior health care management for many years until I took early retirement. I had always tried to look after the well-being of the sick and vulnerable. I was very surprised and somewhat hurt and disappointed that, despite the fact that I had voluntarily served the sick of the diocese for over three years, no one from the diocese ever phoned me to see how I was when I was seriously ill. Or course, I would not have expected the bishop to call me, as he was a very busy man, but I would have at least expected my parish priest to give me a call on behalf of the parish team. However, I never heard from anyone, and I was quite shocked about this. I did begin to get the feeling that things were not quite the same between myself and the clergy as they had been before the lockdown, perhaps due to the fact that I had not seen either of them for some months and any communication had occurred by email. I was quite worried about this and wrote to the parish priest about it and also tried to phone him, but he was not in on the two occasions when I phoned, and my calls were never returned. All I actually received from my parish priest was a sharp email asking me not to bother him and a copy of the rite for consecration, which he stated he had edited and which he asked me to familiarize myself with. There was no inquiry about my health whatsoever and no empathy. Neither the bishop nor my parish priest seemed to think that it might be rather awful to be living alone in a lockdown with a very serious illness. They showed me no love, concern, or compassion despite the fact that I had done my utmost to give the same to their parishioners for over three years.

At the beginning of July, the government began to look toward an easing of restrictions, but I was still desperately ill at this time. I was no better at all. My liver was still not functioning and I could still eat nothing but bread, fruit, and vegetables. I felt frequently sick and nauseous and remained orange in color. I still had no idea whether I would survive this illness and had never been so seriously ill in my entire life. I wrote to the bishop and asked him what would happen in regard to my consecration now that restrictions were going to be eased. I said that personally I would prefer an earlier rather than later consecration and a very small ceremony but obviously I knew that it was his decision and I would accept whatever he decided to do. I suggested some potential dates from mid-August onward for his consideration. I hoped I might have recovered a little by then.

The bishop replied and asked if we could meet on July 16, 2020, after restrictions had been lifted. Actually, I was dismayed that he wanted to meet me in person to arrange a date, as I was still extremely ill and not at all up to a face-to-face meeting. However, I did not want to upset him and so I agreed to the meeting and simply told him that I was looking forward to seeing him again after such a long period. I had already received by email the rite of consecration from my parish priest and began to familiarize myself with it in case the bishop wished to discuss it.

On July 16, I drove over to the bishop's residence. I was really sick and looked awful; in fact, I had actually received a blood test that morning from my private consultant that showed me to be very dangerously ill. No one could possibly have not realized how sick I was, as I was still orange in color. The door was opened by the administrator, who showed me into the parlor, where I awaited the bishop. He arrived, asked me how I was, and sat down. I told him that I was still very unwell, as he could probably tell from my color. The bishop then launched into a long monologue.

The bishop stated that he had called me in to see him because he had decided he was no longer going to consecrate me. He stated that I could do everything I wanted to do as a laywoman and there was no need for me to be consecrated. He went on to state that he did not believe my consecration was meant to happen, as it had been canceled by the pandemic. He also stated that I must be "obsessed" with my vocation, as I had asked him several times during the lockdown when my consecration was going to happen. To say I was simply gobsmacked would be an understatement. I sat stunned and paralyzed and unable to say anything for the moment.

Eventually, I managed to speak. "But I am ill," I said. "I thought I was going to die, and I am still by no means in the clear. That is why I asked you if we could go ahead with my consecration earlier."

The bishop shrugged his shoulders. I will never forget that moment. He acted as if I were less than human, as if my life didn't matter. He treated me with no compassion or respect whatsoever.

"I have decided," he said, emphasizing the *I* as if he were God Almighty himself. "I am not going to do it." He repeated, "I am not going to do it. I am not going to do it."

I was in no fit state to argue with him, and I got up to leave. He followed me to the door and I left. I was feeling very nauseated. I had noticed with my illness that whenever something upset me emotionally, it made my symptoms even worse. I went home and sat stunned in the lounge. As I began to think about what had occurred, I realized that the bishop had consulted no one about his decision. He had certainly not discussed it with my spiritual director, as she would have told me and would never have agreed to my consecration's being canceled in such a way.

A few hours later, I called one of several priest friends of mine and told him all about what had occurred. He was horrified and said that the way the bishop had acted was completely out of order. To call in a very sick woman out of the blue and advise her that her consecration was canceled for reasons that were highly flimsy was simply unacceptable.

"Couldn't he have at least waited until you were better?" He said, "This is outrageous! And we have all been locked down for months and have only just opened up. Is this the right time to make such a decision, straight after a lockdown? And why didn't he consult anyone? He hardly knows you. I suspect you can count on two hands the number of times you have met him face-to-face. He should have consulted your spiritual director about this decision, and if he had any issues with you, he should at least have advised you of his issues and given you time to address them. No one cancels a consecration like this unless a serious sin has been committed, and you have not committed any serious sin! He should have called you in, told you of any concerns he may have had, and given you a chance to address them. He should have at least given you three months before making such a decision."

My friend and I discussed the matter further, and we began to wonder if the reasons I had been given for the cancellation of my consecration were the real reasons. My friend could not believe that a bishop would cancel a consecration for such trivial reasons, i.e., that I had requested an earlier consecration date when I was very seriously ill and that I was supposedly obsessive and overenthusiastic. Weren't people meant to be enthusiastic about their consecrations? The idea that my consecration had been canceled by God due to the pandemic was also completely ridiculous. Did this mean that every wedding or baptism that didn't go ahead during the pandemic was also canceled by God? The idea was completely ludicrous, and we wondered if there were other reasons for this cancellation that I had not been told about. Perhaps another cleric who was against the consecration of widows had "got to" the bishop during the lockdown, or perhaps he did not like the idea that I was a writer. The given reasons for the cancellation of my consecration did not ring true, and it all seemed very odd.

I simply could not believe that the bishop had behaved in this way. I had always believed him to be a perfectly reasonable person. I realized that, as I had been so ill and so shocked, I had not actually argued the issue through with him. I therefore decided to send him a very nice letter putting my own case and hoped that he would change his mind. I had been on the consecrated path for nearly six years at that point and had given it my all. I truly believed that I had a genuine call. I had also generated a lot of interest in the vocation within the parishes and was certain that if I were consecrated more people would want to come forward to take up this path. I passionately believed in my vocation and very much hoped to find a way forward.

I drafted a letter to the bishop and duly sent it. However, I had already made up my mind that if the bishop did not respond positively to my letter, then I would never go to any church in his area ever again and would move house. This was because I had done absolutely nothing to warrant this kind of treatment. Perhaps I may have inadvertently irritated him in some way—I don't know. But I was very seriously ill, and we had been in a lockdown. I had committed no serious wrong, and nothing could justify this kind of action toward me. I knew that if I remained in the parish and was not consecrated my reputation would be completely destroyed. Everyone would wonder why I had not been consecrated and would assume I had done something terrible. I hadn't done anything seriously wrong, and I was not going to have my reputation destroyed in this way. Extracts of my letter to the bishop are below:

> Dear Bishop [X],
> Thank you for meeting with me this morning. I must admit to being very shocked and surprised by your decision as it was only about 3 weeks or so ago, I received from Fr [X] the rite for the service and was asked to familiarize myself with it. I have not spoken to either of you since then . . . so I am naturally left wondering what has happened between then (3 weeks ago) and now to bring about this change of course . . .
>
> In regards to your comments that I can do all the things that I wanted to do as a lay woman I do not think that this is the case. There are lay vocations and there are consecrated vocations. Both may be equal but they are not the same. For the last 6 years I have been in formation for the consecrated life. As a footnote to this letter, I will add what the Church says about consecrated virgins in its universal rite and how they differ from lay people. As you know the universal rite for widows has not been published yet but is in the pipeline. I think they (widows) will be viewed by the Church in a similar manner . . .
>
> I do feel a little betrayed in regards to this as I actually left the institute to follow this path. At no time did the institute ever ask me to leave. I asked to leave because I loved this diocese and my parish community and wanted to serve in this diocese and I also wanted to promote the restored and new consecrated vocations which have not taken root in Great Britain in the way they have in the rest of Europe. I felt I would be better placed to do this in this diocese and in the English group (with Lyn). Yourself and Fr [X] indicated support. The institute actually asked me to remain but I refused

and left because I thought the diocese would better support my vocation. Now my consecration has been cancelled after I had been given official approval by yourself. Naturally I will not be looking to return to the institute now. That time has gone . . .

It is highly unusual for a consecration to be cancelled after official approval has been given unless a great sin has been committed. That is why I was so shocked. As you are aware this approval (your approval) had been published on the Church newsletter and if I return to the parish now everyone will be asking me when my consecration is going to happen. I don't know what I am supposed to say. The bishop doesn't want to consecrate me anymore? They will all be wondering what I have done. I have never gossiped or been the subject of gossip and this situation would now place me in a position where I would be a focus of gossip. It therefore makes it impossible for me to return to this community (I will have to find another one) and I am deeply saddened. It was a community that I loved deeply and I gave my ministries in that community my all. My daughter and others close to me (outside this parish) knew how much I valued that community and they are deeply shocked at how this has been taken away from me at the last minute when I have tried to love God and serve all the community here.

You stated something along the lines that I was too enthusiastic or fixated on my vocation and obsessive. I don't know what I am supposed to be. Does the Church only want people who are lukewarm to follow a vocation these days then, I ask?

In regards to myself I have been very seriously ill the last few weeks but I feel I have done my best to follow the vocation during the pandemic with a life of prayer. At one point about 8 weeks ago I thought there was maybe some kind of misunderstanding between us when I was questioning why private ceremonies were not allowed. . . . I have been extremely worried about my health throughout this lockdown and remain so. I am saddened that I have been given no leeway for my very poor health at the moment when I have tried so hard to serve the sick people of this parish over the past almost four years . . .

I will keep yourself and Fr [X] in my prayers. Thank you so much for the privilege of being part of that community. Below is the

note on the restored rite for Virgins. The restored rite for widows is
in the pipeline as you know.
Yours ever in Christ,
Debra

It was a very nice letter and I did my best to give him the benefit of the
doubt. I felt sure that he would reflect and contact me, but I received
no reply. In the meantime, I had advised my spiritual director of the
situation, but, sadly, she had now been told that her cancer was terminal
and so she was not in a position to assist me. I also phoned my parish
priest and asked him if he was aware that my consecration had been
canceled. He said that the bishop had advised him of the same and
suggested that when I was better, I should continue to attend the church
and carry out all my ministries as a laywoman. I said that I would not be
doing so, as I had done nothing to warrant this action; and if I returned
to the parish and advised people that I was no longer being consecrated,
they would all assume I had committed some kind of serious wrong and
my reputation would be ruined. I was actually amazed that my parish
priest thought I would be prepared to humiliate myself in this way.
Yes, there is a Christian teaching that we should be humble, but being
humble is rather different to lying down and accepting spiritual abuse.

As the bishop did not respond to my letter, I wrote to him again
and this time asked him directly to reverse his decision. He refused to
do so. The tone of his email suggested that he believed that his decision
to cancel my consecration was right even though he had made it all
on his own and consulted no one. He suggested that he had the divine
authority to do this because he was a bishop of the church and therefore
had no need to consult anyone and could never be wrong. He also said
that it would be "irresponsible" of him to change his decision, as though
I was some kind of wicked, sinful pariah. I have my faults, like everyone
else. I am not perfect. But I had done nothing to warrant this. All I had
done prior to the lockdown was try my hardest to serve God and the
community. There had been a lockdown and I was very ill. How could
a lockdown and my illness have changed anything? It didn't make sense.

By this time, the bishop was also pressurizing me to accept his
decision and to agree that I did not have a vocation. He suggested that

his decision was inviolate, and I even began to doubt myself and believe I was wrong. Perhaps I didn't have a vocation after all? Looking back now, I can see that I was spiritually abused, although I still have no idea why the bishop did this. There was never any suggestion that it was my illness (from which I later made a full recovery) that had caused the cancellation of my consecration. On reflection today, I simply feel that he had taken a sudden disliking to me during the lockdown (perhaps due to misunderstandings in email conversations) and was determined to humiliate me at all costs. It was suggested to me by others that this might also be due to the fact that I was an intelligent, strong-minded woman who was writing a book and that I did not fit his image of how a woman should be. Perhaps he had initially believed me to be a limp, docile, and compliant person, but when he realized that I was actually passionate and assertive he no longer wanted me in his circle. Who knows? I really have no idea why he suddenly changed his mind, although there does seem to be very little room for passion and enthusiasm within the church these days.

Whatever the reason for the bishop's behavior, the following extracts from Oakley's and Johnson & Van Vonderen's definitions of spiritual abuse certainly applied to my situation:

> the suggestion that the abuser has a "divine" position, isolation as a means of punishment, and superiority and elitism. (Oakley)

> It's possible to become so determined to defend a spiritual place of authority, a doctrine or a way of doing things that you wound and abuse anyone who questions, or disagrees, or doesn't "behave" spiritually the way you want them to. When your words and actions tear down another, or attack or weaken a person's standing as a Christian—to gratify you, your position, or your beliefs while at the same time weakening or harming another—that is spiritual abuse. (Johnson & Van Vonderen)

I never went back to the parishes, and I placed my property on the market. There was no obligation to attend Mass at that time due to the lockdown, and so I was able to watch online services that were broadcast from more enlightened places. I was strongly supported by various friends of mine who were both priests and laypeople, and they pulled me through. Eventually, I recovered from my illness and completed my first book, which was later published. I also moved house, but before I did so, I wrote to the bishop again. By this time, I had reflected on my experience at his hands and I strongly believed that I was a victim of a great injustice. My consecration had been taken away from me for no good reason, and I had felt forced to move house and to leave the community I had loved in order to save my reputation. Extracts of my final letter to the bishop follow:

Dear Bishop [X],

I have been urged for some time to write to you about the events that occurred just after the lockdown earlier this year leading me to see a side of the Church I had not previously witnessed. Up until that point I had been blessed with many happy years in the Church and many positive experiences which included my study of theology in Oxford; my many friendships with members of the clergy; meeting my husband in Oxford and my long association of many years with three religious orders. God had truly blessed and enriched my life through the Church. Your actions however were destructive and may have been intended to be so. This was the first time I had been subjected to such actions from a member of the Church and I find that very sad. Fortunately, God is good and others stepped in to ensure there was no lasting damage to my life . . .

In regards to your decision not to consecrate me; you are of course entitled to consecrate whoever you wish and this letter is not really about your decision at all but rather about the way the decision was made and the lack of due process. I was also very much aware of your failure to see me as a person created in the image of God and I believe that I was treated in a way that was less than human . . .

Prior to the lockdown you had not indicated in any way that you were unhappy to consecrate me and you had also given me your official approval. Fr [X] had therefore announced my forthcoming consecration to the three parishes on the newsletter. By this time, I still did not know you very well nor did you know me and I therefore assumed that you were granting this approval on the basis of my spiritual director's reports and also on the basis that I had given two to three days of my time each week to serving the sick people of five parishes for in excess of three years. Whatever the reasons for your approval if you were unsure of it, you should not have granted it so as not to renege on something later and at the last minute which is simply unheard of . . .

During the lockdown I was extremely ill and when I say extremely ill, I mean that I was at death's door for part of the time . . . You knew I was seriously ill as well. I had told you this prior to that meeting and asked for your prayers.

You may wonder why I bring this up here. Well for the following reasons: Firstly, if a person is seriously ill, they do not behave in the way they normally would. One day when you are seriously ill, I hope God will ensure that you remember my words. Secondly, if I had been in a secular position in the secular world, you would not have been allowed to dismiss me from my secular post when I was ill precisely for those reasons. I would have had a case for wrongful dismissal. The secular state it seems has more compassion and is more loving than a bishop of the Church. It is not surprising that many people are now leaving the Church in droves. Thirdly, St. Ignatius advises that when a person is trying to discern something they should never make a decision in a time of trouble or desolation as the decision could be unsound—they should wait until circumstances return to normal. Fourthly, I recently attended a service at a church of another denomination (I do still of course attend the Catholic Church but not in this diocese) and the preacher actually stated that during this time of pandemic we should be gentle on ourselves and on others. I am afraid I received no such gentleness from you. Quite frankly I would not have treated an animal the way you treated me yet alone a human being. You called me in when I was desperately sick and made a serious life changing announcement that you knew would upset me without showing the slightest bit of compassion. I have visited sick people for years and am a nurse. I could never have treated anyone who was sick in the way you treated me. You treated me like a subhuman. Where was the love of Christ that you preach every Sunday from the pulpit my Lord Bishop? Where was your heart? Do you have one at all? Do you? I was left with the impression that for you, human life is incredibly cheap . . .

Moving on from there I was also dismayed that my three and a half years' service to the parishes and all the good work that I had done here was completely forgotten and brushed aside due to the fact that you were apparently not happy with me when I was ill during a few weeks in lockdown . . .

The way you treated me was also unacceptable. I am a scrupulous person and am always willing to confess if I feel I have done anything wrong. I used to go to Fr [X] for confession and I can remember asking him after confession if he thought I was suitable for consecration and always being told "yes" (that is another thing that disappointed me—I would have expected him to have supported me bearing in mind his previous glowing endorsements) and so I am not a person who is unwilling to admit a fault. However, on this occasion I can say in good conscience that I did nothing wrong. I had served the parishes extremely well and I was ill during the lockdown. Yes, I may have irritated you due to asking for a new date but did this really warrant the cancellation of a consecration in such a rash manner when I was so ill? I think not. What you did was done without due process and callous in extreme and I would like to point out to you that your office will not protect you from the consequences of sin. You will be held to account just like the rest of us. I refer you to Mark 12:38–40 . . .

My letter may seem to be very harsh but I am not going to be afraid to express some home truths just because I am a woman. No doubt you will dismiss me as a mere woman and wonder why I have the audacity to write to you in such a way but that will be your problem not mine. I do pray every day that you will experience some remorse for your actions but if you do not then that is again your problem and not mine. I ask that you do not contact me again unless it is to express some remorse. I do not wish to read any kind of justification for your actions. I have sought the advice of many who know me and all think your actions were completely unjustifiable.
Yours sincerely
Debra Maria Flint (Mrs)

I think the extracts from this letter clearly express how I now felt about this bishop's previous actions toward me. I felt they were spiritually abusive and unjustified. Of course, he had the right to consecrate whomever he wished; but in regard to consecrating me, he should have been absolutely sure that was what he wanted to do before he agreed to do it. Having officially approved a consecration, if he then later had some doubts, he should at least have consulted my spiritual director and asked her if she had any concerns as well. He also should have advised me of any concerns he might have had and given me time to address them. As it was, I was simply thrown out straight after a lockdown, and the reasons given did not warrant such actions. I have never believed that these were the real reasons for the cancellation of my consecration. I have always believed that this cancellation was due to something else. I have often wondered if, during the lockdown, the bishop came to the conclusion that I was not the person he had initially thought me to be. Perhaps he did not want a strong woman on his team, and this may have been why this action was taken. This may also have been why the reasons I was given for the cancellation of my consecration were so lame. There were no real good reasons for this action, as I had never done anything seriously wrong. But the bishop could not tell me that my consecration had been canceled because he did not like me, and so, perhaps, I was given some flimsy reasons for its cancellation.

In the event, the bishop never responded to this letter. He did not express any remorse. I could only assume that he believed himself to be incapable of any sin or error of judgment due to the "divine" authority that the church has given him.

I moved house and was very sad to have to go through this upheaval. By now I was sixty years of age, and I had hoped that my last move would be my final one and that I would have settled into this community for the rest of my life. I had a very beautiful, quaint old cottage in a lovely village where I had put down some very good roots. I had also made many friends in the parishes and felt very much part of the wider community. I had given the last six years of my life and the best years of my later middle age following this consecrated path. It broke my heart to have to uproot myself in order to protect my reputation and to have to leave this life that I had forged for myself behind me. I was deeply saddened to walk away, but I saw no alternative. I was simply not prepared to be humiliated without just cause. This was not about pride. It was about justice. I had not deserved to be treated in the way that the bishop had treated me, and to have remained would have suggested that I concurred with the way that I had been treated. However, in no way did I concur.

Time passed, and several months after I had sent the letter to the bishop it became clear to me that he was never going to respond or express any remorse in regard to the way I had been treated. I therefore began to explore ways in which I might possibly bring the bishop to account. I thought that it was very important that he be brought to account as I had been treated so unjustly. I also felt sure that had I been a man, I would not have been treated in such a manner. I wanted to bring this bishop to account not only for my own vindication but also for all other women in the church. I wanted to ensure that no other woman would ever again be spiritually abused in this manner.

I consulted a solicitor and asked her if I had any legal redress. She appeared to think that I did and said that I could possibly sue for breach of contract and defamation of character. I have legal insurance and still reserve the right to take legal action, but this was not really the way I wanted to go. I began to explore whether I could make a complaint against the bishop, and this is when I discovered that a Catholic bishop is solely responsible for teaching doctrine, governing Catholics in his diocese, sanctifying the world, and representing the church in his area. There is no way anyone can make any complaint against him unless it is for sexual abuse or covering up sexual abuse, and, therefore, he can treat people any way he likes. He is regarded by the church as having divine authority, and therefore it is assumed he can never be wrong. It is not right that anyone should be given this kind of power without safeguards being put in place to protect those he governs. Power can corrupt. Everyone knows that. To allow someone this kind of power without any accountability is abusive. Yes, there are some good and dedicated bishops, but there will always be some who fail their people either deliberately or unintentionally, and people are placed at risk by the assumption that bishops will not do things that are wrong.

After I moved house, I went on to publish my first book, which was a considerable success for a new author, and I spent a lot of time promoting this. Like many other women before me, I managed to reinvent myself in writing following an incident of spiritual abuse. However, I was unable to get involved in the church within my area because although I had moved forty miles, I still lived in the same diocese, and I found out that other priests in this diocese appeared to have been warned to beware of me. My reputation appeared to have been deliberately besmirched by this bishop, and I had done nothing whatsoever to warrant it. I believed that he simply could not stand having his authority challenged. He was used to people agreeing with his every suggestion and hanging on to his every word, and when I had questioned his decision in regard to the cancellation of my consecration he was likely very surprised to meet such opposition. Due to my daring to stand up to him and challenge him he had become even more hostile toward me.

I approached the chairman of the Catholic Bishops' Conference in the country in which I lived. He had read my book and said he found it insightful, and I thought he might be sympathetic toward me. I told him what had happened in regard to the bishop and how he had treated me. I said I only sought peace, and I asked if he might approach this bishop and ask him if he would apologize to me for his previous actions and agree to my becoming involved in another parish in his diocese. He stated that he was unable to do this, as he had no jurisdiction over this bishop. It therefore seems that spiritually abusive patriarchal bishops are free to damage lives, and no one can bring them to account.

I still think there is value in the vocation of a consecrated widow, but when I look back on what happened to me, I believe that my spiritual call was stamped upon and suppressed. Everything could have been so different if the bishop hadn't acted precipitously and canceled my consecration on a whim. When I recovered from my illness I would have gone back to the parishes, reconnected with my friends, and picked up my ministries again. There would have eventually been a consecration, and this would have been an uplifting event in the parish after a period of lockdown and desolation. There had been a lot of interest in this vocation, and I am sure more women would have come forward and asked to be considered for this path. The vocation would have flourished. As it was, everything was destroyed on the whim of one man, the diocesan bishop. How many times have some diocesan bishops stamped on vocations and movements of the Spirit? Are some of them suffocating and stifling the spirit of God within the church? Are some of them killing the church?

After my consecration was canceled, many friends sought to rescue me and to offer me alternative paths. I could still have been consecrated in the Catholic Church had I had wished to be so. This could have happened through an order or an institute willing to help me, or I could have moved to a diocese in another country where friends would have given references to another bishop to enable my consecration to go ahead there. However, I chose not to do this and am now considering leaving the Roman Catholic Church and being consecrated in another Christian denomination that has apostolic succession through the Old Catholic Church. The reason why I am considering this is because, sadly, this bishop's actions have really changed my perception of the Roman Catholic Church. Prior to these actions, the church had always been my rock. It was a place to which I flew for protection whenever anyone hurt me or if I, myself, hurt anyone and wanted to discuss it with someone to enable me to put it right. Now a man of this church seems to have deliberately sought not to heal me, but to harm me. I have seen another side of the church, and I have felt the need to explore that side of the church—the dark side of the church that hurts and silences women.

Sadly, I have also found out that I am not the only person to have had an unfortunate experience with this bishop. Someone brought to my attention some media reports that pertained to a period some years back, shortly after this bishop was appointed to his diocese. A priest in the diocese had whistle-blown against a fellow priest who had been sexually abusing young men. When the new bishop was appointed, he was reported as being extremely harsh to the whistleblower who, due to this, felt forced to sue the diocese for unfair dismissal. It seemed the new bishop thought the whistleblower was destroying the reputation of the church! Then the story was suddenly dropped and disappeared from media attention. It was therefore assumed that the new bishop had been forced to pay off the whistleblower, as no case of unfair dismissal involving this priest ever came to court.

This book has come about because, after experiencing spiritual abuse, I could find no way to make a complaint about the bishop concerned and to have my concerns examined by an impartial person within the church. The church has no local diocesan policies or procedures in place for anyone to make any complaints about any bishop unless the complaint is one of sexual abuse. This has led to me feeling a need to explore the dark side of the Catholic Church, and that is why I have written this book and am now considering leaving the church to be consecrated elsewhere. Of course, if I do leave, I will become just one of the many millions of women who have left the church in recent years because they feel that they do not matter in the eyes of the Catholic hierarchy and that they have no voice.

I sometimes go on the Facebook page of the cathedral parish to which I once belonged have and noticed that there has been a significant fall in Mass attendance in recent years and also some fall in financial offerings. This is, of course, due to a number of reasons that include the pandemic itself. However, I also wonder if the Holy Spirit has been suppressed in this diocese due to a very controlling bishop. One young woman left the parish because she was not allowed to start up a young person's prayer group. I also wonder if the cancellation of my consecration had some small effect on the fall in Mass attendance because I do know some people who stopped attending the church because of this. I take no joy in this. It is very sad indeed when one man is given so much despotic power that he can stifle the church. Pope Francis has stated that clericalism is a failure to realize that the mission belongs to the entire church, and not to the individual priest or bishop, and limits the horizon, and, even worse, stifles all the initiatives that the Spirit may be awakening in our midst. He has stated that laypersons are not meant to be peons or employees of the clergy and that they don't have to parrot back whatever they say. Clericalism, says Pope Francis, far from giving impetus to various contributions and proposals, gradually extinguishes the prophetic flame to which the entire church is called to bear witness. The Pope says this, but when, if ever, will the church act on it?

Conclusion

Jesus was not a misogynist, and he accorded to women exactly the same respect as he accorded to men. While Jesus chose twelve disciples to travel with him during his ministry, many women also followed Jesus throughout towns and villages. These women included Mary Magdalene, Joanna, Salome, and Susanna. Later, during the Passion, it is the women followers of Jesus who are depicted in the Gospels as being the most loyal. They would also have been the bravest of his disciples. They followed Jesus to the cross and stood near him as he was crucified, while the male disciples ran away. Jesus also chose Mary Magdalene to be the first witness of the resurrection, and she was instructed to tell his brothers that they must leave for Galilee, where they would see him. Mary Magdalene has never been officially recognized by the Catholic Church as an apostle, although she was regarded as an apostle within the very early church. She has recently been given the title of "apostle of the apostles" by Pope Francis. This title would seem to imply that without her, nothing would have been done, as she was chosen to take the good news of the resurrection to the disciples. Why, then, has her status always been regarded by the Catholic Church as lower than that of the apostles? And why has this "lower" status been used to justify not ordaining women?

In its early stages, Christianity was made up of a variety of communities around the eastern Mediterranean that were often isolated from each other. These communities did not possess all the same documents, and different church traditions grew up around different groups and individuals. These church traditions sometimes had very different perspectives on essential elements of Christian belief and practice. Early Christianity was diverse, and Gnostics and proto-Orthodox Christians shared some beliefs; initially, both of these groups were hard to distinguish from each other. Early Gnostic writings included the Gospel of Thomas, the Dialogue of the Savior, the Gospel of Philip, Pistis Sophia, the Apocryphon of John, and the Gospel of Mary. All of the early Gnostic writings recognized Mary Magdalene as an apostle. It is likely that there was an early church that grew up around the persona or teaching of Mary Magdalene and that this church was suppressed sometime around the fifth century.

In the early church there were three ministries: episcopoi (elders), presbyteroi (priests), and diakonoi (deacons). Originally, the roles of overseer and priest were interchangeable, and the idea of one man leading a church of deacons and elders did not appear until the second century. However, when it did appear, bishops were chosen and elected by the people.

Women were ordained as deacons within the early church, and this practice was universally accepted. Some women were also ordained as priests within the early church, but this practice was not universally accepted. Tertullian, an early church father, was one of the first people to criticize the ordination of women as priests in his "Demurrer Against the Heretics." Later, in the fourth century, the Council of Laodicea ruled out the ordination of women as priests and also stated that women were not to come anywhere near the altar. Nevertheless, the ordination of women as deacons was never suppressed and did continue in some places in the world until well into the tenth century. It eventually died out due to the establishment of infant baptism.

Despite the fact that the ordination of women to the priesthood was suppressed in the fourth century, women still managed to hold positions of influence within the European church. In Britain, there were Anglo-Saxon abbesses who ruled over double monasteries of men and women, and these women held positions of jurisdictional governance. They had many responsibilities, such as teaching theology to men who were training for the priesthood, giving spiritual counsel, and voting at church synods. These double monasteries also existed in France, Belgium, Germany, and Ireland, and the abbesses had similar responsibilities there. The most famous Irish abbess was St. Brigid of Kildare.

The early church synods were attended by eminent royal statesmen and by women. They were not just attended by bishops, and neither was the synodal vote just reserved for bishops. Everyone voted at these synods, and some women exercised a great influence at them. For example, at the Synod of Nidd, the abbess Aelffled persuaded the synod to restore St. Wilfrid to the bishopric. Therefore, at this synod a woman was highly influential in regard to the selection of a bishop.

The double monasteries in Europe disappeared for a variety of reasons. In Britain the main reason for their disappearance was the Danish raids. Viking raids began in England in the ninth century, and monasteries were targeted due to their wealth. The first monastery to be raided was Lindisfarne in AD 793, and from then on, the Vikings continued to raid Britain for almost a hundred years. The monasteries were looted and destroyed, and a great many shrines dedicated to the female Anglo-Saxon saints were lost. The great abbesses were disposed, and with them went their unique and influential role. The system seems to have also died out in other countries at about the same time, and it was not revived until the end of the eleventh century, when the order at Fontevrault was created in France. However, the double monasteries never took off again in the way they had before, and by the eleventh century misogynism was on the rise in Europe.

One of the main heralds of a more misogynistic era within the Catholic Church was almost certainly the schism between the East and the West in 1054. At the heart of this break was the Roman Pope's claim to universal jurisdiction and authority. The two churches had been growing apart for some time, and the churches in the East had been developing distinctive theological differences from those in the West. Five patriarchs held authority in different regions: Rome, Alexandria, Antioch, Constantinople, and Jerusalem. The patriarch of Rome (the Pope) held the honor of "first among equals," but he did not possess authority over the other patriarchs. The Eastern church would not accept that any central authoritarian figure, i.e., the bishop of Rome, could have an absolute last word on church doctrine, which would have meant that many Latin practices would have been forced upon it. These Latin practices included the use of unleavened bread in the Eucharist;

priestly celibacy; the reverence of St. Augustine; and differences on the procession of the Holy Spirit. Problems arose when Norman warriors invaded Southern Italy, which was then part of the Byzantine Empire, and began replacing Greek bishops with Latin ones. The patriarch of Constantinople retaliated by shutting down Latin rite churches, and the East–West Schism was created. Unfortunately, the East–West Schism led to a more misogynistic church in the West. This was because priestly celibacy became the expected norm and it in effect paved the way for Latin priests to be forbidden to marry by the First Council of the Lateran in 1122. Priestly celibacy, as has been demonstrated in this book, has created an elitist and sexist culture.

After priestly celibacy was taken on board by the Latin Church, women began to be perceived as more of a threat to priestly chastity, and their influence began to wane. This was particularly seen in the fact that the First Council of the Lateran not only forbade priests to marry women, it also forbade them to associate with women in any friendly capacity. The Second Council of the Lateran, which was convened in 1139, even forbade nuns from singing the Divine Office in the same choir as monks, and by this time the suppression of women was in full flow. Nevertheless, in the later Middle Ages this misogynism did began to wane a little, and some women still managed to have some influence. These women included the English mystic Julian of Norwich and the Italian mystic St. Catherine of Siena. Julian of Norwich wrote *Revelations of Divine Love*, the first English-language book written by a woman, and St. Catherine of Siena dictated *The Dialogue of Divine Providence*. Both women were also known for the spiritual direction that they gave.

Prior to the Reformation in England there were still some forms of female consecrated life that were flourishing there even though Catholicism as a whole was waning. These forms of consecrated life included the Bridgettine community at Syon Abbey and the independent female vocations of anchoress and vowess.

The Bridgettine double monastery of Syon was led by a woman, Agnes Jordan, and was renowned for its large library. It was regarded as a place of great intellectual learning. The legal corporate identity of the monastery was The Abbess and Convent and Agnes Jordan was its last presiding officer. This abbey was destroyed by King Henry VIII when he seized all the monasteries in England and their land. The independent vocations of vowess and anchoress were still thriving at the time of the Reformation in England, and they were also wiped out. The destruction of these forms of female consecrated life in England did have a long-lasting effect on the Catholic Church as a whole. This is because it can be argued that England had produced a long list of eminent and influential consecrated women, from the time of the Anglo-Saxon double monasteries right through to the independent vowesses and anchorites and the mystic Julian of Norwich, and further through to the final bastion of feminism, the abbess of Syon Abbey. When England's strong Catholic women were eliminated, a feminist light went out in the universal church. In addition to this, many records of pre-Reformation England were also destroyed, as a lot of them were kept in the monasteries. King Henry VIII did not want anyone to remember the pre-Reformation church and reminisce about what once was, so it suited him to destroy all the evidence of the past. Sadly, this made it much easier for previous female influences to be forgotten by the Church of Rome.

The Reformation occurred mainly in northern European countries such as Germany, Switzerland, Austria, Sweden, Czech lands, England, Scotland, and Wales. The English tried to bring about a reformation in Ireland, but it never really took root there. The Reformation was not good for women, because it eradicated all forms of female consecrated life in the countries where it took root, and the only possibility left open for women was that of marriage and family. The Reformation also weakened the female consecrated life within Catholicism itself due to the fact that some forms of consecrated life, such as that of the vowess or anchorite, had been particularly strong in countries that were completely overwhelmed by Protestantism and therefore completely died out.

The Catholic response to the Reformation began with the Council of Trent, which was convened in Trent for three periods between December 13, 1545, and December 4, 1563. This council reaffirmed the Niceno–Constantinopolitan Creed; created the canon of the New and Old Testaments; declared that the official Bible was the Latin Vulgate;

reaffirmed the practice of indulgences, although bringing about various reforms in regard to them; reaffirmed the veneration of the saints and the Virgin Mary; declared that justification was offered on the basis of faith and good works; and reaffirmed the seven sacraments. In regard to the seven sacraments, the council gave great weight to these, as it wanted to stress that they were necessary vehicles of grace, in opposition to Luther's view that justification was by faith alone. This led to priestly celibacy, being reaffirmed and to ordination's being defined as imprinting an indelible character on the priest's soul. This teaching was very unfortunate, as it continued the Catholic trend of elevating priests to a superior status above the rest of humanity. This trend had, of course, already been an issue in the previous schism with the Orthodox Church, as the Orthodox had never agreed with enforced celibacy. Now, with the Council of Trent, not only were priests "special" because they were celibate, they also had an indelible mark placed on their souls at consecration that neither women nor married men could obtain. A priestly celibate cult had been further reinforced, and naturally this further demeaned the status of women, who were seen as a threat to the myth of the "pure" celibate priest. The Orthodox Church has never, to this day, accepted the Catholic notion of *in persona Christi capitis* and states that it is the Holy Spirit, not the priest, that consecrates the Eucharist.

Following the Council of Trent, some new religious orders were founded in Europe, and the Carmelite order was also reformed by the Spanish mystics St. John of the Cross and St. Teresa of Avila; however, all of the female religious orders that existed post-Reformation were enclosed. In England, Mary Ward tried to found an active religious congregation for women on the lines of the Jesuit religious order for men, but her efforts were suppressed. This rule was eventually approved by Pope Clement XI in 1703. Afterward, many active female religious congregations were founded in both Britain and Europe, and most of these were involved in educating girls and providing social care. These religious movements did have a very positive effect in some European countries, but the religious women involved did not possess anything like the influence that women had enjoyed in the Catholic Church pre-Reformation. They did not have the jurisdiction that the abbesses of double monasteries had enjoyed, and they had no voting rights at church synods. Eventually, once they had achieved their social reforms, these religious congregations began to die out. Some of these congregations also died out because they were eventually drawn into a web of organizational, spiritual, and (less frequently) sexual abuse, particularly in countries such as Ireland, where church and state worked hand in glove. In that country the religious orders provided services on behalf of the state, and this made organizational abuse much more likely, as the congregations became incorporated into a large political regime rather than remaining more independent, as in England.

In the nineteenth century, the First Vatican Council was convened by Pope Pius IX. This council sat between December 8, 1869, and October 20, 1870. Its main purpose was to condemn rationalism, secularism, naturalism, modernism, materialism, and pantheism and also to pronounce that the Pope was infallible. The dogmatic constitution stated that the Pope had "full and supreme power of jurisdiction over the whole Church" and that when he "speaks ex cathedra, that is, when, in the exercise of his office as shepherd and teacher of all Christians, in virtue of his supreme apostolic authority, he defines a doctrine concerning faith or morals to be held by the whole Church, he possesses, by the divine assistance promised to him in blessed Peter, that infallibility which the divine Redeemer willed his Church to enjoy in defining doctrine concerning faith or morals." Unfortunately, this council only served to increase the stranglehold of the celibate few over the people of God and to further remove the church from the people. Later, in the early twentieth century (1917), the hierarchy produced the Pio-Benedictine Code of Canon Law. This code ended the practice of laypeople being created cardinals and enhanced the hold of celibate men on the Catholic Church even further.

During the mid-twentieth century, after many centuries of removing the teaching of the church further and further from the people of God, the hierarchy of the church began to develop the idea that some kind of reform was needed to give the church back to its people. With this in mind, Pope St. John XXIII opened the Second Ecumenical Council of the Vatican, usually known as Vatican II, on October 11, 1962. The council was closed three years later by Pope St. Paul VI on December 8, 1965. This council differed from earlier councils such as the Council of Trent and Vatican I in that it had been called to actually look critically at the church rather than to make further triumphalist doctrines and decrees.

Vatican II instigated many reforms, including the following: the widespread use of the vernacular languages (instead of Latin) in the Mass; the revision of Eucharistic prayers; the abbreviation of the liturgical calendar; the ability to celebrate Mass with the priest facing the congregation; an emphasis on laypeople as the "people of God"; a new emphasis on biblical theology; a new emphasis on ecumenism; recognition of the rites of Eastern Catholics in communion with Rome to keep their distinct liturgical practices; a new recognition of the apostolate of the laity; a call for the adaptation and renewal of the religious life; and a call for priests to become brothers as well as fathers and teachers. In addition to this, there were also some reforms that were made in the wake of Vatican II, such as the restoration of the permanent diaconate and the restoration of the order of consecrated virgins.

After Vatican II and the reforms that immediately followed in its wake, there was a great air of optimism and expectation among laypeople who expected further reforms to take place, such as the approval of birth control for all married Catholics; the ending of enforced priestly celibacy; and the opening up of the female diaconate to women. However, these reforms did not occur; and in 1968 Pope St. Paul VI produced *Humanae Vitae,* which not only directly contradicted the eminent gynecologist who had produced the oral contraceptive pill but also went against the conclusions of the Pope's own papal birth control commission. In 1966 this commission had voted overwhelmingly to allow Catholic couples to decide for themselves about birth control. After the production of this 1968 encyclical, the church in the West began to experience a dip in Mass attendance. And later on, when Pope St. John Paul II produced *Ordinatio Sacerdotalis*, this hemorrhaging of members further increased. Millions became disappointed with the church and began to leave en masse. This exodus was not helped by the emergence of the Society of St. Pius X and the church's failure to deal with this challenge; the rushed canonization of Pope St. John Paul II; and the involvement of a substantial number of the clergy in sexual abuse.

The current Synod of Bishops was established in 1967. Following on from this, in 1983, a new Code of Canon Law was produced that situated the Synod of Bishops as part of the hierarchical constitution of the church. Canon 342 of this new Code of Canon Law states that the Synod of Bishops is a group of bishops selected from different parts of the world who meet together at specified times to promote the close relationship between the Roman pontiff and the bishops. These bishops assist the pontiff in the defense of faith and morals; in the preservation and strengthening of ecclesiastical discipline; and in the consideration of questions concerning the activity of the church in the world.

The creation of the current Synod of Bishops did not represent any step forward and was highly unfortunate. This is because, while early synods within the church were composed of both laypeople and women, this synod comprises only of celibate men. Thus, a new power structure has been created to "be" the church and to tell everyone in the church what to do, and there are no married people or women within its membership. The Orthodox Church also has a Synod of Bishops within each of its autonomous churches, but in that church lesser clerics and laypeople are also delegated to attend these synods. Anglican synods consist of elected clergy and lay members and are not just confined to bishops. This new Synod of Bishops has, however, once again placed more power into the hands of an elite celibate few.

Pope Francis decided that the XVI Ordinary General Assembly of the Synod of Bishops would be dedicated to the theme "For a Synodal Church: Communion, Participation and Mission." What this essentially meant was that this was a synod on synodality, and laypeople were invited to give their views to their bishops, who would then feed them back to the Assembly of Bishops. The bishops would then decide where the Holy Spirit was leading the church. Recently Pope Francis has also decided that five religious sisters and 70 lay people will also be able to vote at this synod. This is a very welcome attempt by the Pope to make the church more inclusive but laypeople will still be a very small minority at this synod.

The Synod on Synodality may not be able to herald any major changes within the church because the lay voice, although now present, will be very weak due to the numbers of laypeople involved in the voting process. What has actually happened here is that laypeople have merely been consulted by their bishops, who are now meant to take their views back to the Ordinary General Assembly of Bishops, where up to 5,600 celibate bishops along with a very small number of laypeople will then decide where the Holy Spirit is leading the church. This process is far from perfect because diocesan bishops can easily omit to discuss or bring forward to that assembly any views of laypeople in their dioceses with which they do not agree. Why should one billion lay Catholics, who are male or female, single, married, or gay, have such a small voice at a synod of the church? Who or what is the church? Is the church the 5,600 celibate men who are eligible to sit on the Synod of Bishops? Or is it the one billion male, female, single, married, and gay Catholics who make up the people of God? How is it that only celibate men can discern the way in which the Holy Spirit is moving in the church, when celibacy is not a natural, God-given state? We read in Genesis that God created them male and female and he blessed them and named them mankind when he created them (Genesis 5:2). God did not create the human race celibate. Also, nowhere do we read in the New Testament that only celibate men can discern the workings of the Holy Spirit. As has previously been stated in this book, the first Pope was married, and the first witness of the resurrection was a woman.

Over the past thousand years since the East–West Schism, the Roman Catholic hierarchy has, through a series of synods and councils and through the creation of Canon Law, moved itself further and further away from the people of God and turned itself into an elitist, hierarchical, celibate group that is far removed from both society and reality. It is a disconnected group that has failed to keep up with modern advances in many areas, such as medicine, biology, existentialist philosophy, psychology, anthropology, sociology, astronomy, and, of course, human rights. This hierarchical, celibate group also does not comprehend the people among whom it lives, and it fails to properly consult with or speak with these people. Its lack of comprehension comes from the fact that there isn't a single woman or married man in its midst. Over the years, this hierarchical, celibate group has failed to listen to and discounted many lay specialists in many fields, and it has learned nothing from doing so. For example, despite having discounted Copernicus and Galileo and having been forced to admit it was wrong in both instances, it has gone on to discount the voices of many others, such as those of existentialists, psychologists, gynecologists, liberation theologians, and feminist theologians. However, the hierarchy of the church does not merely discount those voices with which it does not agree. It sometimes stamps on them and oppresses them in a cruel and callous way. The Catholic hierarchy has no room for debate and is often abusive to any people it perceives as threatening its power. It is abusive to women because it has no desire to share its power with this sex and also because it has produced within itself an ingrained culture of misogynism due to its distancing from the female sex, which has now gone on for over a thousand years.

It is hard to see how the Catholic Church can survive long term without radical changes to its organization and structure. Of course, it will survive for a while yet in some third-world countries, where there are some members of religious orders working to bring about reforms in social care. However, in the West, the church is losing all credibility. This is very sad, because following Vatican II the church had initially restored its credibility and was being taken very seriously by the whole world. However, the reforms were not allowed to continue, and once again the church began to sink back into regressive stagnation. The church of Vatican II was beginning to offer to a broken world a Jesus of hope and healing. As a convert who joined the church in the wake of that inspired council, I have found it heartbreaking to watch the church attempt to sink back into its previous pyramidal hierarchical mode. Sadly, this mode will not work anymore, because both society and education have moved on. People have learned to think for themselves, and they will not be coerced. Any organization that attempts to coerce will be rejected, and there can be no turning back. In addition to this, women in particular have proved their competence now in all walks of life and can be found in every work discipline. Women have discovered that they are not mere sexual reproductive machines to be used by men for sex or procreation and then discarded. Women have a spiritual side that is as important to them as the physical, and they can find fulfillment in pursuing careers or spirituality just as much as they can find fulfillment in motherhood. Today's married Catholic woman uses the natural contraceptive pill, created by the eminent Catholic gynecologist John Rock, to regulate her childbearing, and in doing so she is able to have time both for a career and a family and to ensure that her children are brought up in relative comfort rather than in suffering and poverty. The modern Catholic woman will never be returning to the kitchen sink at the behest of a few celibate men.

In order for the Catholic Church to survive long term in the West, it needs to start promoting and sanctifying a healthy model of family life as most lay thinking and spiritual beings today understand it. This would be a family life where sex is used as a beautiful expression of love as well as a means of procreation and where the couple is free to regulate their childbearing as they both see fit. It would also be a family life led by two parents who have mutual respect for each other and are both free to work and seek fulfillment in other pastimes as well as within the marriage. No person owns another person, and successful marriages are based on mutual discussion, discernment, and compromise. They are not based on coercion. The church needs to develop a theology of marriage that respects women rather than demeans them by viewing them as mere childbearing machines. The old icon of woman as a reproductive machine is dead.

Furthermore, if the church is to retain women in its midst as members of its organization, a complete overhaul of its history and organizational structure is required. Misogynistic saints, such as St. Thomas Aquinas, should not be venerated as doctors of the church. One can understand how men such as these were saints in their own time, as they did have some great achievements. However, they did not have the knowledge available to them then that we have today. Saints of their time they certainly were, but role models for today they are not, and it is neither healthy nor holistic to revere men such as these as great intellectual doctors.

In addition to this, if misogyny is to cease in the Catholic Church, the only way to end it is to end the practice of enforced priestly celibacy. This practice is not only cruel to the men forced to embrace it, but has also created an elitist sexist cult of men who have been encouraged to keep women at a distance and regard them as inferior. Furthermore, it has created a perverse view of natural God-given sexuality within the hierarchy of the Catholic Church. There is a value in celibacy, and there will always be men who will choose to be celibate. The problem is not celibacy itself. The problem lies with forcing men who wish to be priests to take celibacy on board. This not only creates failing celibates, it also creates a group of men who are completely out of touch with those who live a normal, healthy married sexuality.

Finally, the church will only retain both women and married men in its midst if they are included in its magisterium. The people of God who are overwhelmingly not male celibates will no longer be dictated to by a small group of celibate men. They require the synodal vote at every synod (not just the forthcoming one) if they are to remain in the Catholic Church. One simple way to do this would be to return to the practice of appointing lay cardinals.

There are two ways that reform could be brought about in the Catholic Church. One way would be through a merger with the Eastern Orthodox Church, and another way would be through the church hierarchy voluntarily instigating reform. In regard to a merger with the Eastern Orthodox Church, this could be used by the hierarchy as a means to undo papal infallibility and put the bishop of Rome back on a level with the other church patriarchs; cease compulsory celibacy; allow lay delegates at all church synods; and restore the female diaconate. However, the Orthodox Church is doing really well without the Catholic Church, and one wonders whether it would actually want to be bothered with all this, particularly when it would probably take years of discussion and debate. The other route would be through the church hierarchy voluntarily instigating reform, and this reform should include both lay cardinals and the setting up of independent panels in every diocese to investigate all complaints including complaints about the bishops themselves. But will they have the courage to do so? The celibate hierarchy of the Catholic Church has a choice—it can instigate reform and save the church or it can hold on to its own power and allow the church to die, bringing about its own suicide. Whatever happens, the Orthodox Church will survive, as it has never brought upon itself the problems that the Catholic Church has done due to not embracing some aspects of a theology that incorporates both misogynism and a perverse sexuality.

Epilogue

In July 2020, immediately after the first lockdown for COVID-19 and while I was seriously ill, my bishop canceled my consecration out of the blue without any prior discussion with me and without any consultation with my spiritual director. I had been in formation for the consecrated life for almost six years, and the reasons I was given for this cancellation were flimsy and unsatisfactory. I had been allowed no voice in his decision-making, and I was discarded in a cruel and callous manner. For me it was not so much the fact that the bishop canceled my consecration that was the issue; it was the fact that I was treated with no respect and with a complete lack of Christian love. If the bishop had ever had any issues with me, he should have advised me of these and given me a chance to address them. To simply dismiss someone's vocation and ministry without consultation and due process was spiritually abusive—particularly when the person was seriously ill at the time. This experience completely turned my world upside down, and it was this experience that led me to begin to reflect on the subject of the spiritual abuse of women within Catholicism. I began to write *No Place for a Woman* about fourteen months after this experience. I also began to explore another church at the same time as this.

No Place for a Woman was completed in early 2022, and shortly after its completion I was ordained a deacon in another church. I would not have looked for another Christian community had I not been ill treated by someone in authority in the Catholic community to which I had belonged or had that person acknowledged his wrong against me and apologized. As an ordained female deacon who has left the Roman Catholic Church, I am unsure if I was automatically excommunicated from that church on my ordination as the church's position on the female diaconate remains unclear. Roman Catholic women who are ordained as priests are certainly excommunicated. The late Pope Benedict XVI decreed on May 29, 2008, that the ordination of a woman was a "crime" and that any woman who attempted ordination and any bishop who ordained her would be automatically excommunicated. This decree placed the ordination of a woman as an act on a par with child sexual abuse, and it is not only a breach of human rights, it is also a scandalous and perverse disgrace that illustrates the deeply entrenched level of Roman Catholic misogynism. How can any sane person believe the ordination of a woman to be a crime on a par with child sexual abuse? The Vatican may not wish to ordain women, but to call such an act a crime is tantamount to hate speech.

My current Christian denomination claims apostolic succession through the Old Catholic Church. My church has many members who have left the Roman Catholic Church, and a lot of them are now deacons and priests within this church. My church is also led by an archbishop who listens to people and consults with them. This man does not sit on a pedestal and pontificate on his own self-importance. Instead, he treats all human beings with respect and love, and he also tries to spread whatever love he can into a broken world in order to bring about peace and healing. As Jesus continuously tells us in the Gospels, the second commandment is to "love your neighbor as yourself" (Mark 12:31). The second commandment is not to love power and your own ego above all things, and Jesus repeatedly condemned this love of power (Luke 20:46; Matthew 20:16).

Shortly after I was ordained a deacon within our church, a Roman Catholic sister posted on social media that I should repent of my apostacy. I found her action abusive and unnecessary but sadly very typical of the Roman Catholic Church of today.

The Roman Catholic Church states in *Nostra Aetate* that only itself and the Eastern Orthodox Church are in full possession of the truth of the Gospel. Other Christian denominations, it states, have only elements of truth in their beliefs and practices. This document does reprove as foreign to the mind of Christ any discrimination against men or harassment of them because of their race, color, condition of life, or religion. However, notably missing from this list is harassment of persons due to their gender, and the Roman Catholic Church continues to discriminate against women by denying them access to ordination.

In a later document, *Dominus Jesus*, Cardinal Ratzinger (later Pope Benedict XVI) stated that the full revelation of divine truth had been given only to the Catholic Church and even the Orthodox Church did not possess the truth in its complete fullness, although it did have apostolic succession and a valid Eucharist. This document stated that the church did not expect any further revelation and that nothing could be taken from other religions in order to make the faith more complete. It also stated that members of other denominations are "gravely deficient" relative to members of the Catholic Church.

Throughout the ages this has always been how the Roman Catholic Church has dealt with all criticism. It has always stated that it holds the complete truth and refused to enter into proper dialogue with other religions. It has also used fear to keep people in the Catholic Church by stating that those of us who leave the church are in danger of losing our salvation. This way of dealing with other Christian denominations and people of other faiths is not only pharisaical and arrogant, it is also appallingly abusive. That is because using fear or threats to control the actions of individuals is always abusive.

How can a church composed of prelates who have in the past covered up the abuse of Catholic seminarians and innocent children have the audacity to state that members of other Christian denominations are gravely deficient relative to members of its own church? What Ratzinger is actually implying here is that an abusive cardinal, such as the late cardinal Keith O'Brien, is superior to a holy and loving prelate in another Christian denomination. Statements such as these are simply appalling because they ignore the fact that the central message of Christianity is to love your fellow human beings and not to treat them in an abusive manner. St. Paul is quite clear in his writing (1 Corinthians 13) that it is the ability to love that defines a Christian and not adherence to any particular dogma.

In the past, the church has used documents such as those mentioned above to get out of any challenges in regard to the abusive actions of its prelates and to maintain its hold on its members. These documents use a technique of asserting the God-given authority of the (sometimes abusive) prelates to pronounce on all matters of faith and dogma, followed by an attempt to induce fear in those of us who dare to question this authority. We are told that we will become "gravely deficient" if we dare to leave the Catholic Church. The idea is that due to statements such as these none of us will ever challenge or leave the church.

These written statements from the hierarchy no longer work. Many people have experienced abuse at the hands of the Catholic Church, and they refuse to accept that an abusive church is in full possession of the truth of the Gospel. Since the 1990s, millions of Europeans have walked out of the Catholic Church, either to join other denominations or religions or to abandon religion altogether. Sadly, they will continue to do so unless the church reforms its power structure, because it is a love of power rather than a love of God that has brought the church to this state of affairs.

In regard to myself, while I am a person who, like everyone else, possesses some weaknesses, I am also a person who seeks God with a sincere heart, and I do not believe that I have ever abused anyone. In addition to this, I am a person who has given twenty years of my life to working with children who have been abused, and I've also been spiritually abused myself. I believe in good conscience that the current structure of the Roman Catholic Church is abusive. I have fought for victims of abuse all my life and will continue to do so. I fear nothing that any Catholic prelate may say to me about my conduct or my salvation. I trust in the love of God. I would also like to stress that I am not anti-Catholic. I joined the Catholic Church in the wake of Vatican II, and I learned and gained a lot from the church in the years following my initial conversion from agnosticism. I have also had many wonderful Catholic friends who have been a great blessing and an inspiration to me. Sadly, in more recent years, I have watched the church swing away from the teachings of the Second Vatican Council and revert to its previously closed structure. After a very upsetting and spiritually abusive experience that occurred when I was very seriously ill in 2020, I felt I had no option but to leave the church and to write this book. However, I continue to pray for reform, and I pray that one day the Roman Catholic Church will become a caring and loving home for all people.

Afterword

Rev. Paul Murphy-Sanderson

The fact that this book ever had to be written is a travesty. As the author has clearly explained, the original teachings of Jesus Christ regarding the place of women in the Christian community have been distorted by the Roman Catholic Church with the result that numerous bishops and priests still believe and teach that women are a threat and that giving them equal power in the Church would go against nature. This is because they believe that God created men to be leaders, authoritarians, and decision makers, while women were created to be servants, helpers, and nurturers. Pope Francis, along with numerous bishops and priests, has often said that women are entitled to equal dignity, but never that they are entitled to equal power. They want women's voices to be heard in discussions, but it doesn't necessarily follow that they want to entrust them with actually making decisions.

Many people would find it hard to believe that such deeply ingrained beliefs could still be held in our modern world. However, I speak from experience as one who spent five years studying for the Roman Catholic priesthood in the 1980s and '90s, followed by nineteen years as a Cistercian monk (1995–2014), during which time I was ordained as a Roman Catholic priest. I recall with shame the way that women were treated in the seminary. They were simply there to do the cooking, cleaning, and washing. If you put a sock with a hole in it in your laundry bag it would mysteriously come back darned, but you were conditioned to simply take this for granted, almost as something deserved by your position. If you were caught talking to a female member of the "Domestic Staff," as they were referred to, you would get a severe talking too as if they were some sort of "Domestic Danger" (see the quote from St. John Chrysostom below) trying to lure us away from our celibate vocations. No one mentioned the fact that about 60% of the students were homosexual and were more interested in each other than in the cleaning staff. This was and I believe still is the environment in which students are prepared for ordination to the priesthood. Is there any wonder then that such an adolescent mind-set is innate in the celibate/sexual system of power and that furthermore it reinforces traditional attitudes toward women by its inadequate training in the realities of sexuality, celibacy, and the true equal nature of women?

Three recent Popes have actually stressed the equality of women. Pope St. John XXIII, in *Pacem in Terris* (1963), somewhat patronisingly wrote:

Since women are becoming ever more conscious of their human dignity, they will not tolerate being treated as mere material instruments, but demand rights befitting a human person both in domestic and public life.

Pope St. Paul VI (1963–78) also spoke on the issue of equal rights for women, stating that it must still be regretted that fundamental personal rights are not yet being universally honored. Ten years later, in 1988, Pope St. John Paul II (1978–2005) went so far as to issue an apostolic letter entitled *On the Dignity of Women.*

However, words that simply endorse a theory of women's equality will never be enough; what is required is the practical working out of such a theory, a theory that petrifies a celibate male hierarchy.

As the author has demonstrated, there has been little support for women's equality in the celibate tradition since the time of St. Augustine. Witness St. John Chrysostom writing in about 386:

What else is a woman but a foe to friendship, an inescapable punishment, a necessary evil, a natural temptation, a desirable calamity, a domestic danger, a delectable detriment, an evil of nature, painted with fair colours.

I am reminded of a deanery meeting I attended in 2012 where it was brought to our attention that a woman who had been a pupil of the local convent school had brought an accusation of sexual abuse against a past convent chaplain. One of the priests announced, "Typical! Another money grabbing floozy comes out of the woodwork," and they all laughed in agreement.

It is clear that a woman who seeks power, equality, or even acknowledgment within the Church system is perceived as not only malicious but also dangerous.

I recall my years spent within the monastery, which, by its very nature, demands withdrawal from the world. That being said, monks were permitted to bring male guests inside the monastic enclosure but never women. On the day I entered the abbey my father was allowed to see my room in the novitiate but not my mother, and this would have been of great comfort to her, just to see and know that everything was ok. This unwritten rule wasn't something that could be questioned; its roots lie in the deep-seated misogyny that is still prevalent in the Church and the fear that a woman would somehow contaminate and perhaps tempt the monks.

Is there hope for the future? I believe there is! The Church does not belong to a misogynistic group of celibate men clinging on to power for dear life; it belongs to everyone. I don't believe that Jesus ever saw his mission as leading to a separate religious movement called Christianity. His ministry was 'to the lost sheep of the house of Israel' (Matthew 15:24), and this in no way contradicted the truth that God's message is for all people.

As St. Paul wrote in his letter to the Galatians (3:28):

There is neither Jew nor Greek, slave or free, male or female, for you are all one in Jesus Christ.

With equality in mind, it is a shame that there aren't more priests around today like Fr. Robert Banister (1725–1812) of Mowbreck in Lancashire who, in a letter to his nephew, Fr. Henry Rutter, dated July 27, 1789, wrote:

Two very elegant girls, the daughters of one Mr Hall, a Protestant surgeon in Manchester (but his wife is a Catholic), one 10 the other 9 years old, for the first time were my acolytes (assistants) last Christmas Day, being dressed up in fine muslin frocks and very nice tippets, and blue silk bonnets, and red merroquin (sic) slippers. They officiated in the same dress on three or four other festivals . . . (and) several of the congregation were much pleased to see them serving me so becomingly and elegantly.

It is striking that only fourteen years earlier, in his encyclical *Allatae sunt* of July 26, 1775, Pope Benedict XIV had reaffirmed the Church's ruling that:

Women should not dare to serve at the altar; they should be altogether refused this ministry, and one could add "any ministry."

Clearly Fr. Robert Banister didn't think much of such a misogynistic ruling, but it wasn't until March 1994 that Pope St. John Paul II finally gave permission for women and girls to be altar servers.

If a woman can be an altar server, a catechiser, a parish visitor, a safeguarding officer, an organizer of liturgies, a choir leader, a reader at Mass, a gift bearer, and even a distributor of holy communion both in church and in the home, why then can she not be ordained a deacon? As the author has made very clear, there is ample evidence of the ministry of women deacons up until the fifth century in the West. St. Paul calls one of these women, Phoebe, a deacon of the Church in Cencrae (Romans 16:1–2).

Unfortunately, the Roman Catholic Church of today is far removed from the community authorized by Christ, a community reflected in his choice of women, such as Mary Magdalene and the sisters Martha and Mary, to name a few. It is true that the Catholic tradition has honored the lives and writings of many women down the ages, but if we review the history of the Church and the calendar of saints the female heroes are virgins, martyrs, and widows. In other words, the Church holds up as models for women the sexless, the silent, and the dead.

If you wander around Rome, or any Roman Catholic Church for that matter, you will see many monuments and statues to powerful female saints, but power in marble is sadly not reproduced in reality. Our gratitude to the dead does nothing to ease the restriction of the living to roles of subservience. The inclusion and representation that was present in the Gospels and early Church is no more, and the exclusion of women's insights and lived experience has resulted in the institutional hierarchy's being detached and disconnected from the ordinary lives and struggles of women.

Thankfully some members of the current hierarchy are beginning to speak out about Church reform and the true place of women. The Bishop of Parramatta in Australia, Vincent Long, said the following:

> So long as we continue to exclude women from the Church's government structures, decision-making processes and institutional functions, we deprive ourselves of the richness of our full humanity. So long as we continue to make women invisible and inferior in our Church's language, liturgy, theology and law, we impoverish ourselves as if we heard with only one ear, we saw with only one eye and we thought with only one half of our brain— and often the lowest reptilian section thereof. Until we have truly incorporated the gift of women and the feminine dimension of our Christian faith, we will not be able to fully energise the life of the Church.

Hopefully the days of clericalism, with its many abuses of power and lack of accountability, are numbered. The idea that one half of the human race can represent the whole is now a well-recognized fallacy in most of the world's cultures. It is way beyond time that the Roman Catholic Church caught up, because if it doesn't then more and more people will be unable to accept a system that they experience as unreasonable and essentially dishonest, and the misogynistic upper echelons of the Roman Catholic Church will no longer have any lower echelons to lord it over, and what will they do then?

The Rev. Paul Murphy-Sanderson B.D. is a former Cistercian monk, abbey archivist, potter, farmer and regional secretary for formation. He has also served as a Roman Catholic priest in several parishes as well as been a part-time prison chaplain and naval chaplain. In 2014 he left the Roman Catholic Church due the treatment he received for speaking out about clergy sexual abuse, of which he is a survivor. He currently lives in Ireland on a smallholding with his wife.

Selected Bibliography

Allen, Elise Ann. "Peruvian Ex-nuns Report Abuses of Power, Conscience Inside Order." *Crux*, November 27, 2021. https://cruxnow.com/church-in-the-americas/2021/11/peruvian-ex-nuns-report-abuses-of-power-conscience-inside-order.

Amato, Angelo. "Vatican Decrees Excommunication for Participation in 'Ordination' of Women." *Catholic News Agency*, May 29, 2008. https://www.catholicnewsagency.com/news/12780/vatican-decrees-excommunication-for-participation-in-ordination-of-women.

American Experience. "Dr. John Rock (1890–1984)." *PBS.org*. Accessed January 7, 2022. https://www.pbs.org/wgbh/americanexperience/features/pill-dr-john-rock-1890-1984/.

Anson, P. F. *Religious Orders and Congregations of Great Britain and Ireland.* Worcester, UK: Stanbrook Abbey Press, 1949.

Anson, P. F. *The Call of the Cloister.* London: SPCK, 1955.

Aquinas, Thomas. *Summa Theologica.* London: Burns Oates & Washbourne, 1925.

Armstrong, Karen. *The Case for God.* London: Vintage, 2009.

Armstrong, Karen. *Through the Narrow Gate: A Nun's Story.* London: Pan, 1982.

Association of Catholic Priests. "The Children of Priests—Coping International." *Association of Catholic Priests*, August 23, 2017. https://associationofcatholicpriests.ie/the-children-of-priests-coping-international/.

Augustine, St. *Against the Epistle of Manichaeus, Called Fundamental.* Savage, MN: Lighthouse Christian Publishing: 2017.

Baker, Denise N. (ed.). *The Showings of Julian of Norwich.* New York: W.W. Norton, 2005.

Barron, Robert. "What Is Synodality?" *Word on Fire*, February 18, 2020. https://www.wordonfire.org/articles/barron/what-is-synodality/.

Beck, George A. *The English Catholics (1850–1950).* London: Burns & Oates, 1950.

Bede. *Ecclesiastical History of the English People (673–735)*, revised edition. London: Penguin Classics, 1990.

Black, Henry C. *A Law Dictionary*, 2nd edition. Minneapolis, MN: West Publishing Co., 1910.

Brockhaus, Hannah. "Pope Francis Establishes New Commission to Study Women Deacons." *Catholic News Agency*, April 8, 2020. https://www.catholicnewsagency.com/news/44137/pope-francis-establishes-new-commission-to-study-women-deacons.

Brown, Raymond. *The Community of the Beloved Disciple*. New York: Paulist Press, 1978.

Bunting, Madeleine. "Bitterness of Priest's Women Painfully Clear." *Irish Times*, September 21, 1996. https://www.irishtimes.com/culture/bitterness-of-priest-s-women-painfully-clear-1.88198.

Bürger, Martin. "Former Vatican Doctrine Head Corrects Modern, Wrong Understanding of 'Synodality.'" *LifeSiteNews*, May 1, 2020. https://www.lifesitenews.com/news/former-vatican-doctrine-head-corrects-modern-wrong-understanding-of-synodality/.

Carmelite Sisters of the Most Sacred Heart of Los Angeles. "St. Teresa and St. John of the Cross." Accessed December 11, 2021. https://carmelitesistersocd.com/2015/stteresaandstjohnofthecross/.

Clement of Alexandria and Origen. *Alexandrian Christianity: Selected Translations of Clement and Origen*. Edited by Henry Chadwick and J. E. L. Oulton. Louisville, KY: Westminster John Knox Press, 2006.

Daly, Mark. "Fresh Claims Over Catholic Church Sex Abuse." *BBC News*, July 26, 2013. https://www.bbc.co.uk/news/uk-scotland-23459459.

Danaher, Dan. "Clare Bishop of Ferns Says He Is in Favour of Women Priests." *Clare Champion*, June 19, 2021. https://clarechampion.ie/clare-bishop-of-ferns-says-he-is-in-favour-of-women-priests/.

David, Ariel. "Byzantine Basilica with Graves of Female Ministers and Baffling Mass Burials Found in Israel." *Haaretz*, November 15, 2021. https://www.haaretz.com/archaeology/2021-11-15/ty-article-magazine/byzantine-basilica-with-female-ministers-and-baffling-burials-found-in-israel/0000017f-e722-dc7e-adff-f7af11070000.

Dearie, James. "Orthodox Move for Women Deacons Is 'Revitalization' Not 'Innovation.'" *National Catholic Reporter*, November 30, 2017. https://www.ncronline.org/news/theology/orthodox-move-women-deacons-called-revitalization-not-innovation.

Denysenko, Nicholas. "Shared Ministry and Divine Grace: Restoring the Diaconate in Orthodoxy." *Public Orthodoxy*, March 7, 2017. https://publicorthodoxy.org/2017/03/07/restoring-the-diaconate/.

Deutsche Welle. "Doris Reisinger: 'I Was the Perfect Victim.'" *Deutsche Welle*, February 7, 2019. https://www.dw.com/en/doris-reisinger-for-clergy-i-was-the-perfect-victim/a-47414759.

Devlin, Brian. *Cardinal Sin*. Dublin: Columba Books, 2021.

Edwards, David L. *Christian England.* London: Collins, 1981.

Fairchild, Mary. "The Great Schism of 1054 and the Split of Christianity." *Learn Religions,* last updated July 31, 2019. https://www.learnreligions.com/the-great-schism-of-1054-4691893.

Falardeau, Ernest. "The Eucharist in Eastern Orthodoxy." Ecumenical Corner, Congregation of the Blessed Sacrament, Cleveland, OH. September 3, 2012. https://blessedsacrament.com/the-eucharist-in-eastern-orthodoxy/.

Farmer, David Hugh. *The Oxford Dictionary of Saints,* 3rd edition. Oxford: Oxford University Press, 1992.

Flannery, Tony. "The Story of Lavinia Byrne and the CDF." Accessed December 14, 2021. http://www.tonyflannery.com/the-story-of-lavinia-byrne-and-the-cdf/.

Flint, Bill. *Edith the Fair: Visionary of Walsingham.* Leominster, UK: Gracewing, 2015.

Flint, Debra Maria. *Look Back to the Future: Consecrated Women in Britain 597 AD to Date.* Kula, HI: DWM Press and Debra Maria Flint, 2021.

Gnostic Society Library. "Gnostic Scriptures and Fragments: The Gospel According to Mary Magdalene." Accessed November 4, 2021. http://www.gnosis.org/library/marygosp.htm.

Godfrey, John. *The Church in Anglo-Saxon England.* Cambridge: Cambridge University Press, 2009.

Heneghan, Tom. "Pope Explains Why He Accepted Aupetit Resignation." *The Tablet,* December 6, 2021. https://www.thetablet.co.uk/news/14772/pope-explains-why-he-accepted-aupetit-resignation.

Herrin, Judith. *The Formation of Christendom.* London: Fontana Press, 1987.

Horowitz, Jason, and Elisabetta Povoledo. "Vatican's Secret Rules for Catholic Priests Who Have Children." *New York Times,* February 18, 2019. https://www.nytimes.com/2019/02/18/world/europe/priests-children-vatican-rules-celibacy.html.

Hylen, Susan E. *Women in the New Testament World.* New York: Oxford University Press, 2018.

IICSA (Independent Inquiry into Child Sexual Abuse). *Ampleforth and Downside (English Benedictine Congregation Case Study) Investigation Report, August 2018.* London: HMSO, 2018. https://www.iicsa.org.uk/document/ampleforth-and-downside-investigation-report-august-2018.

Johnson, David, and Jeff Van Vonderen. *The Subtle Power of Spiritual Abuse: Recognizing and Escaping Spiritual Manipulation and False Spiritual Authority within the Church.* Bloomington, MN: Bethany House, 2005.

Jones, Ruadhán. "New Bishop of Ferns 'Daunted' but Eager to Get Started." *The Irish Catholic*, June 24, 2021. https://www.irishcatholic.com/new-bishop-of-ferns-daunted-but-eager-to-get-started/.

Jurgens, William. *The Faith of the Early Fathers, Volume 1*. Collegeville, MN: Liturgical Press, 1970.

Jurgens, William. *The Faith of the Early Fathers, Volume 2*. Collegeville, MN: Liturgical Press, 1979.

Kempe, Margery. *The Book of Margery Kempe*. Harmondsworth, UK: Penguin Classics, 1994.

King, Karen L. *The Gospel of Mary of Magdala: Jesus and the First Woman Apostle*. Santa Rosa, CA: Polebridge Press, 2003.

Knowles, David. *The Religious Orders in England*. Cambridge: Cambridge University Press, 1950.

Lamb, Christopher. "Pope Chooses 'Synodality' as Next Synod Theme." *The Tablet*, March 7, 2020. https://www.thetablet.co.uk/news/12563/pope-chooses-synodality-as-next-synod-theme.

Mares, Courtney. "Pope Francis Says He Accepted Paris Archbishop's Resignation 'on the Altar of Hypocrisy.'" *National Catholic Register*, December 6, 2021. https://www.ncregister.com/cna/pope-francis-says-he-accepted-paris-archbishop-s-resignation-on-the-altar-of-hypocrisy.

Molinari, Paul. *Julian of Norwich: The Teaching of a 14th Century English Mystic*. London: Longmans Green, 1958.

O'Driscoll, Mary. *Catherine of Siena*. London: Catholic Truth Society, 2007.

Oakley, Lisa. "Understanding Spiritual Abuse." *Church Times*, February 16, 2018.

Ombres, Robert. "The Synod of Bishops: Canon Law and Ecclesial Dynamics." *Ecclesiastical Law Journal* 16, no. 3 (2014): 306–318. https://doi.org/10.1017/S0956618X14000519.

Peters, Edward N., ed. *The 1917 or Pio-Benedictine Code of Canon Law*. San Francisco: Ignatian Press, 2001.

Ramsey, Michael. *The Gospel and the Catholic Church*. Peabody, MA: Hendrickson, 2009.

Rees, Elizabeth. "Consecrated Widows." *Pastoral Review*, November/December 2015.

Reisinger, Doris. "Testimony Against Sexual Abuse." Wijngaards *Institute for Catholic Research*, June 29, 2019. https://www.wijngaardsinstitute.com/doris-reisinger-testimony-against-sexual-abuse/.

Ridyard, Susan J. *The Royal Saints of Anglo-Saxon England: A Study of West Saxon and East Anglian Cults*. Cambridge: Cambridge University Press, 1988.

Robinson, Maurice A., and Pierpont, William G. *The New Testament in the Original Greek*. Scotts Valley, CA: CreateSpace, 2016.

Sanders, Margaret. *Intimate Letters of England's Queens*. Stroud: Amberley Publishing, 2014.

Scudder, Vida Dutton, trans. and ed. *Saint Catherine of Siena as Seen in Her Letters*. London: Imperium Christi Press, 2014.

Sherbrook, Michael. "The Falle of Religiouse Howses, Colleges, Chantreyes, Hospitalls, &c." In *Tudor Treatises*, edited by A. G. Dickens, 89–14. Wakefield: Yorkshire Archaeological Society, 1959.

Stenton, Frank M. *Anglo-Saxon England*. Oxford: Oxford University Press, 1943.

Thompson, James. "Ministry in the New Testament." *Restoration Quarterly* 27, no. 3 (1984): article 1, https://digitalcommons.acu.edu/restorationquarterly/vol27/iss3/1/.

Upjohn, Sheila. *In Search of Julian of Norwich*. London: Darton, Longman and Todd, 1989.

Vatican, The. *Dominus Jesus*. 2000. https://www.vatican.va/roman_curia/congregations/cfaith/documents/rc_con_cfaith_doc_20000806_dominus-iesus_en.html.

Vatican, The. *Evangelii Gaudium*. 2013. https://www.vatican.va/content/francesco/en/apost_exhortations/documents/papa-francesco_esortazione-ap_20131124_evangelii-gaudium.html.

Vatican, The. *Humanae Vitae*. 1968. https://www.vatican.va/content/paul-vi/en/encyclicals/documents/hf_p-vi_enc_25071968_humanae-vitae.html.

Vatican, The. *Lumen Gentium*. 1964. https://www.vatican.va/archive/hist_councils/ii_vatican_council/documents/vat-ii_const_19641121_lumen-gentium_en.html.

Vatican, The. *Nostra Aetate*. 1965. https://www.vatican.va/archive/hist_councils/ii_vatican_council/documents/vat-ii_decl_19651028_nostra-aetate_en.html.

Vatican, The. *Ordinatio Sacerdotalis*. 1994. https://www.vatican.va/content/john-paul-ii/en/apost_letters/1994/documents/hf_jp-ii_apl_19940522_ordinatio-sacerdotalis.html.

Vatican, The. *Vademecum for the Synod on Synodality* (General Secretary of the Synod of Bishops). 2021. https://www.synod.va/en/news/the-vademecum-for-the-synod-on-synodality.html.

Vatican, The. *Vita Consecrata*. 1996. https://www.vatican.va/content/john-paul-ii/en/apost_exhortations/documents/hf_jp-ii_exh_25031996_vita-consecrata.html.

Walter, Katherine Clark. *The Profession of Widowhood: Widows, Pastoral Care and Medieval Models of Holiness*. Washington, DC: Catholic University of America Press, 2018.

We Are The 51. "Dr Lavinia Byrne." Accessed December 14, 2021. http://www.the3rdimagazine.co.uk/2012/02/influential-women-dr-lavinia-byrne/.

West's Encyclopedia of American Law, 2nd edition. Minneapolis, MN: West Group, 1998.

Wijngaards, John. "The Priesthood of Mary." https://www.johnwijngaards.com/priesthood-mary/.

Wood, Laura Mary. "Vowesses in the Province of Canterbury, c. 1450–1540." PhD thesis. Royal Holloway University of London, 2017. https://pure.royalholloway.ac.uk/portal/files/27904553/2017woodlmphd.pdf.

Zagano, Phyllis. "Pope Francis Is Asking the US Bishops to Listen to the People. Will They?" *National Catholic Reporter*, December 6, 2021. https://www.ncronline.org/news/opinion/pope-francis-asking-us-bishops-listen-people-will-they.

About the Author

Debra Maria Flint was born in Birmingham, UK, to an agnostic family. She converted to Catholicism at twenty-two years of age in the wake of Vatican II. She lived in Greece from her late teenage years into her early twenties and speaks and writes fluent Greek.

On her return to the United Kingdom, Debra studied theology in Oxford. She met her late husband, Bill, at that time, and they moved to Somerset. Debra later went on to qualify as a nurse. She also obtained a bachelor of science in health, with safeguarding children and adults as her specialism. She has postgraduate qualifications in management and investigative research.

Debra spent over twenty years safeguarding children and vulnerable adults. She managed both children's homes and care homes and later went on to work as a social care inspector for Ofsted. She was the first Ofsted social care inspector in England to represent Ofsted in court when a company failed to have robust safeguarding practices in place. Ofsted won the case.

Debra was married for twenty-nine years. Her late husband died in 2014, and she decided to follow a consecrated path within the Catholic Church. She spent six years exploring the new and restored forms of consecrated life before experiencing difficulties in 2020.

Debra's first book, *Look Back to the Future: Consecrated Women in Britain 597 AD to Date*, was published in April 2021. *No Place for a Woman: The Spiritual and Political Power Abuse of Women within Catholicism* is her second book. Since writing this book, Debra has sadly found it necessary to leave the Roman Catholic Church and is now serving as an ordained deacon within another Christian denomination that has apostolic succession through the Old Catholic Church. Debra still considers herself to be part of the One Holy Catholic and Apostolic Church.

About the Publisher

Lantern Publishing & Media was founded in 2020 to follow and expand on the legacy of Lantern Books—a publishing company started in 1999 on the principles of living with a greater depth and commitment to the preservation of the natural world. Like its predecessor, Lantern Publishing & Media produces books on animal advocacy, veganism, religion, social justice, humane education, psychology, family therapy, and recovery. Lantern is dedicated to printing in the United States on recycled paper and saving resources in our day-to-day operations. Our titles are also available as e-books and audiobooks.

To catch up on Lantern's publishing program, visit us at www.lanternpm.org.

facebook.com/lanternpm
instagram.com/lanternpm
twitter.com/lanternpm